OTHER DICKENS

For my parents,

VIVIAN AND NESTA BOWEN

OTHER DICKENS

Pickwick to Chuzzlewit

JOHN BOWEN

OXFORD
UNIVERSITY PRESS

OXFORD
UNIVERSITY PRESS

Great Clarendon Street, Oxford OX2 6DP

Oxford University Press is a department of the University of Oxford.
If furthers the University's objective of excellence in research, scholarship,
and education by publishing worldwide in

Oxford New York

Athens Auckland Bangkok Bogotá Buenos Aires Calcutta
Cape Town Chennai Dar es Salaam Delhi Florence Hong Kong Istanbul
Karachi Kuala Lumpur Madrid Melbourne Mexico City Mumbai
Nairobi Paris São Paulo Singapore Taipei Tokyo Toronto Warsaw
and associated companies in Berlin Ibadan

Oxford is a registered trade mark of Oxford University Press
in the UK and certain other countries

Published in the United States
by Oxford University Press Inc., New York

British Library Cataloguing in Publication Data
Data available

Library of Congress Cataloging in Publication Data
Bowen, John.
Other Dickens : Pickwick to Chuzzlewit / John Bowen.
Includes index.
1. Dickens, Charles, 1812–1870—Criticism and interpretation. I. Title.
PR4588 .B69 1999 823'.8—dc21 99-16104
ISBN 0-19-818506-5

1 3 5 7 9 10 8 6 4 2

Typeset by Best-set Typesetter Ltd., Hong Kong
Printed in Great Britain
on acid-free paper by
Biddles Ltd., Guildford and King's Lynn

Acknowledgements

MANY PEOPLE HAVE helped in the preparation and writing of this book. I should most like to thank Richard Godden, Grahame Smith, and Anthea Trodd who read the whole book in typescript and commented in detail on it, Jim McLaverty who first told me to write about Dickens, and Charles Swann. Jonathan Dancy has been a great source of encouragement, and Sarah Dancy of good sense. Dr David Parker of the Dickens House Museum and the librarians of Keele University, the New York Public Library, and Birmingham Central Library have been most helpful. I should also like to remember and thank the late John Goode and Allon White, to whom I owe so much.

The author and publishers gratefully acknowledge permission to reprint copyright material in this book as follows: Chapter 4 was first published as 'Performing Business, Training Ghosts: Transcoding "Nickleby"', *English Literary History*, 63 (1996), pp. 153–75. © 1996 The Johns Hopkins University Press. Parts of Chapter 2 were first published as ' "Pickwick" and the Postal Principle', *Imprimatur: A Journal of Criticism and Theory*, 1, 2/3 (Spring 1996), pp. 180–5. Another version of this appeared as 'Posts, Ghosts, and "Pickwick"', in Joe Andrew and Robert Reid (eds), *Neo-Formalist Papers: Contributions to the Silver Jubilee Conference to mark 25 years of the Neo-Formalist Circle* (Amsterdam: Rodopi, 1998), pp. 65–77.

Earlier versions of parts of this book were given as papers at the Centre for Critical and Cultural Theory, University of Wales, Cardiff; the Victorian Literature Research seminar, Oxford; the Centre for Social History, Warwick; the Goethe-University, Frankfurt; and the 'Dickens, Childhood and Empire' Conference at Rhodes University, South Africa. I should like to thank Laurent Milesi, Kate Flint, Carolyn Steedman, Harald Raykowski, and Wendy Jacobson for their hospitality, and my hearers for their patience.

My greatest debt is to my wife, Sally Gray, without whom nothing is possible.

Contents

Abbreviations

Pilgrim: M. House, G. Storey, K. Tillotson *et al.* (eds), *The Pilgrim Edition of The Letters of Charles Dickens* (Oxford: Clarendon Press, 1965–in progress)

Introduction

READERS HAVE IN Dickens's work an embarrassment of riches, and if the lover of Shakespeare can feel justified in not knowing the finer points of Act Four of *Cymbeline* or not having the plot-twists of *Two Gentlemen of Verona* at his or her finger tips, so the reader of Dickens may well feel content with the familiar features of *Great Expectations, Bleak House, Hard Times, Little Dorrit,* and *Our Mutual Friend*. These are the most widely taught of Dickens's works and those most familiar to the literary profession, if not to the common reader. Common readers, though, have over the decades admired Dickens's earlier novels—*Pickwick Papers, Oliver Twist, Martin Chuzzlewit*—at least as much as their successors. It is the contention of this book that they were right to do so and that literary critics have an obligation to say why. If Nature was prodigal in her gifts to Dickens, and Dickens was prodigal in their exercise, then we should be grateful that we have in his oeuvre not four or five major novels, but a dozen or more. To read all Dickens's works may be a long party, but the best bits are not all late in the evening.

Dickens's early novels present interesting problems for many of the customary practices of contemporary literary criticism. His mix of directness and popular appeal with profound inventiveness and subtlety, while delighting the reader, can frustrate critics in their task of explaining what is going on and why. The challenge is not only to our aesthetics and to the divisions we customarily make in the field of culture, but also to many of the more deeply held convictions of the modern period—to our understanding of the process of history, for example, or what it is to be a human being or to be natural. Dickens's narrators are not content with merely appreciative audiences; they want their readers to sob, rage, see visions, and then to do things about them. The books are performative, concerned to make their readers different people from the ones who began the book. When it succeeds, this process of change is as disturbing as it is frequently hilarious.

This is not then a study of a particular theme in Dickens's

novels, nor the illustration of how a particular theory or method might help us to understand the books. It is a reading in sequence of all of the novels and some of the minor writing published by Dickens between 1836, when the first instalment of *Pickwick Papers* appeared, and the final episode of *Martin Chuzzlewit* in 1844. It is a very heterogeneous group of texts and Dickens is a deeply experimental and self-conscious writer from his earliest years. No one could have predicted *Oliver Twist* on the basis of *Pickwick Papers* or *Martin Chuzzlewit* after *Barnaby Rudge*. At each stage there is major generic, linguistic and narrative invention, and it has often seemed to this critic that he has had to begin all over again with each new text to be even minimally faithful to it. The best method seemed to be that of reading all the novels in order, not to show Dickens's 'development' or growth to maturity, but to witness to each text's singular force. No critic can ever do justice to the texts he or she discusses, but this way I hope to avoid some of the more flagrant kinds of injustice. J. Hillis Miller has rightly said that 'one of the most obvious characteristics of works of literature is their manifest strangeness'.[1] Dickens, as the epigraph to his journal *Household Words* tells us, wanted to be not a strange but a familiar writer, as 'familiar in their mouths as Household Words'.[2] I have tried to show how he can be both familiar and strange at the same time, and often in the same words.

Some of the very mixed bunch of texts that go by the name of 'theory' or 'literary theory' have been helpful to me in writing this book, and I try to acknowledge my debts in the text, but I cannot claim a proper theoretical coherence to my argument for I do not believe that a secure and grounded theory or method on which to base the reading of major literary texts is possible. Indeed, literary texts' inability to be interpreted by a consistent set of principles and methods may well be the (paradoxical) condition of their (impossible) existence.[3] Unless the reader is open

[1] J. Hillis Miller, *Fiction and Repetition: Seven English Novels* (Cambridge: Harvard University Press, 1982), 18.

[2] Charles Dickens, *The Uncollected Writings of Charles Dickens: 'Household Words' 1850–1859*, ed. Harry Stone (London: Allen Lane, 1969), I, 18.

[3] 'Similar blind forks or double binds are encountered in the attempt to develop a general "theoretical" terminology for reading prose fiction and, on the other hand, in the attempt to eschew theory', J. Hillis Miller, *Ariadne's Thread: Storylines* (New Haven: Yale University Press, 1992), 23. See also Jacques Derrida, *Acts of Literature*, ed. Derek Attridge (London: Routledge, 1992), 42–3.

to the possibility in each encounter with them that some or all of his or her most cherished and fundamental assumptions may be transformed or thrown into radical doubt, then the reading of the text cannot be said to have taken place. This of course can be a pleasurable as well as disturbing affair, and in the course of writing these pages I have often found the theory futilely lumbering behind the Dickens text, like a pantomime elephant trying to pick up°a pea, or indeed, at times, like a pea trying to pick up an elephant.

Most critics of Dickens in this century have placed a higher value on his later novels than those that I consider in this book. There are two main grounds for this preference: first, that the later novels are better plotted, more integrated and symbolically coherent than their precursors; second, that their darker vision is a more truthful and plausible one, providing a comprehensive indictment of (Victorian) (capitalist) society. These judgements, as is well known, differ in some important ways from most contemporary assessments, in which the later novels were often seen as sad and laboured fallings away from the world of Sam Weller and Mr Bumble. Recent decades have seen at least one conceptual revolution in literary studies and correspondingly dramatic changes in idiom, objects of attention, and evaluative criteria. In particular, criticism has come to question both the possibility and desirability of the kinds of unity that have been claimed for the later novels of Dickens and has given renewed attention both to rhetorical analysis and the relation between popular and literary art. Together they may provide the grounds for a different account of these novels, the possibility of valuing them at a different rate, and the chance to be less troubled (or troubled differently) by their alleged incoherences and lapses.

There is little we can take for granted in the genres, forms, or narratives of Dickens's early novels, for they enact one of the more sustained projects of textual experimentation in the language, one which seems to undo in the process so many of the distinctions—between popular and high culture, between fictional and non-fictional writing, between social and political thought, and, more radically still, between past and present, self and other, life and death—within which its readers move. And to say that Dickens's texts are disturbing, radical, and transgressive is also to say that they are intensely pleasure-giving, the most wildly funny books in the language. Samuel Johnson, writing of that 'licentious and vagrant faculty', the Imagination, saw it as 'unsusceptible of limitations, and impatient of restraint', always liable 'to baffle the logics, to perplex the confines of distinction, and burst the inclosures of regularity'.[4] Of no author is this more true than Charles Dickens, and one is constantly struck how strongly his writing outplays and subverts the critical norms and presuppositions both of his day and our own. In this book I have tried to be faithful to this licence and vagrancy, and to the baffled logics, perplexed distinctions, and burst inclosures that ensue.

In Dickens's final, uncompleted novel, *The Mystery of Edwin Drood*, Rosa Budd finds herself in an apartment in Staples Inn which the narrator compares to 'the country on the summit of the magic beanstalk'.[5] In the fairy tale which Dickens invokes, Jack's mother casts his beans away, only to see them sprout into a great plant whose tip is in the clouds. The beanstalk, like the tale of which it is a part, unites two very different countries: that of Jack's and his mother's poverty and hunger and, high above it, a fantastical place beyond human reason and sense. The story is thus very like the fiction that this book discusses, whose stories connect (and thus displace) a world of poverty and exploitation with one of sublime and wonderful imaginings. The critical challenge is to be true to them both, and to the promise of the writing from which they come. Raymond Williams once said of Christopher Caudwell's work that it 'was not specific enough to be wrong'.[6] I have tried to be specific enough.

[4] Samuel Johnson, *The Rambler*, 125, Tues 28 May 1751, in *Works*, 4, ed. W. J. Bate and B. Strauss (New Haven and London: Yale University Press, 1961), 300.

[5] Charles Dickens, *The Mystery of Edwin Drood*, ed. Margaret Cardwell (Oxford: World's Classics, 1982), 188.

[6] Raymond Williams, *Culture and Society 1780–1850* (Harmondsworth: Penguin, 1963), 268. See also Raymond Williams, *Politics and Letters: Interviews with New Left Review* (London: Verso, 1979), 127–8.

CHAPTER ONE

Arbitrary and Despotic Characters

A Christmas Carol starts with the ambiguous words, 'Marley was dead: to begin with.'[1] Like many storytellers, Dickens begins with what appears at first to be a simple and unequivocal death, but as so often in his work there is no simple end to the life, or beginning to the story, for, as Scrooge and we learn, Jacob Marley will not stay dead. He returns to tell Scrooge to change his life, bringing with him three Christmas Spirits, festive and demanding in equal measure. Scrooge is made to visit his own grave, to appear at his own wake as it were, an event which is also his awakening. Dickens's fiction is fascinated by what is dead but will not lie down, in things or people or people-things who cross or trouble the boundaries between what was, what is, and what may be living. The novels are full of living people thought to be dead, inanimate objects made animate, human beings who become things before our eyes, and ghosts, spirits, and spectres of all kinds. The books are saturated with what Freud will later call the 'uncanny', in which the most unfamiliar event or presence will turn out to be our most familiar and disturbing acquaintance.[2] This is not simply one theme in Dickens's work, one strand in the tapestry. On the contrary, Jacob Marley's condition—being dead, but only to begin with— may be the necessary condition of all themes and all interpretation, all writing and reading of fiction, a matter of ghosts and their kin, of people or things like Scrooge, Marley, and ourselves that are dead and not dead at the same time. At important moments, Dickens's narrators encourage the reader to see the whole business of creating fictions and fictional characters as a matter of conjuring and living with ghosts, of believing-and-not-

[1] Charles Dickens, *A Christmas Carol*, in *The Christmas Books Volume One*, ed. Michael Slater (Harmondsworth: Penguin, 1971), 45.
[2] Sigmund Freud, 'The Uncanny' in *The Pelican Freud Library Volume 14: Art and Literature* (Harmondsworth: Penguin, 1985), 335–76.

believing in the existence of Sam Weller, Sim Tappertit, Mrs Gamp, and their imaginary friends. Indeed, the novels will often stage scenes of mourning in their prefaces and conclusions for their own characters, or rather for their ghosts, which is all they ever are. And we as readers will often experience the emotion of knowing or caring more for someone who never existed, in a place and time that never were, than for those we believe to be alive around us every day. This is the perfectly normal and utterly strange effect of that activity we call reading fiction, or reading Dickens's fiction at least.

The writing of criticism shares in these effects, in its desire to conjure up its own pale ghosts: ghosts of other critics ('as Marcus has argued . . .'), ghosts of the author ('Dickens is here showing . . .'), ghosts of the work ('*Martin Chuzzlewit* is . . .') and ghosts of you, 'the reader', who feels, knows, and intuits so much, as we tell you. These 'ghost effects' of criticism are not merely one theme among many but a condition of the criticism of fiction. And as the ghost of Marley does not come alone, or simply to disturb or question Scrooge, but obliges him to witness the poverty and exploitation of the working people and the abject poor who surround him and who suffer by his deeds, so all Dickens's fiction bears with it ethical demands upon its readers. Perhaps the best-known painting of Dickens—R. W. Buss's *Dickens's Dream*—is of the writer asleep in a chair, surrounded, haunted as it were, by his creations. In his childhood Dickens was already, he tells us, a 'strange little apparition', already haunting and haunted.[3] Many of his later critics, even the most robustly pragmatic, will find themselves reaching at key moments for the word 'haunt' or one of its derivatives.[4] Dickens will often think of dreams and other psychological processes as forms of haunting by both the living and the dead, and, as Marx will a little later in the century, think of history and historical fiction as complex and multiple hauntings and doublings of the past by the present and the present by the

---

[3] John Forster, *The Life of Charles Dickens*, ed. A. J. Hoppé (London: Dent, 1966), I, 23.

[4] Angus Wilson, 'Charles Dickens: A Haunting', in George H. Ford and Lauriat Lane Jr (eds), *The Dickens Critics* (Ithaca: Cornell University Press, 1961), 374–86; Malcolm Andrews, Introduction to Charles Dickens, *The Old Curiosity Shop* (Harmondsworth: Penguin, 1972), 11; Peter Ackroyd, *Dickens* (London: Sinclair Stevenson, 1990), 18, 34.

past.[5] As I begin now to write of 'Dickens', I seek to conjure a ghost in and from the traces of language that surround me in the name of an ethical demand and a history which has as yet no name. Like Scrooge, I am certain that Dickens is dead: to begin with.

I

Let me begin with a scene of writing. It is taken from the first book of John Forster's *The Life of Charles Dickens*, in which Forster weaves or grafts together sections from the lost manuscript now known as the 'Autobiographical Fragment' with passages from *David Copperfield* to tell a story that has come to dominate later interpretations of the character called 'Dickens'. Dickens, Copperfield, or some ghost or hybrid of the two is a shorthand reporter in the old House of Commons whose hand is tracing signs—'arbitrary characters, the most despotic characters I have ever known'—to represent the workings of arbitrary and despotic power.[6] He writes absurd signs—'a pen-and-ink skyrocket stood for disadvantageous', 'a thing that looked like the beginning of a cobweb meant expectation'—to stand for absurd rhetoric in a scene of representation where success is judged by the strict transcription of politicians' words. It is an extraordinary beginning to a writer's career, such a writer's career, this writing that is not writing, endless and dull. The biographer can find in it the roots of Dickens's industry, punctuality, reporter's eye, and his lifelong hatred for Parliament and cant, and can make it stand as the gate or pillar at the head of Dickens's imperial, republican progress through the novel: in the gallery the spectating, silent youth, at five guineas a week, an ear and hand reproducing endless repetition, helping the hot air circulate a little further, enough to cool the warmest heart. It can be contrasted with another scene taken from the end of his life in which Dickens is not a writer but a reader, not pegged

[5] Karl Marx, 'The Eighteenth Brumaire of Louis Bonaparte', in David Fernbach (ed.), *Surveys from Exile* (Harmondsworth: Penguin, 1971), 143–249; Jacques Derrida, *Specters of Marx: The State of the Debt, the Work of Mourning, and the New International* (London: Routledge, 1994).

[6] Forster, *The Life of Charles Dickens*, I, 46. Compare Charles Dickens, *David Copperfield*, ed. Nina Burgis (Oxford: World's Classics, 1983), 444.

to others' words, but now lodging his own familiar characters in the hearts of his readers; not just an ear, but the often remembered eye, a body and voice; not witnessing but witnessed, actor of his own fictions come alive as theatre—*A Christmas Carol, The Poor Traveller, Sikes and Nancy*.[7] One can draw a moral from this contrast and trace the story it implies, the triumph of creation over mechanical reproduction and of full, authentic speech over constrained and imitative writing, the hilarious victory of performance and the creating act over mere surveying passivity, a victory for Dickens but also for us, as the truth of art defeats the lies of politicians in the festive, communal laughter of one audience against the insufferable ennui of the other. Representative scenes, then, concerned with representation and theatricality, speech and writing, politics and laughter.

If only it were so. Yet Dickens's work tells no such story, never moves from empty words to full authentic speech, never escapes from the tyranny and absurdity of arbitrary and despotic characters. The scene Dickens saw in the Commons was as much theatre, as much a scene of representation, as his later readings were, his writing as embedded in rhetoric as the politicians' speech. The two adjectives he uses—arbitrary and despotic—are significant, for Dickens throughout his writing both demonstrates and exploits the despotism and arbitrariness of human languages, cultures, social structures, and power. Not that despotism is arbitrary in the sense that it can be wished away by thought or that the arbitrariness of the sign is so despotic that any change or difference is absurd or futile, but that Mr Bumble and Wackford Squeers, the House of Commons, and his own writing hand are engaged alike in the exercise of a power both arbitrary and despotic. Arbitrary because social and political power like the power of writing is not grounded or given in any way—by God or Nature or the authentic self—however often it claims to be; despotic because, while language and the powers invested by and through it continue to exist, they remain the sources of terror or pleasure, forces that cannot be withstood either by the sobbing and hysterical audiences of the sobbing, self-terrorized Dickens or by poor little Oliver Twist about to be beaten by the beadle Bumble. Dickens is sometimes

<hr />

[7] Charles Dickens, *Sikes and Nancy and Other Public Readings*, ed. Philip Collins (Oxford: World's Classics, 1983).

thought to be condemning social injustice in his books, but he is doing something far stranger and better than that, for Bumble is an arbitrary and despotic character, but he is also a mere collection of arbitrary and despotic characters—six small squiggles, in short, absurd as a pen-and-ink skyrocket or the beginning of a spider's web. Writing is not outside arbitrariness and despotism, but another use of it, found in these early days in a thing that looks like the beginning of a cobweb, meaning expectation. Dickens's writing is a kind of web, endlessly re-spun in our readings and rewritings, but the skyrocket matters too. Dickens himself is a pen-and-ink skyrocket and an early reviewer wondered whether Dickens, having risen like a rocket, would come down like the stick.[8] The sign for that absurd politicians' word 'disadvantageous' sends us shooting off into laughter, by simple attendance to the process of signification. It is astonishing that such a little thing can make such a difference, but it is characteristic of the art we call Dickens, whose characters, like Mr Squeers's clothing in *Nicholas Nickleby*, are often astonishing themselves (and thereby us, their readers) by the arbitrariness of their respectability or power, by how easily they and we naturalize and take for granted the marks of character and the signs and tokens of office.[9] Not just linguistic signs, but the whole work of cultural inscription and re-inscription to be found in such things as Mr Bumble's hat, deposited with phallic pride on Mrs Corney's table, or the bundle of rags that finally bring home to Scrooge his possible fate, or 'the excellent example of the power of dress' that is the naked and defenceless Oliver Twist.[10]

Most people would prefer to sob at a Dickens reading than after a Bumble beating, which reminds us that there are better and worse despotisms, different and better uses of writing and power. The writing constantly does this work of evaluation, valuing one source of authority (humanity, tenderness) against another (bigotry, brutality), one use of language against another;

[8] Abraham Hayward [?] from an unsigned review of *Pickwick*, nos I–XVII, and *Sketches by Boz*, in the *Quarterly Review*, lix (October 1837) 484–518, reprinted in Philip Collins (ed.), *Charles Dickens: The Critical Heritage* (London: Routledge and Kegan Paul, 1971), 62.

[9] Charles Dickens, *Nicholas Nickleby*, ed. Paul Schlicke (Oxford: World's Classics, 1990), 31.

[10] Charles Dickens, *Oliver Twist*, ed. Kathleen Tillotson (Oxford: World's Classics, 1982), 3.

this ethical or theoretical stance against that, this deed or action against another, mobilizing the powers of rhetoric to subvert or delete the languages and voices of exploitative authority, to value this factory child or street urchin over that beadle or drunken aristocrat. But it is the double recognition that matters; that this evaluation is absolutely necessary and valuable, but that there is nothing, but nothing, we can take for granted in the process: not language, the self, or any source or ground of authority. This is a liberating insight, and there can be few (at least outside of educational establishments and examination halls) who have not felt liberated by these novels' overwhelming and continuing practical sense that the world is profoundly, radically open to change. It is also terrifying, something akin to the sensation we feel when Monks opens the trapdoor in the mill beneath Bumble's feet to reveal the abyss beneath. Bumble walks home that night 'looking nervously about him for hidden trap-doors'; it is a common feeling in reading Dickens, as it was, perhaps, in writing Dickens.[11]

This liberating terror stems perhaps from the work his texts do to make the powers of language and the world both familiar and strange to us. The board of workhouse guardians considers Oliver's career:

In great families, when an advantageous place cannot be obtained either in possession, reversion, remainder, or expectancy, for the young man who is growing up, it is a very general custom to send him to sea. The board, in imitation of so wise and salutary an example, took counsel together on the expediency of shipping off Oliver Twist, in some small trading vessel bound to a good unhealthy port. This suggested itself as the very best thing that could possibly be done to him: the probability being, that the skipper would flog him to death, in playful mood, some day after dinner, or would knock his brains out with an iron bar; both pastimes being, as is pretty generally known, very favourite and common recreations among gentlemen of that class.[12]

Here the power over Oliver is made strange, defamiliarized we might say, and registered, as so often in Dickens, by a joke, albeit an unusually black one, stemming from the gap between the brutal truth and the playful pastimes. But it is not only distanced and made strange, but also made unnaturally close and

[11] Dickens, *Oliver Twist*, 242.   [12] Ibid., 68.

familiar. This is true of so much of Dickens's writing: the search
for the odd angle or appositely unfamiliar detail—Mr Sowerberry, the undertaker, has a snuff-box in the form of 'an ingenious little model of a patent coffin'—brings the object close
for our inspection, like carnival laughter, but also pushes it
away so that we can understand and criticize it better, through
knowing that it can be different, radically so.[13] To put it alle-
gorically, his readers are in the web and off on the skyrocket
at the same time, and it is only language that can make this
happen. It is a quality that Chesterton catches well when he says
of Dickens's optimism:

> The pessimist can be enraged at evil. But only the optimist can be sur-
> prised at it. From the reformer is required a simplicity of surprise. He
> must have the faculty of a violent and virgin astonishment. It is not
> enough that he should think injustice distressing; he must think injus-
> tice *absurd*, an anomaly in existence, a matter less for tears than for a
> shattering laughter.[14]

'Violent and virgin astonishment' captures the sense both of the
absolute wrongness of certain human creations, like the workhouse and the blacking-factory, and of the knowledge that there
is no theory that could justify or ground that sense of wrongness; the belief that the world can be made known and familiar
by being made strange and uncanny; the possibility of wholesale change and the conviction that there is nothing in any
divine, transcendental or metaphysical order that prevents or
guarantees that change.

Before and between these episodes, between the blacking
factory and the work for the *Mirror of Parliament* and *The True
Sun*, are many other scenes, each of which could be taken for
some sort of beginning. Edgar Johnson begins his book with the
boy Dickens and his father seeing the great house on Gad's Hill,
where Dickens was later to live, Fred Kaplan with the burning
of his letters, Peter Ackroyd with his death, and Chesterton with
no scene at all but a distinction between the word 'vague' and
the word 'indefinable'.[15] We could have begun with Dickens's

[13] Ibid., 69.

[14] G. K. Chesterton, *Charles Dickens* (London: Methuen, 1906), 6–7.

[15] Edgar Johnson, *Charles Dickens: His Tragedy and Triumph* (New York: Simon
and Schuster, 1952), 3; Fred Kaplan, *Dickens: A Biography* (London: Hodder and
Stoughton, 1988), 17; Peter Ackroyd, *Dickens* (London: Sinclair Stevenson, 1990),
xi; Chesterton, *Charles Dickens*, 1.

grandmother telling tales at Crewe Hall, a female, oral lineage; with his absconding criminal grandfather or errant, indebted father. Or from his own life, his first published piece of fiction 'A Dinner at Poplar Walk', or before that, the little tragedy 'Misnar' which he writes as a child about a prince who utters wisdom when surrounded by monsters and demons.[16] Or his calling card 'Charles Dickens, Resurrectionist. In search of a Subject'.[17] But my choice is a third scene in Forster's *Life*, one both of writing and of labour, which stands behind and ahead of Dickens's later career. A small boy works in a cellar near Fleet Street; he later moves to a room near Covent Garden, sticking labels on pots of shoe blacking, prey to sudden cramps and pains in the side of his chest, his father a bankrupt in the Marshalsea Prison, his mother, when he has a chance to escape, 'warm for my being sent back'.[18] There are few major literary figures who have had what Forster calls such 'Hard Experiences in Boyhood', that will make him write so differently, so radically differently, both from his contemporaries and from most of his later critics about poverty and labour, childhood and families, about suffering and education. For they are a kind of education, these months in the blacking factory, a lesson in what we can call the insecurity of economic life under capitalism, or the prevalence of child labour in the late Regency period, or the appalling pressures that poverty (or profligacy, one can moralize it) can place upon a family. Or, in a different idiom, a story about envy and revenge; of an inadequate father, successful sister, and unforgiven mother. But they all seem inadequate to the writing that Dickens made of this *episode*, which was so much more than an episode, that word which derives from the Greek for a coming-in-besides, an entrance or a passage, in tragedy an underplot, in comedy an interlude. A singular event, which was nevertheless typical and representative; which was almost unspeakable, literally so, even to the closest members of

[16] 'A Dinner at Poplar Walk', later revised as 'Mr Minns and his Cousin', Charles Dickens, *Sketches by Boz and Other Early Papers 1833–1839*, ed. Michael Slater (London: Dent, 1994), 306–15. See also *The Dickensian*, 30 (1934), 3–10. For 'Misnar', see Forster, *The Life of Charles Dickens*, I, 8.

[17] J. C. Hotten, *Charles Dickens: The Story of his Life* (London: J. C. Hotten, 1870), 36–7, cited in Andrew Sanders, *Charles Dickens: Resurrectionist* (London: Macmillan, 1982), ix.

[18] Forster, *The Life of Charles Dickens*, I, 32.

his family, and yet which was so often written about that one foolishly sometimes wonders if every thread cannot be taken back, somehow, to a boy in a cellar labelling pots, in what seem absurdly prescient and symbolic names—Warren, Hungerford, the blacking factory—to this entrance or passage into this extraordinary writing, this interlude, this underplot.

If parliamentary reporting is a repetitive, secondary, painful business, of constraint and disciplined writing, how much more so is the labelling of pots. The same words—Warren's Blacking, 30, Hungerford Stairs, Strand—day after day, week after week, month upon month, a name and a label, a trademark which is hardly a trademark, swiped as it was from the 'better-known establishment' of Warren's Blacking, 30, Strand. This too in its own way is a scene of writing, the circulation of an imitative, misleading name on a label held on with string. But it is also a scene of labour, of the petty extraction of a small surplus value from a hungry child who fears he will never escape, part of the history of primitive accumulation and child labour, a 'speculation' to 'make a great business', as Dickens puts it in the 'Autobiographical Fragment', a story about shiny shoes and suffering.[19] Dickens's account of these years returns to scenes of eating or of not eating enough, and of journeying hungry to work, looking in shop windows at food. He writes about the work of reproducing himself in the most simple material sense: the need to arrive at the same place every day, to do the same work, having eaten enough food not to faint, in order to stick labels on pots. He tells of scenes of consumption, imaginary consumption for the most part, stories of a small boy dreaming of rich puddings, on the wrong side of the shop-window's glass. They are also stories of masculinity and enforced maturity, of a boy forced to behave like man ('I was so young and childish . . . to undertake the whole charge of my existence') and a man ('My old way home by the Borough made me cry, after my eldest child could speak') who says that 'I often forget in my dreams . . . that I am a man'.[20] They are also tales about haunting, about how the blacking factory haunts him, as it haunts all sorts of busy and abandoned corners of his writing: in a great house called the Warren in *Barnaby Rudge*, in blacking bottles

---

[19] Ibid., 20–1.   [20] Ibid., 24, 33, 23.

carrying medicine to a pauper family in *Oliver Twist* and holding a crippled boy's flowers in *Nicholas Nickleby*, in Sam Weller cleaning a pair of boots.

The concern with food and drink—the necessary bare fact of human subsistence in the brutal early nineteenth-century city—is embedded in a story about a consciousness constitutively haunted and about the strangeness of writing. For Chesterton, 'the whole secret' of Dickens's later work is held in an anecdote recounted in the 'Fragment' about a coffee shop in St Martin's Lane, where:

> there was an oval glass plate, with 'COFFEE-ROOM' painted on it, addressed towards the street. If I ever find myself in a very different kind of coffee-room now, but where there is such an inscription on glass, and read it backward on the wrong side 'MOOR-EEFFOC' (as I often used to then, in a dismal reverie), a shock goes through my blood.[21]

Of all things in the world, it is two words, spelt backwards, that return to haunt the adult writer, two words which through their simple capacity to be repeated can puncture the continuities of mature subjectivity and shock the blood. The return of this writing takes the adult Dickens back to the hungry reveries in which he lost himself as a child; the adult, as the child did, loses himself for a moment on the wrong side of the glass, a place like the tain of the mirror. The writing is inverted as well as repeated and 'MOOR-EEFFOC' are not really words at all, but neologisms, like the language of dreams or the unconscious. They appear and reappear in many coffee-rooms and texts—Dickens's, Forster's, Chesterton's—and are not subordinate to a particular place or a single moment of time. Chesterton is right to insist on the paradox: 'That wild word, "Moor Eeffoc" [*sic*] is the motto of all effective realism . . . the principle that the most fantastic thing of all is often the precise fact.'[22] Except that 'MOOR-EEFFOC' or 'Moor Eeffoc'—those exotic, eerie words—are not quite strange enough. No coffee-room would have read like that, but rather 'mooЯ-ɘɘʇʇoƆ' or 'MOOЯ-ƎƎꟻꟻOƆ', more strange, secret, and unreadable.

[21] Chesterton, *Charles Dickens*, 47, quoting Forster, *The Life of Charles Dickens*, I, 25.

[22] Chesterton, *Charles Dickens*, 47–8.

When Dickens tells the story of his family's time in prison, he includes a final scene of writing, a tale of his imprisoned father writing a petition to the King 'for the . . . boon of a bounty to the prisoners to drink His Majesty's health on His Majesty's forthcoming birthday':

To everybody in succession, Captain Porter said, "Would you like to hear it read?" If he weakly showed the least disposition to hear it, Captain Porter, in a loud sonorous voice, gave him every word of it. I remember a certain luscious roll he gave to such words as "Majesty— gracious Majesty—your gracious Majesty's unfortunate subjects—your Majesty's well-known munificence"—as if the words were something real in his mouth, and delicious to taste; my poor father meanwhile listening with a little of an author's vanity and contemplating (not severely) the spikes on the opposite wall. Whatever was comical in this scene, and whatever was pathetic, I sincerely believe I perceived in my corner, whether I demonstrated or not, quite as well as I should per- ceive it now. I made out my own little character and story for every man who put his name to the sheet of paper . . . I would rather have seen it than the best play ever played; and I thought about it after- wards, over the pots of paste-blacking, often and often.[23]

It is a childhood memory and trauma, held at bay and mastered by a narrative gift. It is also a scene of writing and authorship, which creates a document to be signed over and over again, with one author and many signatories. John Dickens writes a peti- tion which is also a paean to the king, a pathetic grandiloquent beggary. He watches 'with a little of an author's vanity'—from the wings as it were—this scene that is better than a play. His son watches too, from a corner, also writing or preparing to write. The whole scene is a performance, a little piece of theatre, barely consented to by an audience whose members are also authors or signers of a petition to a distant, brutal authority only a few years after Peterloo. Writing a dead letter to an absent authority in a collective act and performance in which the two authors wait in the wings, writing that seems 'delicious in the mouth, and good to taste', the most fantastic writing, reading, listening, performance imaginable. Repetition upon repetition; Captain Porter carrying all before him with a lus- cious roll. Something to be remembered in the blacking factory, never to be polished off.

[23] Quoted in Forster, *The Life of Charles Dickens*, I, 30–1.

II

There is a revealing letter from Dickens to one of his most atten-
tive early readers, George Henry Lewes, the philosopher, biographer, and critic.[24] Lewes was planning 'a treatise on the mind'
and was intrigued by a passage in *Oliver Twist*. Dickens replied
to Lewes's letter:

> I scarcely know what answer I can give you . . . I thought that passage
> a good one *when* I wrote it, certainly and I felt it strongly (as I do
> almost every word I put on paper) *while* I wrote, but how it came I
> can't tell. It came, like all my other ideas, such as they are, ready made
> to the point of my pen—and down it went. Draw your own conclu-
> sion and hug the theory closely.[25]

It is an interesting reply, and one that refuses to give Lewes what
he wanted, which was a theory or hypothesis of the mind. There
is a long history in the nineteenth century of attempting to found
both the practice of novel-writing and its criticism on the emerg-
ing science of psychology, an ambition that has perhaps done
more to damage Dickens's critical reputation than anything
else.[26] For if a novel cannot create psychologically plausible
characters, what else can it do? After Dickens's death, Lewes
wrote one of the more influential articles on the novelist's work,
in the idiom of a nascent psychology, comparing some of his
characters to 'frogs whose brains have been taken out for physiological purposes' and invoking madness, insanity, and hallu-
cination to read these texts in a framework of knowledge that
claims to be able to understand them.[27] Dickens's, he concludes,
was 'merely an animal intelligence . . . He never was and never
would have been a student.'[28] The dominant tone of Lewes's
article is caught in the phrase 'Psychologists will understand',

[24] Pilgrim, I, 402–4. On Lewes's 'half-jealousy of CD's "genius" and success', see
Pilgrim, V, 190n.

[25] Ibid., 403.

[26] On the connection between Victorian narrative and materialist sciences of the
self, see Jenny Bourne Taylor and Sally Shuttleworth (eds), *Embodied Selves: An
Anthology of Psychological Texts 1830–1890* (Oxford: Clarendon, 1998).

[27] George Henry Lewes, 'Dickens in Relation to Criticism', *Fortnightly Review*
(February 1872), 141–54, reprinted in Ford and Lane (eds), *The Dickens Critics*,
65.

[28] Ibid., 69.

and against this knowledge is set the merely popular reputation
of Dickens:

> readers to whom all the refinements of art and literature are as mean-
> ingless hieroglyphs, were at once laid hold of by the reproduction of
> their own feelings, their own experiences, their own prejudices, in the
> irradiating splendour of his imagination . . . Only the cultivated who
> are made fastidious by cultivation paused to consider the pervading
> commonness of his works, and remarked that they are wholly without
> glimpses of a nobler life; and that the writer presents an almost unique
> example of a mind of singular force in which, so to speak, sensations
> never passed into ideas.[29]

But psychologists and the fastidiously cultivated will not understand, cannot understand (at least within psychology), the
absolute, immaculately polite, refusal, which Dickens had
returned, bearing not a theory of the mind ('I am a very modest
man', he adds later in the letter), a justification, or speculation,
but strong feelings and the point of the pen, force and
inscription.

Dickens's fictions frequently question the easy confidence that
there are psychological processes which can be readily separated
from physiological ones, and thus make us doubt whether we
can take for granted the distinctions—between frogs and men,
sense and nonsense, sane and insane, incomprehensible hiero-
glyphs and scientific truth, animate and inanimate processes,
organic and mechanical life, cultivated and uncultivated people,
between 'sensations' and 'ideas', 'perception' and 'reflection',
'experience' and 'education'—that Lewes so confidently assumes. What if there is no psychology in the sense that Lewes
thinks there is? What if the human itself was also at stake in
these novels, not a given but a question? What if many of the
things Lewes and many of his successors have pushed around
in novel-criticism—character, plot, realism, plausibility, psychological development, the idea of language as expression,
the differences between past and present, human and
animal, life and death even—were all at stake, under question
or simply (or complexly) forgotten or erased in this extraordinary writing?

The passage that Lewes wrote to Dickens about is most likely

[29] Ibid.

to have been from chapter 34 of *Oliver Twist*, in which Dickens describes Oliver within 'a kind of sleep' in which 'we have a consciousness of all that is going on about us' and in which 'reality and imagination become so strangely blended that it is afterwards almost a matter of impossibility to separate the two', where, 'although our senses of touch and sight be for the time dead, yet our sleeping thoughts, and the visionary scenes that pass before us, will be influenced, and materially influenced, by the mere *silent presences* of some external object'.[30] It is one of the strangest episodes in the book, a passage between sleeping and waking, about senses that are dead and alive, an event that is neither and both real and imaginary, a visionary scene and a material influence, of writing and silent, speaking presences. In this state, Oliver hears (or does not hear, or hears and does not hear) Fagin and Monks at the window, who appear to him 'as firmly impressed upon his memory, as if . . . carved upon stone, and set before him from his birth'.[31] Having thus inscribed themselves, they instantly disappear, leaving no tracks or traces on the soil. Draw your own conclusions and hug the theory closely.

Lewes's partner George Eliot was similarly troubled by Dickens's writing, in particular its unwillingness or inability to conform to the norms of psychological complexity. In 'The Natural History of German Life' she writes:

> We have one great novelist who is gifted with the utmost power of rendering the external traits of our town population; and if he could give us their psychological character—their conceptions of life, and their emotions—with their same truth as their idiom and manner, his books would be the greatest contribution Art has ever made to the awakening of social sympathies. But . . . he scarcely ever passes from the humorous and external to the emotional and tragic, without becoming as transcendent in his unreality as he was a moment before in his artistic truthfulness.[32]

If it were not for Dickens's humour, she writes, his works would be:

> as noxious as Eugene Sue's idealized *proletaires* in encouraging the miserable fallacy that high morality and refined sentiment can grow out

---

[30] Dickens, *Oliver Twist*, 216–17.   [31] Ibid., 217.

[32] George Eliot, 'The Natural History of German Life', in Rosemary Ashton (ed.), *Selected Critical Writings* (Oxford: World's Classics, 1992), 264, first published in the *Westminster Review*, lxvi (July 1856), 51–79.

of harsh social relations, ignorance and want; or that the working classes are in a condition to enter at once into a millennial state of *altruism,* wherein everyone is caring for everyone else, and no one for himself.[33]

There is a good deal at stake in Eliot's essay, which is as programmatic in its way as her *Adam Bede* of the same decade.[34] Like many who have followed her, Eliot sees Dickens's portrayal of moral goodness as the great weakness of his fiction. For a criticism which identifies moral goodness with moral growth and subjectivity with psychological growth, Dickens's characters seem flat and unconvincing. It seems difficult or impossible to defend the Cheerybles' cheery cheer or Rose Maylie's asinine charm against Eliot's strictures. Yet in recent years it is precisely the ethical dimension of Dickens's writing that has appealed to contemporary philosophers.[35] For Richard Rorty, Dickens can be taken as a figure almost paradigmatic of 'the West' who can stand 'as a sort of anti-Heidegger', and for Martha Nussbaum, a novel such as *David Copperfield* can embody a 'more complicated' moral exploration of love and moral judgement than that of the canonical theorists—Hume, Kant, Adam Smith—of philosophical ethics.[36]

The virtues that Dickens's novels most admire—benevolence, reciprocity, selflessness, compassion, trust—are essentially collective ones that depend on the existence of a community of others in which to develop and flourish.[37] There are of course

---

[33] Ibid., 264–5.

[34] John Goode, 'Adam Bede', in Charles Swann (ed.), *Collected Essays of John Goode* (Keele: Keele University Press, 1995), 45–63, first published in Barbara Hardy (ed.), *Critical Essays on George Eliot* (London: Routledge, 1971), 275–92.

[35] Richard Rorty, *Contingency, Irony, and Solidarity* (Cambridge: Cambridge University Press, 1989), 145–50; Martha Nussbaum, 'Steerforth's Arm: Love and the Moral Point of View', in *Love's Knowledge: Essays on Philosophy and Literature* (Oxford: Oxford University Press, 1996), 335–65.

[36] Richard Rorty, *Essays on Heidegger and Others: Philosophical Papers*, vol. 2 (Cambridge: Cambridge University Press, 1991), 68; Nussbaum, *Love's Knowledge*, 338.

[37] On communitarianism, see, for example, Alasdair MacIntyre, *After Virtue: A Study of Moral Theory* (2nd edition, London: Duckworth, 1985). On the nineteenth-century novel and community, see Raymond Williams, *The English Novel from Dickens to Lawrence* (London: Chatto, 1970), 11: 'I would choose one bearing as central: the exploration of community: the substance and meaning of community.' For a more nuanced account, see Raymond Williams, *Keywords* (London: Fontana, 1976), 65–6, and the important reservations in Raymond Williams, *Politics and Letters: Interviews with New Left Review* (London: Verso, 1979), 119: 'community . . . is unusable as a term that enables one to make distinctions . . . It was when I realised that no one ever used "community" in a hostile sense that I saw how dangerous it was.'

many examples of individual virtue in Dickens's novels—of courage and perseverance, for example—but they take their significance from the much wider and communal ethical action of which they are a part. There is an assumption, almost an insistence, on the socially embedded nature of human life in these novels, on the social nature of human identity and the necessity of communal and public goods. The community of the novels is not merely a fictional one, however, for the novels try to mobilize a wider community of readers to share their experience of hope and fear, compassion and trust. This is more than a simple belief in civic responsibility and virtue; it is a commitment to essentially collective moral values, in particular the need for reciprocity, trust, and solidarity across and between individuals and classes divided by wealth and class. Such a commitment to community does not by any means exclude a deep interest in the life of individual characters or subjects. Nor does it try to disguise the different opportunities or fates that communities grant to their members, or the cruel way communities can behave—Oliver Twist is a member of a community at the workhouse, for example. Nor does it discount the exclusions, scapegoatings, and expulsions which communities carry out and by which they constitute themselves.[38] Dickens's fiction is repeatedly drawn to figures—like Smike in *Nicholas Nickleby*, or Barnaby Rudge—who are at or beyond the margins of the communities of the novel they inhabit. Often the novels present a testing of communal values and goods, through limit-cases of exclusion and transgression. In particular, they are interested in that essentially social transgression: the breach of solidarity called crime.

Yet moral life in general and ethical goodness in particular in Dickens's early fiction are often thought to be a peculiarly simple-minded or unconvincing affair, belonging as they do almost entirely to characters who possess a natural benevolence. The Cheerybles in *Nicholas Nickleby*, Brownlow in *Oliver Twist*, and Mrs Jarley and the schoolmaster in *The Old Curiosity Shop* all seem motivated by an unthinking goodwill towards the heroes of their respective novels. There is nothing reflexive

---

[38] On scapegoating, see René Girard, *The Scapegoat* (Baltimore: Johns Hopkins University Press, 1986), and Michiel Heyns, *Expulsion and the Nineteenth-Century Novel: The Scapegoat in English Realist Fiction* (Oxford: Clarendon, 1994).

about their goodness, nor is it motivated by religious or other principles.[39] Convictions or beliefs, where they exist, seem to follow the benevolence rather than cause it. Nor is the benevolence altered or moderated very much by experience or moral ideas. It is not a world of moral choice. This is in sharp contrast to Kantian ethics, for example, where benevolence is seen as intrinsically inferior to principled virtue: benevolence is an 'adoptive virtue' which, although 'beautiful and charming', does not compare with the 'sublime and venerable' nature of the 'genuine virtues'.[40] For Kant, the weakness of benevolence is its mutability and variation. It is not to be relied on, whereas virtue based on principle is not based on whim, and is not subject to change. The stories Dickens tells move to very different conclusions. Benevolence never fails in early Dickens. The Cheerybles do not get bored with Nicholas, and Brownlow does not find a more picturesque orphan than Oliver to patronize. That does not mean that benevolence is infallible—the Maylies do not save Nancy, and nothing can help Little Nell—but it is not fickle. Benevolence is not a caprice in these novels, but a trait so strongly engrained that it can never fail of itself. It may not prevail, but it will not fail.

Acting on moral principle is, by contrast, a much more tricky affair in early Dickens. Almost anyone who expresses a moral principle, particularly the clergy, is a hypocrite of one sort or another. Although the specifically Christian ethical virtues, such as faith and piety, are an ingredient in Dickens's work, they play a role subordinate to benevolent and communitarian virtues. Those who claim to know and speak for the moral law are invariably selfish and egotistical. Seth Pecksniff, simultaneously the most morally articulate and Nietzschean character of these books, is also the most hypocritical, and Scrooge, when he reforms, is not made to obey a principle but to become benevolent. These may appear naive characterizations, but it is better to think of benevolence as a *critical* idea in these

---

[39] On the relation between benevolence and evangelical thought, see Boyd Hilton, *The Age of Atonement: The Influence of Evangelicalism in Social and Economic Thought* (Oxford: Clarendon, 1988), 279.

[40] Immanuel Kant, *Observations on the Feelings of the Beautiful and the Sublime*, trans. John T. Goldthwait (Berkeley: University of California Press, 1960), 61.

novels, as the sign of a determinate absence in a social order or moral practice. In particular, Dickens's use of it questions the dominant ethical programme of the nineteenth century, utilitarianism, which sought precisely the calculative consistency that the novels so distrust, and the subordination of metaphor and figure (which Dickens sometimes calls 'Fancy' but is much more than that) to the norms of its reason. Against the commensurability, aggregation and maximizing principles of utility, the novels oppose the virtues of situated, pragmatic, and benevolent moral action.[41] More importantly, they produce disturbing and uncanny textual-moral effects, which are not reducible either to the felicific calculus or the pragmatic benevolence that opposes it, through a figurative, paradoxical, and hyperbolic language, a discourse 'from outside logical space' which is also a call to 'change one's language and one's life'.[42]

For the majority of at least one generation of critics, George Eliot's remarks appeared to be an unanswerable criticism of Dickens, not least because of their claim to a 'scientific' knowledge, confirmed and tempered by her remarkable fictions. Knowing through such writing that there is a human psychology, and something of what that psychology is, not finding anything similar in the works of Dickens, his novels must consequently give us knowledge only of 'idiom and manners'. In one way it is impossible or foolish to try to adjudicate this dispute, the differences resting as they do on two of the most different and impressive bodies of prose fiction in the language. It seems enough to be pleased that the century or the literature can hold such different talents. Except that Eliot's objection to Dickens's morality is also a *political* one, which raises at its heart the question of the causes and possibilities of social change. For Eliot, 'high morality and refined sentiment' cannot grow out of harsh social relations, and Dickens is foolish to pretend they can. In this century, the question has been asked in a different idiom in two forms: what links ideologies or popular culture and their economic base?

[41] See Martha Nussbaum, *Poetic Justice: The Literary Imagination and Public Life* (Beacon: New York, 1996), 14.
[42] Rorty, *Essays on Heidegger and Others*, 13.

what are the possible agencies to change or destroy the brutal-
ities of industrial capitalism, or (to use the words of Eliot, which
she takes from the two apparitions who appear to Scrooge)
'ignorance and want'?

Eliot makes Dickens sound both like an impossible dreamer
and like Karl Marx. Her description of the implicit claim made
in these novels—that the working people they depict seem immi-
nently able to enter 'a millennial state of *altruism*, where everyone is caring for everyone else, and no one for himself'—is close
to the Marx for whom it was not only possible but necessary
for workers to create such a society. Several later critics have
argued that this is indeed the case and that Marx makes explicit
in political terms what Eliot sees as implicit in Dickens's fictions:
that there is a potential for radical social change for the better
through the self-activity of working people. Macaulay, for
example, found 'a sullen socialism' in *Hard Times*, and from a
very different political position Edwin Pugh claimed Dickens as
'a Socialist without knowing it'.[43] For George Gissing, Dickens's
work displayed 'in essence a *class* feeling', and for Shaw, he
was an unwitting 'revolutionist', to be classed with Marx.[44] Yet
a simple assimilation of Dickens's work to an already-known
socialism is not really possible or desirable, and Eliot's charges
against Dickens—of idealization, millennialism, and altruism—
are distrusted by Marx as much as by Eliot.[45] Marx was,
though, an inveterate reader of Dickens, who 'increasingly
joins Shakespeare in transforming, illuminating and carica-
turing Marx's world'.[46] Of passages in Marx on 'Pecksniff-stil',

[43] 'One excessively touching, heart-breaking passage, and the rest sullen social-
ism.' T. B. Macaulay, *Journal*, 12 August 1854, printed in G. O. Trevelyan (ed.),
Life and Letters of Lord Macaulay (London: Longman, 1959), 614, cited in Philip
Collins (ed.), *Dickens: the Critical Heritage*, 300.

[44] George Gissing, *Charles Dickens: A Critical Study* (London: Gresham, 1902),
2. George Bernard Shaw, 'Preface' to the Limited Editions Club edition of *Great
Expectations* (London, 1937), reprinted in Stanley Weintraub (ed.), *Bernard Shaw's
Nondramatic Literary Criticism* (Lincoln: University of Nebraska Press, 1972),
49–65: 57. For Gissing's relation to Dickens, see also John Goode, *George Gissing:
Ideology and Fiction* (London: Vision, 1978), 13–40.

[45] For Marx's views on Eugene Sue, see Lee Baxandall and Stefan Morawski (eds),
Marx and Engels on Literature and Art (New York: International General, 1974),
77–9, and S. S. Prawer, *Karl Marx and World Literature* (Oxford: Oxford
University Press, 1976), 86–102.

[46] Prawer, *Karl Marx and World Literature*, 203.

S. S. Prawer has written ' "Read your Boz", they would seem to say to their readers, "and you will understand".'[47]

George Eliot's work of writing took her to pessimistic conservatism; Dickens's to a continuing, if contradictory, radical anger. His writing, which almost exactly spans the Reform Acts of 1832 and 1867, is often close to that of contemporary radical discourses.[48] In the idiom of biography, this is relatively straightforward to narrate. Dickens the public man was sympathetic to political reform, hostile to the aristocracy as a class, anticlerical, impatient with parliamentary delay, and sympathetic to the poor and destitute. He was thought to be a radical by his contemporaries and thought himself one. His journalism was mainly in Whig or Radical publications such as the *True Sun* or *The Examiner* and he 'participated with zest in the Tory-bashing that characterised the [*Morning*] *Chronicle*'.[49] He was as hostile to class-based or class-interested politics, whether bourgeois, aristocratic, or proletarian, as to utilitarian philosophical radicalism.[50] Particularly sharp anger was reserved for the magistracy and that 'conjunction of evangelical retribution and utilitarian optimism' that was so strongly in evidence among the framers of the New Poor Law.[51] Although the owner of *Bentley's Miscellany*, the first magazine he edited, was a Tory, Dickens's main personal allegiances were to the aristocratic Whigs who

[47] Prawer, *Karl Marx and World Literature*, 174. The most important of Marx's tributes to Dickens is a passage from 'The English Middle Class' of 1854, praising the 'splendid brotherhood [*sic*] of fiction-writers in England, whose graphic and eloquent pages have issued to the world more political and social truths than have been uttered by all the professional politicians, publicists and moralists put together': Baxandall and Morawski (eds), *Marx and Engels on Literature and Art*, 106.

[48] See Michael Slater, Introduction to Charles Dickens, *The Amusements of the People and Other Papers, Essays and Reviews 1834–51* (London: Dent, 1996), xi–xxiii, and Norris Pope, *Dickens and Charity* (London: Macmillan, 1978), 53–4. More generally on Dickens and contemporary radicalism, see Forster, *The Life of Charles Dickens*, I, 163–5, and Graham Storey, 'Dickens in his Letters: The Regress of the Radical', in Joanne Shattock (ed.), *Dickens and Other Victorians* (London: Macmillan, 1988).

[49] Slater, Introduction to Dickens, *The Amusements of the People*, xiv.

[50] He is, for example, willing to share a platform with both Disraeli and Cobden at Manchester in 1843. See K. J. Fielding (ed.), *The Speeches of Charles Dickens* (Oxford: Clarendon, 1960), 44–52.

[51] 'The object of this series [*Master Humphrey's Clock*] . . . would be to keep a special look-out upon the magistrates in town and country, and never to leave those worthies alone': Forster, *The Life of Charles Dickens*, I, 113. See also Hilton, *The Age of Atonement*, 245.

returned to power in the 1830s.[52] As the last of the Holland House lions, he shared their theatricality and populism, as well as their opposition to Benthamism and sense of responsibility to the popular classes. He had a particular affection for Lord John Russell, the Prime Minister who carried through the First Reform Act and gave the Tolpuddle Martyrs first-class passages home.[53]

Political radicalism at this time was placed at the 'confluence of . . . Benthamism, socialism, Mazzinian nationalism, anti-clericalism, and Whiggery' within an essentially pre-democratic system without modern party allegiances.[54] It is a mobile space and the place of Dickens's writings within it is uncertain and fluid. Biography and history as genres scarcely touch the ways in which his work displaces, exceeds, and transforms radical discourses of this and later periods.[55] The fact that his contemporaries and followers often felt it necessary to qualify his radicalism by one or another epithet—sentimental, unphilosophic, sullen—points to something (which may be everything) in his writing that goes beyond a tidy ascription to a known political position.[56] Indeed, the history of later attempts to appropriate this body of writing to one or another political programme or to domesticate it within the pantheons of liberalism

---

[52] Kathryn Chittick, *Dickens and the 1830s* (Cambridge: Cambridge University Press, 1990), 74.

[53] Peter Mandler, *Aristocratic Government in the Age of Reform: Whigs and Liberals 1830–1852* (Oxford: Clarendon, 1990), 82. Of Russell, Dickens said that there was 'no man in England whom I more respect in his public capacity, whom I love more in his private capacity': Dickens, speech at banquet in his honour at St George's Hall, Liverpool, 10 April 1869, in Fielding (ed.), *The Speeches*, 388–9.

[54] Miles Taylor, *The Decline of British Radicalism 1847–1860* (Oxford: Clarendon, 1995), 13.

[55] The accounts of radicalism signed in Dickens's name are comic. In his childhood, he heard of 'the existence of a terrible banditti called the *radicals*, whose principles were that the prince regent wore stays, that no one had a right to any salary; and that the army and navy ought to be put down': Forster, *Life of Charles Dickens*, I, 10. 'The Boarding House' in *Sketches by Boz* includes John Evenson who 'was a thorough radical and used to attend a variety of public meetings, for the express purpose of finding fault with everything that was proposed', 294, and 'The Parlour Orator' contains Mr Rogers, a radical and a '[w]eak-pated dolt', 288.

[56] 'Sullen': see Macaulay, above, note 43; 'a sort of unphilosophic Radical': Shaw, 'Hard Times', in Weintraub (ed.), *Bernard Shaw's Nondramatic Literary Criticism*, 57; 'sentimental': Walter Bagehot, 'Charles Dickens', *National Review*, 7 (October 1858), reprinted in R. H. Horne (ed.), *Literary Studies* (London: Longmans, Green, 1911), II, 157.

and socialism is one of repeated failure.[57] Orwell described Dickens's work as 'almost exclusively moral', but it is more than this, as it implicates and undoes the distinctions between the moral, the political, and the textual.[58] As Chesterton put it: 'he was not only larger than any of the old factions he satirised; he was larger than any of our great social schools that have gone forward since he died.'[59]

The most interesting of the more directly political texts of Dickens's early years is 'Sunday Under Three Heads'.[60] In 1836 Sir Andrew Agnew had introduced a bill to ban Sunday travelling, recreation, and work. Dickens, under the name of Timothy Sparks, writes a hostile and funny criticism of the bill in a pamphlet which he ironically dedicates to the Bishop of London, a supporter of Agnew. Dickens's/Sparks's principal objection is that the bill for Sabbath observance 'is directed exclusively . . . against the amusements and recreations of the poor', that the life of the wealthy and powerful will be unaffected, while that of the poor will suffer enormously.[61] It is often the case that, as Stallybrass and White have argued, 'participation in the public sphere . . . demanded a withdrawal from popular culture and its translation into negative and even phobic representations', but the opposite is the case here.[62] It is an issue and a bill about the law and religious faith, but Dickens/Sparks takes his stand on another ground, on a defence of those terms that chime through the text: 'pleasure . . . desire . . . happiness . . . cheer . . . affection'. It is a defence of popular life and pleasure, and of the needs of the poor to eat and drink and be merry. The 'Three

---

[57] 'The pantheon of Liberalism and radicalism was the pantheon of socialism—Dickens, Bunyan, Carlyle, Ruskin': Patrick Joyce, *Visions of the People: Industrial England and the Question of Class, 1848–1914* (Cambridge: Cambridge University Press, 1991), 77. On Dickens as a socialist, see T. A. Jackson, *Charles Dickens: The Progress of a Radical* (New York: Haskell House, 1971, first published 1937) and Edwin Pugh, *Charles Dickens: The Apostle of the People* (London: New Age Press, 1908).
[58] George Orwell, 'Charles Dickens', in Sonia Orwell and Ian Angus (eds), *The Collected Essays, Journalism, and Letters Volume One: An Age Like This 1920–1940* (London: Secker and Warburg, 1968), 416.
[59] G. K. Chesterton, *The Victorian Age in Literature* (London: Williams and Norgate, 1913), 123.
[60] Charles Dickens, 'Sunday Under Three Heads', in *Sketches by Boz*, 475–99.
[61] Ibid., 486.
[62] Peter Stallybrass and Allon White, *The Politics and Poetics of Transgression* (London: Routledge, 1986), 99.

Heads' of the pamphlet—'As it is', 'As Sabbath bills would make it', 'As it might be made'—are concerned with possible futures which can promise an everyday happiness. Dickens defends the rights, the political rights, of those he calls 'pleasurers' (a term that dates from only a little earlier in the decade), which describes those people who take pleasure but also add to it, just as Dick Swiveller will add to life when he promises to become a 'liverer'.[63]

In 1841, in the middle of the 'longest and worst depression of the nineteenth century',[64] a time of terrible unemployment and severe political partisanship, Dickens wrote a song, 'The Fine Old English Gentleman, to be said or sung at all Conservative Dinners':

I'll sing you a new ballad and I'll warrant it first-rate,
Of the days of that old gentleman who had that old estate:
When they spent the public money at a bountiful old rate
On ev'ry mistress, pimp and scamp at ev'ry noble gate,
    In the fine old English Tory times;
    Soon may they come again!

The good old laws were garnished well with gibbets, whips and
    chains,
With fine old English penalties and fine old English pains,
With rebel heads and seas of blood once hot in rebel veins:
For all these things were requisite to guard the rich old gains
    Of the fine old English Tory times.
    Soon may they come again!

The story continues through seven more stanzas, listing the historical miseries of England—spies, starvation, and massacres—and ends not, as might be expected, with a contrast between the past and present, but with the continuing threat of fine old English pains re-appearing in the present and future:

The bright old day now dawns again; the cry runs through the
    land,
In England there shall be—dear bread. In Ireland—sword and
    brand!

[63] Charles Dickens, *The Old Curiosity Shop*, ed. Elizabeth M. Brennan (Oxford: World's Classics, 1998), 49.

[64] Jonathan Parry, *The Rise and Fall of Liberal Government in Victorian Britain* (Yale: Yale University Press, 1993), 141.

>And poverty, and ignorance, shall swell the rich and grand,
>So, rally round the rulers with a gentle iron hand,
>   Of the fine old English Tory days;
>   Hail to the coming time![65]

'The Fine Old English Gentleman' is concerned, as many of Dickens's texts are, with the threat or promise of the return of things from the past that were thought to be safely buried, a threat here held and mastered by the ironic invocation: 'Hail to the coming time!' In 1839, for example, Dickens was particularly struck by the discovery of a skeleton in a Strand sewer, ironically suggesting it to Forster as 'a famous subject for an illustration by George [Cruikshank]'.[66] Such an interest in returnings, revisitings, and recyclings are often thought of either as gothic survivals, imaginative quirks in an over-imaginative author, or as a figuring of psychological or unconscious processes, a way of talking about the return of the repressed. But, as 'The Fine Old English Gentleman' suggests, they have as much to do with social and political processes as psychological ones. Marx famously likened political thought and activity to the process of being haunted in *The Communist Manifesto*, where communism is 'a spectre haunting Europe', and in the opening to *The Eighteenth Brumaire* he figures historical memory and political activity as a matter of haunting, dressing up, and farce.[67] Dickens shared these interests in the farcical nature of political and historical processes, the politics of old wardrobes and the multiple hauntings of the present by the past. We are not free from such hauntings, farces, and old clothes today, and have seen in recent years how effectively some varieties of political tyranny and folly have re-animated themselves and found new spirits to haunt, new figures to dress.

A question remains in reading these novels, of the future of Dickens's writing. This often becomes the theme of the eternal life of Dickens's fiction and the passage of his characters into immortality, but it is possible to think of it differently.[68] If the

[65] Quoted in Forster, *Life of Charles Dickens*, I, 163–5.

[66] Pilgrim, I, 582.

[67] Karl Marx and Friedrich Engels, *The Communist Manifesto*, with an introduction by A. J. P. Taylor (Harmondsworth: Penguin, 1967), 78. Marx, 'The Eighteenth Brumaire of Louis Bonaparte', in Fernbach (ed.), *Surveys from Exile*, 146–9.

[68] Chesterton, 'A Note on the Future of Dickens', in *Charles Dickens*, 288–97.

novels outstrip Lewes's psychology, lie beyond the reach of
Eliot's natural history, and resist attempts to give them a safe
home or destiny on the map of criticism, it is because they continue to be radical in quite other ways, through a representa-
tional radicalism.[69] Reading Dickens's last book, Edith Simcox,
author of *Natural Law* and 'devoted admirer of George Eliot',
wrote:

The first thing that strikes a reader is the absence of all familiar boundaries and landmarks: class distinctions are ignored or obliterated;
different ages and sexes assume the prerogative of their opposites;
people transact incongruous business in impossible places; and with
it there is no apparent consciousness that the social order is confused
and inverted. It is still more curious to watch this levelling tendency applied to matters of intellect . . . In such books as *Dombey*
and *Martin Chuzzlewit* we seem lost in a millennium of illogical
goodwill.[70]

Simcox here links Dickens's offences against good social order,
its inversion and confusion, with offences against plausibility
and good mimesis. His fiction, for Simcox, exists in a space
without boundaries or clear limits, in which social class (but
also classification in general) is obliterated, and sexual difference and temporal ordering are inverted. The texts cannot be
assimilated to any logic, congruity, or order, either in social or
mimetic terms, and do not obey any law, either 'natural' or
aesthetic. They are both heterotopic and heteronomian. It is an
extremely accurate account of some of these texts' virtues,
which are, for Simcox, mere vice.

   The chance is that these writings bear not something less than
psychologically coherent, complexly motivated, realistic individuals existing within coherent plots, but something more:
the signs of complex, popular hopes, which stretch our notions
of psychology, aesthetics, and politics alike. Chesterton writes
about the character of Toots, Dr Blimber's senior pupil in
Dombey and Son, a character, as he puts it, 'of all conceivable
human figures, the most futile and the most dull':

[69] Terry Eagleton describes it as 'a veritable traffic-jam of competing fictional
modes . . . which permits realism no privileged status': *Criticism and Ideology: A
Study in Marxist Literary Theory* (London: Verso, 1978), 126–7.
[70] 'H. Lawrenny' [Edith Simcox] from a review in *The Academy*, ii (22 October
1870) 1–3, reprinted in Collins (ed.), *Dickens: The Critical Heritage*, 545–7.

Dickens does not alter Toots in any vital point. The thing he does alter is us. He makes us lively where we were bored, kind where we were cruel, and above all free for an universal human laughter where we were cramped in a small competition about that sad and solemn thing, the intellect.[71]

Writing for Chesterton here is not something that depicts or represents known psychological or other qualities or processes in the world or the self, but a force that remakes them at each moment in a work of radical freedom, even if we must add that freedom is never universal, not always laughing, and not at all human. This force enables the novels to figure a justice beyond that of the law, an opening to difference and to the other in and through writing. This is often and too readily called compassion for other people, but is much greater than this, and does not eschew or fear emotion—no, not tears or rage or anything.

III

Dickens was well known as a conjuror in his lifetime, an accomplished amateur magician. But he used the word in a very different sense in his will, that first piece of posthumous writing. After remembering Ellen Ternan, making his legacies, and saying the things his lawyers had told him were 'necessary to the plain objects of this my Will', he wrote: 'I conjure my friends on no account to make me the subject of any monument, memorial, or testimonial whatever.'[72] Here he is using the word 'conjure' in its more archaic sense, meaning to adjure or implore. It comes from the French 'conjurer', meaning 'to plot or conspire'. All reading is a sort of conspiracy or conjuration between writers and readers and Dickens's will here conjures a particular kind of compact between them. He clearly wants to avoid some of the grosser excesses of Victorian public mourning, a distaste for which runs throughout his work. Yet his posthumous injunction cannot be held simply to this sense. Each of the words he uses—monument, testimonial, memorial—is at least double in meaning, referring both to something written

---

[71] Chesterton, *Charles Dickens*, 257–9.
[72] In Forster, *The Life of Charles Dickens*, II, 422.

and not written. 'Testimonial' comes from the Latin for 'witness', and signifies a letter or writing that bears witness to one's qualifications, as well as a subscription or a gift from the public. A memorial can be either a written memoir or a statue, and a monument is a document as well as a sepulchre. On the one hand, Dickens is determined to be his own testimonial, and no one else can do it for him. The will insists that there should be no repayment: his writing is a free gift and his name needs no external support, statue, or fund to keep it alive. On the other hand, it insists on appropriate forms of repayment and remembrance: through the memory of friends, upon 'my published works', and to a name which is to be inscribed 'in plain English letters . . . without . . . addition' on the tomb.[73] These are all forms of memorial, testament, and monument. Credit must and must not come back to Dickens's writing and to his name, which must and must not be preserved by an exterior prop or support. This is the oath to which his friends are conjured and the double bind through which readers have passed ever since: both to memorialize and not to memorialize Dickens's writing and name. Criticism is testimonial, memorial, and monumental; it is both demanded and forbidden.

Henry James met Dickens twice and wrote a review of *Our Mutual Friend* in 1865, the year of his own first signed tale and a few years before his first novel. It is written before Dickens's death, yet is haunted by the possibility that Dickens may have already in some way passed away. The book, writes James, is 'poor with the poverty . . . of permanent exhaustion' and the characters are 'lifeless, flat, mechanical'.[74] This is a death that precedes death, a writing that continues after the final exhalation, like a machine. Throughout the review James bases his case on a set of oppositions—between spirit and letter, life and death, the natural and the artificial, the true and the false, the spontaneous and the forced, the deep and the superficial, and many more—which are familiar from a long history of aesthetic theory. The novel contains, writes James, 'the letter of his [Dickens's] humour without the spirit' and the book itself is 'so

---

[73] Ibid., 421.
[74] Henry James, 'Charles Dickens', in *Literary Criticism* (Cambridge: Cambridge University Press / Library of America, 1984), 853, first published in *Nation*, I (21 December 1865), 786–7.

intensely *written*, so little seen, known or felt'.[75] It is an important review, which will grow in stature as James's own reputation rises and which is marked by a deep anxiety about the practice of writing in which Dickens is engaged. The invocation of these oppositions at this moment in the aspiring novelist's career demonstrates the depth of the challenge with which Dickens's final novel confronts him, and indeed the entire conception of criticism to which James became such a distinguished contributor. A school writing master in 'Sentiment', one of Dickens's earliest sketches, later collected in *Sketches by Boz*, is called Mr Dadson, and Dickens liked to parody the distinctive speech of his own father.[76] When he does so, his style sounds like nothing so much as that of late Henry James: 'We are very sorry to lose the benefit of his advice—or, as my father would say, to be deprived, to a certain extent, of the concomitant advantages, whatever they may be, resulting from his medical skill, such as it is, and his professional attendance, in so far as it may be considered.'[77] This is more than coincidence, for James overcame (at least in part) his indebtedness or anxiety of influence towards Dickens by writing his fiction in an idiom which in its endlessly circumlocutory politesse comes increasingly to resemble that of both Dickens's father and Wilkins Micawber from *David Copperfield*. Micawber is, of course, both Copperfield's substitute father and the most famous fictional portrait of Dickens's own father. In style at least, James, like Hamlet in Stephen Dedalus's account, attempted to become his own fictional father's fictional father, another writing master, another Dad's son.

Nearly half a century later, near the end of his writing career, James returned to the topic of Dickens, which was so much more than a topic for him, to pay back in different form the debt he owed. In his autobiographical *A Small Boy and Others*, James writes of the performances of Dickens's plays he had witnessed as a child, and particularly those of Micawber (who else?) and Smike, that large boy among others.[78] James's account

---

[75] James, 'Charles Dickens', 853.   [76] Dickens, 'Sentiment', in *Sketches by Boz*, 322.
[77] Pilgrim, IV, 243–4.
[78] Henry James, *A Small Boy and Others* (London: Macmillan, 1913), 118–22. See also pp. 153–6.

testifies to the strangeness of memory, and to 'the force of the Dickens imprint' (which both was and was not a matter of print) upon him.[79] There is no one scene of revelation, no hushed, awed first reading, or a simple progress from early rapture to more just discrimination in James's account. Nothing comes directly to him: all is relayed, diverted, repeated, and indirect.

The nearest thing to a primal scene of reading Dickens is the well-known anecdote of the seven-year-old James, who, having been sent to bed, hid below a table to listen to the reading aloud of the first chapters of the newly published *David Copperfield*. Overhearing young David's travails with the Murdstones, James burst into audible sobs and was promptly 'banished'.[80] The identification in this retrospect of the seventy-year-old public man is clear: tearful, banished David; tearful, banished Henry. James reaches for paradox and more than paradox to express what he elsewhere called 'the immense pressure of Dickens', to register the force and significance of his memories of these Dickens readings and actings, representations of representations of representations, memories which seem to pre-exist memory.[81] 'The great actuality of the current imagination' is his repeated characterization of Dickens, both the thing that is there, actually there, but also a potential power, something latent or in reserve.[82] The territory of criticism when it comes to Dickens is 'both sacred and boundless', a little grove and a space beyond measure in which 'the presence and power' of Dickens's writing 'warn us off even while they hold'.[83] When he reads Dickens 'today', writes James, 'I simply stop: not holding off, that is, but holding on'.[84] He reads by not reading Dickens, possessing him without possession. The writing, he writes, has given him a 'ply' that is 'ineffaceable', a textual folding in which James finds himself enfolded and which seems to belong neither to the past nor the present, neither an inside nor an outside.[85] It is a property simultaneously of the texts, his own mind, and the 'contagious consciousness' of the time, like a disease from which he cannot escape infection or mark the

[79] Ibid., 122.   [80] Ibid., 124.

[81] Henry James, 'London Notes', July 1897, in *Literary Criticism*, 1402, first published in *Harper's Weekly*, XLI (31 July 1897), 754.

[82] James, *A Small Boy and Others*, 126.

[83] Ibid., 122.   [84] Ibid., 123.   [85] Ibid., 124.

necessary distance by which a critical judgement or apprecia-
tion could ever take or have taken place.[86] Dickens, writes
James with a generosity not without reserve, 'did too much for
us surely ever to leave us free—free of judgement, free of
reaction, even should we care to be, which heaven forbid: he
laid his hand on us in a way to undermine as in no other
case the power of detached appraisement.'[87] James returns once
more to the paradoxical figure of being held or bound by
Dickens, in which to be touched is to be undermined, to be
held is to be warned off, and to hold on is to hold off. They are
quite beautiful pages, this registering of the Dickens imprint by
James, as well as the ruin of an aesthetic which is not James's
alone.

James registered in writing, as many have done before and
since, his debt and bond to Dickens. There were other bonds
in Dickens's childhood, documents which bound his father to
repay money he had borrowed, and imprisoned him when he
did not.[88] Such deeds were also both to free and bind the
child and the adult Dickens, and to become a central concern
of his fiction. Dickens's father was, notoriously, always getting
into debt. He did this by spending money he had not got and
signing his name to various bills and promissory notes, which
he often found impossible to repay. He made promises to the
future, affirmed and signed in his own name (and later in his
son's name) in order to gain credit, which in time became
debt for which he was responsible and could be summoned
before the law and punished. Debt, credit, the bond, the name,
the signature, and the law are also central matters of the many
economies of reading and criticism, and readers and critics of
Dickens have been paying their debts and gaining credit in
various ways for many years. It would be an impossible task
to map the many promises, deeds, and signatures by which
these economies have been sustained. The exfoliation of
Dickens's works into what is called modernity—into Joyce and
Van Gogh, T. S. Eliot and Kafka, Nabokov and Adorno,
Beckett, Marx, Freud, and countless other readings, adaptations, plagiarisms, and expropriations—multiply and dissemi-

[86] James, A Small Boy and Others, 124.   [87] Ibid., 122–3.
[88] Forster, The Life of Charles Dickens, 10.

nate the texts, the debt, and the name in an interminable mourning and bond.[89]

There are, of course, other positions to adopt in relation to this work and this debt: of creditor, inheritor, and, often enough, of custodian and enforcer of the law. Criticism often attempts to regulate the proper course and destinations of texts, and the diffuse circulations of Dickens's writing, the strangeness of both its 'internal' and 'external' economies, is for some readers the provocation to a more or less simple regulation or punishment. 'Dickens', his ghost or his name, is arraigned for lacking credit or credibility, for breaking this or that fictional or mimetic law, for tangling up his plots and making promises he could not keep. His readers too are disciplined or punished for being uncritical or naive, for giving him credit where none is deserved. These charges, which bring Dickens's works before this or that tribunal, this or that scene of judgement—for characters who seem too flat or too large, for plots that seem too restless or disordered, for generic hybridity, for hyperbolic and paradoxical language, for domesticating, depoliticizing or disciplining their readers—claim to speak in the name and with the title of a certain law.[90] It is a law

[89] James Joyce, 'The Centenary of Charles Dickens', in L. Berrone (ed.), *James Joyce in Padua* (New York: Random, 1977), 33–7, and Jay Clayton, 'Londublin: Dickens's London in Joyce's Dublin', *Novel: A Forum on Fiction*, 28, 3 (Spring 1995), 327–42; *The Complete Letters of Vincent Van Gogh*, trans. J. van Goch-Bonger and C. de Dood; rev. C. de Dood (London: Thames and Hudson, 1958), III, 374, and Martin Bailey, *Van Gogh in England: Portrait of the Artist as a Young Man* (London: Barbican Art Gallery, 1992), 85–93; T. S. Eliot, *The Waste Land: A Facsimile and Transcript of the Original Drafts including the Annotations of Ezra Pound*, ed. Valerie Eliot (London: Faber and Faber, 1971), 5; *The Diaries of Franz Kafka 1914–1923*, ed. Max Brod (London: Secker and Warburg, 1949), 188–9; Mark Spilka, *Dickens and Kafka: A Mutual Interpretation* (Indiana: University of Indiana Press, 1963); Gilles Deleuze and Felix Guattari, *Kafka: Towards a Minor Literature* (Minneapolis: University of Minnesota Press, 1986), 77–8; Vladimir Nabokov, 'Bleak House (1852–3)', in Fredson Bowers (ed.), *Lectures on Literature* (London: Weidenfeld and Nicolson, 1980), 62–124; T. W. Adorno, 'On Dickens' *The Old Curiosity Shop*: A Lecture', in *Notes to Literature* (Columbia: Columbia University Press, 1992), II, 170–7; Victor Sage, 'Dickens and Beckett: Two Uses of Materialism', *Journal of Beckett Studies*, II (summer 1977), 15–39; Ernest Jones, *Sigmund Freud: His Life and Work* (3rd edition, London: Hogarth, 1972), I, 116, 190; Ned Lukacher, 'Dialectical Images: Benjamin / Dickens / Freud', in *Primal Scenes* (Ithaca and London: Cornell University Press, 1986), 275–336.

[90] 'In the hands of . . . Dickens, domestic fiction carried the process of suppressing political resistance into the domain of popular literature': Nancy Armstrong, *Desire and Domestic Fiction* (Oxford: Clarendon, 1987), 163; see D. A. Miller, *The Novel and the Police* (Berkeley: University of California Press, 1988), xii–xiii.

that distrusts division, multiplicity, and heterogeneity, and cannot think responsibility in ways other than through their elimination. Dickens's characters, like his plots, are self-divided and proliferating, his rhetoric excessive, his forms unstable—and this must not be allowed. Such scenes of critical judgement often belong to a critical melodrama in which a good and bad Dickens, good and bad characterization, readers, plots, parts of plots, parts of novels, parts of texts, and parts of characters are partitioned one from another, and some sent home and some to gaol. They are also scenes in a romance of rescue and forgiveness, in which one or another Dickens can be taken home or sent out to wander the streets. This is a familiar and familiarizing drama, not limited to Dickens by any means, which tries to locate or domesticate 'an essential, persisting *Unheimlichkeit*' of writing, and simultaneously and impossibly to be quit of debt and to lay all ghosts safely to rest.[91]

One of the first of Dickens's critics, already worried by the debts and the name that might come with him, attempted to control him in a particular way. The mother of Dickens's first love, Maria Beadnell, meeting the young Dickens out walking, allowed him to escort her and Maria to the door of a dressmaker's before dismissing him with the words: 'And now, Mr Dickin . . . we'll wish *you* good morning.'[92] Determined to defend her daughter from the possibility of marriage with Dickens, she partitions and abuses his proper name, cutting it off short to make it safe. It was a brave if futile gesture, for Dickens's name was already hard at work disseminating and proliferating itself from well before his birth. 'Dickens' was, then as now, a proverbial name in interjections or exclamations such as 'What the Dickens!' or 'Go to the Dickens!' The first usage recorded in the *OED* is from *The Merry Wives of Windsor*, where Mistress Page asks the page the name of his knight. The answer, serendipitously, is 'Sir John Falstaff', the fat knight, perhaps the best known of all Shakespeare's characters, the most famous episode in whose life occurred at Gad's Hill, where Dickens was later to live. The first example of its second usage, in a phrase such as 'Play the Dickens'

---

[91] Geoffrey Bennington and Jacques Derrida, *Jacques Derrida* (Chicago: Chicago University Press, 1992), 252.
[92] Pilgrim, VII, 534.

(meaning to cause mischief or to play havoc) is equally happily from the prologue to Urquhart's translation of Rabelais, the great anthology and thesaurus of carnival laughter and practice. More darkly, 'Dickens' in such phrases was a substitute for 'the devil', or the deuce (a card or a dice with two spots), the doubling of the devil in short, the devil's dummy, the thing you find in the place where the devil should be, a kind of ghost or shadow of the devil, his absent presence. So the devil, the deuce, haunts Dickens, just as Fagin (who is called the devil) haunts Oliver Twist; unless Dickens haunts the devil. Causing mischief, playing havoc; warding off the devil: playing the Dickens.

Dickens's life and writing accelerated these divisions and transformations so much that a hostile critic of Dickens's final Christmas story *The Haunted Man* wrote that 'Mr Dickens, as if in revenge for his own queer name, does bestow still queerer ones on his fictitious creations'.[93] His christening ceremony, for example, went wrong. His parents intended to give him 'Huffam' as a middle name but the clerk wrote down 'Huffham' instead, which sounds the same but is different.[94] He never used it again. When Dickens's own son was christened, his father, John Dickens, shouted out 'Boz' in the middle of the ceremony and Charles Culliford Dickens, the nameless infant, became Charles Culliford Boz Dickens, son and heir.[95] These are both slight deviations, slight detours or embarrassments to the successful completion of the performative act of christening, two little supplements, two improper names, but the violence, multiplication, and deviations to which Dickens subjects his name in the fiction is on a different scale altogether. Indeed, at times he resembles no one so much as Major Bagstock in *Dombey and Son*, alias old Joe Bagstock, alias old J. Bagstock, alias old Josh Bagstock, alias Joey B, alias J. B., alias Antony Bagstock, for whom 'to be on the most familiar terms with his own name' was the very 'stronghold and donjon-keep of light humour'.[96]

[93] From an unsigned review of *The Haunted Man*, in *Macphail's Edinburgh Ecclesiastical Journal*, January 1849, vi, 423–31, reprinted in Collins (ed.), *Dickens: The Critical Heritage*, 180.
[94] Johnson, *Charles Dickens: His Tragedy and Triumph*, 9.
[95] Pilgrim, I, 339n.
[96] Charles Dickens, *Dombey and Son*, ed. Alan Horsman (Oxford: World's Classics, 1982), 71.

Dickens's own name and signature implants itself multiply and perversely in his letters and stories. Syllables and phonemes float free to be hunted and crushed into new combinations, uses, and shapes in a continual linguistic perversity which begins with the mad errancy of the name Charles John Huffham (or Huffam) Dickens.[97]

There are, for example, several Charleses or Charlies in the fiction—Charley Bates (more usually, in an old joke, known as Master Bates) in *Oliver Twist*, Charley Bit (an alias) in *Mr Nightingale's Diary*, Charles Fitz-Marshall, Jingle's alias in *Pickwick*, Charles and Louisa, the cool young couple in *Sketches of Young Couples*, Old Charles, the highly respected waiter in *Somebody's Luggage*, Charles Kitterbell, Charles Scarton, amateur actor in *Sketches*, Charles Cheeryble in *Nickleby*, Charles Darnay in *A Tale of Two Cities*, Charley the potboy in *Pickwick*, Charley the narrator of 'The Boots' in *The Holly Tree Inn*, Charley the marine store dealer and Charles Mell in *Copperfield*, Charley, Esther's maid in *Bleak House*, Carlo the performing dog in *The Old Curiosity Shop*, to say nothing of the King Charles's head that gets into Mr Dick's head in *David Copperfield* and Winking Charley who enters the narrator's night thoughts in 'Lying Awake'. There are several Charlottes, including two in *Sketches of Young Couples*, as well as a Caroline, the wife of one of Scrooge's debtors, and a Carolina, the maid in 'At Dusk'. There is truly quite a lot of Charles John Dickens in Giovanni Carlavero in 'Italian Prisoner' in the *Uncommercial Traveller*. John, the name of Dickens's father as well as his own, is equally popular. There are John Dounce and John Evenson the radical in *Sketches by Boz*, John Edmunds and John Smauker in *Pickwick*, John Browdie in *Nickleby*, John Carker in *Dombey*, John Willett, Sir John Chester, and John Grueby in *Barnaby Rudge*, John Owen in *Curiosity Shop*, John Westlock in *Martin Chuzzlewit*, John Chick in *Dombey*, two John Chiverys in *Little Dorrit*, John Jarndyce and John Jasper, John Podsnap and John Nandy. There are twelve characters

---

[97] '[P]honetic word play had often a . . . structural role in his art': Randolph Quirk, 'Charles Dickens and Appropriate Language', in Stephen Wall (ed.), *Charles Dickens: A Critical Anthology* (Penguin, 1970), 410. On the proper name, see Bennington and Derrida, *Jacques Derrida*, 105–6.

simply called John, including several servants, a labourer, a twin brother who appears as a phantasm, a waiter, a pantomime clown, a boilermaker, an inventor, and a tenant of a haunted house. There is Johnny, a dead child in *Our Mutual Friend*. There are endless Janes and Jacks, a couple of Jeans, and several interesting Jacksons and Johnsons, including Nicholas Nickleby's stage name of Mr Johnson.

Dickens often called himself Dick, and there are many Dicks and Richards in the work, including little Dick, Oliver Twist's friend, Dick Datchery in *Edwin Drood*, Dick the sweetheart of Sally in *No Thoroughfare*, Dick the ostler in *Chuzzlewit*, Dick the guard of the coach and Dick the blind blackbird in *Nicholas Nickleby*, Richard Carstone in *Bleak House*, and, doubling everything, Richard Doubledick in *Seven Poor Travellers*. 'Dick' easily becomes Pick, Wick, Chick, and the two Nicks of *Nicholas Nickleby*. With additions it turns into Chickenstalker, Chicksey, Chickweed, and Browndock, whom Mrs Nickleby recalls. One or two more changes take us to Bilkins, the only authority on taste in 'Our French Watering Place', John Dawkins (the Artful Dodger), Blinkins at 'Our School', Chuckster in *Old Curiosity Shop*, Click in *Somebody's Luggage*, Clickett the Orfling in *David Copperfield*, Mr and Mrs Click- ett in *Sketches of Young Couples*, Clocker and Cocker, Dunkle, Edkins, Fladdock, Jilkins, Jinkins, Jinkinson, Jinks, Jock, Jorkins, Kedgick, Krook, Larkins, Lillyvick, Limbkins, Linkin- water, Loggins, Mackin, Macklin, Micawber, Neckett, Nupkins, Orlick, Packer, Packlemerton, Pancks, Pankey, Parkins, Pawkins, Pecksniff, Perkins, Perkinsop, Pickles, Pickleson, Pilkins, Pipkin, Pluck, Pockett, Porkenham, Rickets, Skimpin, Sparkins, Specks, Sprodgkin, Tackleton, Tapkins, Tickit, Tickle, Tiggin, Timkins, Tipkins, Tipkisson, Tomkins, Veck, Watkins, Wickham, Wickfield, Wicks, Wilkins, Winkle, and Winks, to name only the most obvious. They can be supplemented by other signatures of Dickens's letters and writings: Tibbs, Boz, Timothy Sparks, The Proscribed One, Manlius, Grattan, Bully, The Congreve of the Nineteenth Century, The Mask, Villium Gibbons, Anti-Pusey, The Misconceived One, Victoria, Young Dando, Dick the Doomed, Pitchcock, Swabber, Trillington and Dawberry, The Unwaistcoated One, Henry Bluff, Philo

Forecastle, Ariel, The Insolvent One, The Cheer, W. Ferraud, Bobadil, CupiD, Sutherland, B, and CD.[98]

This overnaming of his own queer name does not end with Dickens's characters and signatures, or even with everything we could call 'Dickensian', which means both old-fashioned and sordid, and hilariously funny. 'Dick', that name of Dickens, is also an abbreviation for 'dictionary' and, like the whole string of 'nonce words more or less' found buried half-dead in the *OED*—Dickensy, Dickensesque, Dickensish—is a possible entry in a potentially infinite Dickens dictionary which would contain not only these pseudonyms, signatures, and alibis, but also their relatives and friends, such as 'dicacity', a jesting habit of speech, raillery, pertness, talkativeness, 'dicatectic' meaning doubly catalectic, a line of verse lacking two feet, as if it had two wooden legs, 'dichastasis' meaning undergoing spontaneous subdivision, and 'dichaeology', a plea in favour of the righteous. Each of these words, linked by a seemingly arbitrary alphabetic proximity, names an essential quality of Dickens's writing, which is full of raillery, pertness, and talkativeness, lacks something (two things perhaps), spontaneously subdivides itself, and is a plea in favour of the righteous.

It might be here in this strange Dickens 'dick', that we can glimpse the possibility of another Dickens criticism, which would pay its debts and do its mourning somewhat differently. Such a criticism would not try to avoid the law, for, as Mr Micawber and Dickens's father learned, the law cannot indefinitely be evaded, however ingenious one is in proliferating signatures and names.[99] Indeed the law in many forms—natural, social, juridical, generic, critical—haunts readers of Dickens, as it haunts his characters, who are so often brought before a law which they cannot name or see, yet which finds them guilty or holds them, as did Mrs Beadnell, on a threshold.[100] So many, perhaps all, of Dickens's texts, place us before the law: 'A Visit to Newgate' in *Sketches by Boz*; Bardell versus Pickwick and

[98] Respectively, Pilgrim, IV, 5; II, 91; II, 439; III, 291; III, 511; III, 505; III, 503; III, 498; III, 498; III, 433; III, 315; IV, 528; IV, 529; IV, 407; IV, 515; IV, 18; IV, 61; IV, 910; IV, 138; IV, 139; IV, 404; III, 220; III, 287; III, 285.

[99] Bennington and Derrida, *Jacques Derrida*, 239–53.

[100] Jacques Derrida, 'Before the Law', in Derek Attridge (ed.), *Acts of Literature* (London: Routledge, 1992), 181–220.

the Fleet Prison; Fagin in the condemned cell, Oliver and the Artful Dodger at the Old Bailey; Squeers in gaol; the politics of the law, judicial murder, and the sacking of Newgate in *Barnaby Rudge*; Jonas's suicide in *Martin Chuzzlewit*; further ahead, *Bleak House*, *Little Dorrit*, *Edwin Drood*—trial after trial, judgement upon judgement. In his biography we can mark some of Dickens's more obvious encounters with the law—his grandfather's absconding, his father's bankruptcy, as a lawyer's clerk, as a student at Middle Temple, as a possible police magistrate, in fights over copyright and with publishers, in a son who became a judge—all of which rest just on the edge, before the law. Early the next century, Franz Kafka, whose story 'The Stoker' he calls 'a sheer imitation of Dickens', will write a parable called 'Before the Law' about a man from the country who approaches the Law, but is forever held at its threshold.[101] The law in Dickens is often a bleak and comfortless place, most comprehensively in *Bleak House*, but it can also be something very different, not a solitary vigil at an incomprehensible threshold but noisy and multivoiced. In perhaps the most celebrated scene he ever wrote, chapter 34 of *Pickwick Papers*, the 'Trial of Bardell versus Pickwick', the legal apparatus, in the figure of Mr Justice Stareleigh, seeks to control events through various procedures of administrative justice, such as the accurate recording of names, the provision of oaths and rules of evidence. This is in the service of true testimony and responsible speech. Yet the proceedings of the trial are manifestly false and unjust. One of the few moments of truthfulness, which is also very funny, is Sam Weller's testimony, where Sam follows to the letter the demands of the law and the conventions of the court, but at the same time and in the same gestures turns them against themselves.

It is not accidental that this scene became, for the nineteenth century at least, the most famous of all Dickens's chapters, a privileged metonymy of his work. Its concern with testimony and

---

[101] ' "The Stoker" a sheer imitation of Dickens, the projected novel even more so . . . above all the method. It was my intention, as I now see, to write a Dickens novel, but enhanced by the sharper lights I should have taken from the times and the duller ones I should have got from myself': Franz Kafka from his diary, in Wall (ed.), *Charles Dickens: A Critical Anthology*, 257. Franz Kafka, 'Before the Law', in *Wedding Preparations in the Country and Other Stories* (Harmondsworth: Penguin, 1978), 127–9. See also Derrida, 'Before the Law', in *Acts of Literature*.

the name, the interpretation of documents, the consequences of
indebtedness (Sam Weller's to Pickwick, Pickwick's to Weller,
Dickens to them both) and the law, are central both to Dickens's
writing and any criticism that attempts to do justice to it. Sam
does not succeed in defeating the law or Dodson and Fogg, for
Pickwick goes to prison. But in his double affirmation and grafting of languages, in the laughter he generates in court and out of
court, he provokes the thought of a better justice than the law's.
Dickens is often said to be a social critic, but in scenes like
this he is something better. His is an affirmative writing and
the affirmations are, like Sam Weller's testimony, pragmatic and
plural, willing to take responsibility for what they say and do,
but also self-dividing and multiple. Through grafting together
genres and idioms of discourse, both those proper to literature
and those not, they affirm not a single vision of the good life, a
utopia or a social or political programme, but something more.
There are, to be sure, good lives and programmatic elements in
the fiction, but these are subordinate to more local, heterogeneous, popular, and comic affirmations. One can at times name
them, as when we are told repeatedly in *Martin Chuzzlewit* of
Mark Tapley's 'jollity', but these words are often merely gestures
to a greater force. It is an affirmation that makes a promise to
the future, to which it is willing to sign its name. It is also self-
divided and heterogeneous, a matter of endless pseudonyms and
signatures, of other Dickenses and Dicks.[102]

The most frequent epithet for Dickens among his contemporaries was 'The Inimitable', so much so that it became a noun
and a proper name, one that Dickens himself accepted and
used.[103] 'Inimitable' means, straightforwardly enough, 'surpass-

---

[102] 'What returns to your name, to the secret of your name, is the ability to disappear *in your name*. And thus not to return to itself, which is the condition of the
gift (for example, of the name) but also of all expansion of the self, of all augmen-
tation of self, of all *auctoritas*. In the two cases of this same divided passion, it is
impossible to dissociate the greatest passion and the greatest privation': Jacques
Derrida, 'Passions: "An Oblique Offering"', in David Wood (ed.), *Derrida: A
Critical Reader* (Oxford: Blackwell, 1992), 12.

[103] It is not clear if Dickens gave himself this name. John Forster said that Dickens
took the name from an inscription on a silver snuffbox given him by his old schoolmaster, William Giles (Forster, *The Life of Dickens*, I, 10), but Percy Fitzgerald
claimed that Dickens was already using the name in the 'Answers to Correspon-
dents' section of *Bentley's Miscellany*: 'Boz and his Publishers II: Richard Bentley
and his "Miscellany": II', *Dickensian*, III (1907), 71–2.

ing or defying imitation'. But 'imitation' is also a common English term to translate 'mimesis', that term within Platonic and subsequent aesthetic theories, whose task is to dictate and master the laws by which representations are made.[104] Dickens's novels are, without serious dispute, surpassing imitations—surpassingly good in their quality and force—but in their extravagance which wanders out of bounds, their hyperbole which goes beyond measure, in their many names and signatures, in their protean, exorbitant, impure, vulgar affirmation, the force of what James called their ply, they may also surpass and defy imitation itself.

[104] Plato, *Republic*, trans. Paul Shorey, in Edith Hamilton and Huntington Cairns (eds), *The Collected Dialogues* (Princeton: Princeton University Press, 1963), 575–844.

Adjestin' the Differences:
Pickwick Papers

I

FOR GUSTAVE FLAUBERT, it was not spanking but the poor construction of novels that was the English vice. He wrote in 1872 to George Sand: 'Je viens de lire *Pickwick*, de Dickens. Connaissez-vous cela? Il y a des parties superbes; mais quelle composition défectueuse! Tous les écrivains anglais en sont là. Walter Scott excepté, ils manquent de plan. Cela est insupportable pour nous autres latins.'[1] It is a familiar set of judgements, almost worth including in an updated *Dictionary of Received Ideas:*[2] *Dickens*: Say 'He is superb in parts, but lacks plan.' *Latins*: Say 'We Latins require planning in novels.' *Walter Scott*: English writer of well-planned novels. *Composition, poor*: See *English writers. English writers*: See *Dickens*.

Flaubert's remarks show what a trouble *Pickwick Papers* can be to readers and critics, and to both formally and historically oriented methods of analysis. It seems hard to think of a method or theory that could do justice both to the novel's success and to the apparent 'incoherences' and 'improvisations' that are such a marked feature of the text. Take for example the incident in the first chapter of the book in which Mr Blotton calls

---

[1] Gustave Flaubert, Letter of 12 July 1872, *Œuvres Complètes* (Paris: Club de l'Honnête Homme, 1971–5), vol. 15, 143. Flaubert discusses Dickens's work on a number of occasions. See in particular the reference to *Nicholas Nickleby* ('il y a des choses à prendre') in the letter of autumn 1859 to Ernest Feydeau, *Œuvres Complètes*, vol. 16, 369 and the observations in the letter of July 1862 to Madame Roger des Genettes, *Œuvres Complètes*, vol. 14, 121: 'L'observation est une qualité secondaire en littérature, mais il n'est pas permis de peindre si faussement la société quand on est le contemporain de Balzac et de Dickens.'

[2] Gustave Flaubert, *The Dictionary of Received Ideas*, in *Bouvard and Pécuchet*, trans. A. J. Krailsheimer (Harmondsworth: Penguin, 1976), 291–330.

Pickwick a 'humbug'.[3] Blotton's name is an interesting one: to 'blot' has the archaic meaning of 'to cover with worthless writing' as well as the more common modern one of 'to efface, obscure or eclipse', and a blot is something to be avoided in writing, because it may interfere with sense and meaning. Blotton attempts to blot out Pickwick, whose angry response turns the chapter into a dispute about meaning, and the meaning of Blotton's insult. It is resolved by Blotton saying, when asked if he meant 'humbug' in its usual sense, that he meant 'humbug' in a 'Pickwickian' sense. His is a remarkable speech act, a curious self-cancelling performative utterance, for Pickwick is both the Club's and Mr Pickwick's name, so it can be either a fulsome apology or no apology at all. It is a speech act that means and does something—apologizes—and that does and means nothing at all, because no one knows what a Pickwickian sense is, either in the novel or the world. For Blotton to apologize in a Pickwickian way, just as he has insulted in a retrospectively Pickwickian way, is a remarkably cunning feat of improvisation both from him and from Dickens. Like many such feats it gets repeated and passed from mouth to mouth until eventually it ends up in the *OED*, where we can learn what 'Pickwickian' really means, or so we think: 'Pickwickian sense, language in a technical, constructive or conveniently idiosyncratic or esoteric sense; usually in reference to language "unparliamentary" or compromising in its natural sense.' Which sends us off, as such quests do, to other places in the dictionary, to 'technical': 'belonging or relating to an art or arts', and 'constructive': 'resulting from a certain interpretation; not directly expressed but inferred'. This seems straightforward enough, if we believe that language can ever have a 'natural sense', directly expressed. If we do not, as I do not, then we must ask what meaning does not belong to a certain art or arts, does not rest on acts of inference, does not result from a certain interpretation? What meaning, in short, is not Pickwickian?

If all meaning is Pickwickian, what critical theory or practice could be true to Pickwickian sense? For the book is, as Grahame Smith writes, 'a work not susceptible to a reading in the general

---

[3] Charles Dickens, *The Pickwick Papers*, ed. James Kinsley (Oxford: World's Classics, 1986), 71. All references will be to this edition and placed in the text.

terms established by the classic modern theories of the novel, all of which are marked by some adherence to the idea of organic form, that is an absence of elements in excess of those required for the work's inner aims'.[4] Critical history has, in more and less self-conscious ways, reflected the difficulty, and critics have been pulled by the novel towards two very different and apparently incompatible vocabularies and idioms: to the language of contingency on the one hand and that of transcendence on the other. Contingency because it is so clearly an improvised book, begun impulsively and continued in similar vein, full of interpolated stories, hasty inventions, and awkward transitions. But also because the narrative itself is full of accidents and contingencies: Winkle shooting himself by accident, Pickwick falling through the ice, in the wrong room in the inn at Ipswich, asleep in a wheelbarrow, inhabiting a book full of pratfalls, mistakings, all sorts and kinds of wandering, Mr Pickwick a Quixote in errancy. It seems more the material and method of a variety show or a scrapbook than a formally coherent work of art.[5] Yet critics are often drawn, at times in the teeth of their own resistance, to a transcendental vocabulary to describe the book. For Steven Marcus, Sam and Tony Weller are 'the geniuses of the mythical country of *Pickwick Papers*', 'tutelary spirits' in an idealized world. The book itself gives glimpses, writes Marcus, of 'the ideal possibilities of human relations in community'.[6] W. H. Auden, like Dostoevsky before him, sees it as a Christian allegory, a product of a 'mythopoeic imagination', a story of Eden and the Fall.[7] In the most seductive reading of the text, Chesterton calls it 'not a good novel . . . not a bad

[4] Grahame Smith, *The Novel and Society: Defoe to George Eliot* (Batsford: London, 1984), 179.

[5] Malcolm Andrews describes it as a 'hybrid' and a 'medley' in his edition of *The Pickwick Papers* (London: Everyman, 1998), xxviii, xxix. Kathryn Chittick notes that on its first appearance, it 'fell into no recognizable literary genre': *Dickens and the 1830s* (Cambridge: Cambridge University Press, 1990), 89. On generic instability and mixing, see Alastair Fowler, *Kinds of Literature: An Introduction to the Theory of Genres and Modes* (Clarendon: Oxford, 1982), 45–8, and Jacques Derrida, 'The Law of Genre', in Derek Attridge (ed.), *Acts of Literature* (London: Routledge, 1992), 221–52.

[6] Steven Marcus, *Dickens: From Pickwick to Dombey* (Chatto and Windus: London, 1965), 17, 52.

[7] W. H. Auden, 'Dingley Dell and the Fleet', in *The Dyer's Hand and Other Essays* (London: Faber and Faber, 1963), 407.

novel . . . not a novel at all . . . something nobler than a novel',
part not of literature but 'mythology', of 'folklore, the literature
of the people', a tale of 'the gods gone wandering round
England' and their eternal pagan life.[8]

It is of course possible that a hastily improvised and weakly
plotted book, full of interpolated and seemingly irrelevant
matter, the product of a request for hack letter-press to accom-
pany sporting illustrations, should achieve the transcendence
that is claimed for it. Indeed, in some accounts it is the paradoxical condition of it. Like the bourgeois self, *Pickwick Papers*
seems capable of transforming itself from a bundle of accidents
into a unity, able to cancel and preserve its errancy, and thus
raise the study of Tittlebats, Dodson and Fogg, and the wheelbarrow in the pound to the level of the angels. Such claims are
not hard to satirize and it is easy to see the insistence on the
book's 'epic' or 'mythical' qualities as a sign of embarrassment
at the sheer awkward fact that the most impressive body of
work in nineteenth-century English fiction and its most popular
and triumphant book should have had such profane and humble
beginnings. And then to celebrate, in contrast to the more
achieved formal unity of Dickens's later work, the complex
material imbrication of this text, a literary work so often found
(and finding itself) outside literature: in the French, Danish,
Swedish, Hungarian, Dutch, and other foreign editions; in adaptations, improvements, continuations, selections, plagiarisms,
and imitations, such as *The Pickwick Songster*, *The Pickwickian Treasury of Wit*, *The Penny Pickwick*, *The Peregrinations
of Pickwick*, *Mr Pickwick in America*, *Pickwick in India*,
'Noctes Pickwickianae', and *Marmaduke Midge, the Pickwickian legatee*; in china ornaments, *Sam Weller's Jest Book*, and the
cult of the Pickwick hat.[9]

---

[8] G. K. Chesterton, *Charles Dickens* (London: Methuen, 1906), 79, 83.

[9] On early foreign editions, see Charles Dickens, *The Pickwick Papers*, ed. James
Kinsley (Oxford: Clarendon, 1986), xc. Adaptations and continuations include
George W. M. Reynolds, *Pickwick Abroad: Or, The Tour in France* (London:
Thomas Tegg, 1839); *The Pickwick Comic Almanac for 1838 containing Sam
Weller's Diary of Fun and Pastime* (London: W. Marshall, 1838); *The Pickwick
Songster*, ed. Sam Weller (London, 1837); *Posthumous Papers of the Cadgers'
Club* (London: E. Lloyd, 1838); *The Beauties of Pickwick*, edited and arranged by
Sam Weller (London, 1838: W. Morgan). On these, see Louis James, *Fiction for
the Working Man 1830–1850: A Study of the Literature Produced for the Working
Classes in Early Victorian Urban England* (Harmondsworth: Penguin 1974), 51–82.

For this reason, Pickwick and his papers often seem to be more a part of cultural than of literary history, as the stable object of the text that literary critics invoke seems to slip away into other cultural networks and sites. The text is also internally divided. As Chesterton puts it, Dickens 'tried to tell ten stories at once; he stirs into the pot all the chaotic fancies and crude experiences of his boyhood; he sticks in irrelevant short stories as in a scrapbook; he adopts designs and abandons them, begins episodes and leaves them unfinished.'[10] Pickwick's character seems to change radically in the course of the book, whose design, such as it is, only seems to take shape about halfway through with Mrs Bardell's breach-of-promise suit. It is natural to look for the thread of a story, but the *Papers*, like the Pick-wickians, are always losing their threads.[11] The episodes of the novel, like those of a Brecht play, are written in semi-detached form;[12] and they are immediately adapted, quoted, and plagiarized on innumerable occasions, an iterability with few precedents in the history of the novel and in which Dickens himself participates by reviving or reproducing the most distinctive feature of the text—its signature almost—in Sam and Tony Weller's reappearance in *Master Humphrey's Clock*.[13] It is a novel that often loses its own proper story and direction, full of 'interpolated' tales, absurd and grotesque stories intent on diverting, misappropriating, and misdirecting the characters, the story, and the good reader with their violence, melodrama, and ghosts. What could be the possible thread or threads of such heterogeneous and multiple textualities? Its plot is dispersed and diffuse, its central character divided, its citations innumerable and constantly remade. 'All in a concatenation accordingly' is

[10] G. K. Chesterton, *Chesterton on Dickens* (London: Everyman, 1992), 16.

[11] On the importance of this metaphor, see J. Hillis Miller, *Ariadne's Thread* (New Haven and London: Yale University Press), 1–27.

[12] 'Every number should be, to a certain extent, complete in itself', xxiv. 'With an epic work, as opposed to a dramatic, one can as it were take a pair of scissors and cut it into individual pieces, which remain fully capable of life': Bertolt Brecht, *Brecht on Theatre*, ed. John Willett (London: Eyre Methuen, 1978), 70.

[13] No one has fully mapped the 'Pickwick phenomenon', but on this topic, see George H. Ford, *Dickens and his Readers* (New York: Norton, 1965 [1955]), 3–19; James, *Fiction for the Working Man*; Elliot Engel (ed.), *Pickwick Papers: An Annotated Bibliography* (New York: Garland, 1990), 27–74. Among the more unusual items in the latter, see Claude Debussy's 'Hommage à S. Pickwick Esq. P.P.M.P.C.', 56.

a favourite Dickens quotation, but what could be the accord or concatenation of this text, its harmony, conformity, or linking together as in a chain?[14]

The book has been called 'the greatest of Dickens's mysteries' and its mysteries are of many sorts.[15] It had a messy birth—as letter-press to a book of sporting illustrations by Robert Seymour, who committed suicide after two numbers—and a messier life. It is not unified or defined by its genre: first reviewed as 'a periodical' or a 'magazine consisting of only one article', in later criticism it becomes an epic or a myth, either quotidian ephemera or a member of the most transcendent and dignified of genres, immortal and eternal.[16] Even the title of the book is uncertain. Is it *Pickwick* or *The Pickwick Club* or *Pickwick Papers* or *The Pickwick Papers* or *The Posthumous Papers of the Pickwick Club containing a faithful record of the perambulations, perils, travels, adventures, and Sporting transactions of the Corresponding members, edited by 'Boz' with illustrations*? And what is their relation to *The Pickwick Travels*, *The Pickwick Diary*, *The Pickwick Correspondence*, and *The Transactions of the Pickwick Club*, all of which appear in the book's first announcement, emphasizing the endlessly proliferating and regressive nature of the text, which rests on a wholly fictional and lost original of which there is no copy?[17]

Admirers of *Pickwick Papers* have often seen it as a beginning like no other. Most hyperbolically (and hyperbole, that term for everything that goes beyond or outside boundaries, may be a necessary figure of speech for discussion of this novel), Steven Marcus sees it as the beginning of beginnings, an inaugurating creative act akin to that of the Deity:

[*Pickwick Papers*] dramatizes the fundamental activity of the Logos; it dramatizes the notion of the cosmic creation as a word—which is how God, as the Logos, created the world . . . here too, in this novel,

---

[14] 'in a concatenation ackoardingly': Oliver Goldsmith, *She Stoops to Conquer*, in Arthur Friedman (ed.), *Collected Works of Oliver Goldsmith* (Oxford: Clarendon, 1966), V, 117. 'Dickens's favourite quotation': Pilgrim, II, 62.

[15] Steven Marcus, 'Language into Structure: Pickwick Revisited', in Harold Bloom (ed.), *Modern Critical Views: Charles Dickens* (New York: Chelsea House, 1987), 129.

[16] Chittick, *Dickens and the 1830s*, 64–5. Chesterton, *Charles Dickens*, 79.

[17] Dickens's Address from a publisher's advertisement of 26 March 1836 is reprinted as Appendix A in Dickens, *Pickwick Papers*, ed. Kinsley, 720–1.

we begin the creation with a word, with language . . . Mr Pickwick and Dickens are each of them the Logos . . . each of them is in his separate, distinctive way the Word made flesh.[18]

It is a striking and convincing passage from Marcus, prefigured by Dickens's parodic descriptions of Pickwick and his own novel, but if *Pickwick* is the great inaugurating act of Dickens's writing career, it is also no beginning at all. For Dickens was by 1836 the author of many works of fiction, most of them already collected and revised in *Sketches by Boz: First Series*; before that he had written a mass of semi-anonymous reports on parliamentary debates, and before that the depositions and documents of his years of legal reporting and clerking, any of which could fairly be taken as the beginning of his writing career. *Pickwick* itself is preceded by 'extended prefatory marchings and countermarchings', and is frequently interrupted and interpolated by new beginnings and new stories, each of which points to the inaugurating force of this text, a force 'virtually unexampled in the history of the novel', and at the same time, through the anticipation, retrospection, and repetition that belong to these and all beginnings, demonstrates the impossibility of any beginning or origin to his writing at all.[19]

We seem with *Pickwick* to be in a world both of destiny—the book uncannily prefigures so many of Dickens's later works, from *Oliver Twist* to *Little Dorrit*—and of chance and contingency. Chesterton once tried to explain the power of the book by invoking a strange retrospective causality: *Pickwick*, he writes, is 'the mere mass of light before the creation of sun or moon', a 'pre-natal vision of all the children of Dickens'.[20] Its force does not stem from itself but as a vision of what will follow, which we can only understand in its effects. Its characters only work because of their later reflections, only make sense in the context of their successors, Chesterton argues, in an echo of what Freud called *Nachträglichkeit*, retrospective causality or

[18] Marcus, 'Language into Structure', 133–4.

[19] Ibid., 133, 151. On beginnings, see Geoffrey Bennington and Jacques Derrida, *Jacques Derrida* (Chicago: University of Chicago Press, 1993), 15–19.

[20] Chesterton, *Chesterton on Dickens*, 15–16. In an illuminating discussion, J. Hillis Miller sees *Pickwick Papers* and its illustrations enacting 'a solar drama, involving a doubling of the sun': J. Hillis Miller, *Illustration* (London: Reaktion, 1992), 97. On the metaphor of the sun, see Bennington and Derrida, *Jacques Derrida*, 299–300.

deferred action.[21] Pickwick Clubs do not exist in the world until their minutes and transactions have been published in a novel which was not even intended to be a novel. What was secondary has become primary; what was mere supplementary and derivative matter—Dickens's words—has retrospectively become the inaugurating act, an improbable, parodic repetition of the Logos. We thus have not the divine creative Word, but something belated, strange, and secondary, in which Dickens 'laughs at his own jokes before he has made them . . . laughs at his comedy before he creates it, and . . . has tears for his tragedy before he knows what it is'.[22] It is a wonderfully unsettling, not to say deconstructive, insight to argue that *Pickwick Papers*'s force comes not from its inaugurating power, but through deferred action, paradox, and impossibility. *Pickwick Papers*, that non-originary origin of Dickens's writing, remains both 'his one hack book' and 'his masterpiece'.[23]

II

It has often, and rightly, been said that *Pickwick* is a text peculiarly concerned with language.[24] Yet it is striking how much it is the *written* nature of language that is emphasized: as the title tells us, this is just paper, just papers, the minutes, diary, and other transactions of an imaginary club. The full title's key words—papers, club, edited—speak of a certain fictional impersonality: a club is a collection of individuals, an editor authors nothing, a society's minutes traditionally conceal as much as

---

[21] This is a term in Freud whose importance has been noted in the work of Jacques Lacan. See J. Laplanche and J. B. Pontalis, *The Language of Psychoanalysis* (London: Karnac, 1988), 111–14. It has also been of significance to Jacques Derrida's work and for Geoffrey Bennington it is Freud's 'true discovery': Bennington and Derrida, *Jacques Derrida*, 134. See also Jacques Derrida, *Writing and Difference* (London: Routledge, 1978), 203, 211–12.

[22] Chesterton, *Chesterton on Dickens*, 15.

[23] Ibid., 18.

[24] For Steven Marcus it is a book 'concerned with learning words and with some kind of fundamental or primitive relation to language': 'Language into Structure', 134. See also J. Hillis Miller, 'Sam Weller's Valentine: Dickens', in *Topographies* (Stanford: Stanford University Press, 1995), 105–33; James E. Marlow, 'Pickwick's Writing: Propriety and Language', *ELH: English Literary History*, 52:4 (1985), 939–63, and Garrett Stewart, *Dickens and the Trials of Imagination* (Cambridge: Harvard University Press, 1974), 3–29.

they reveal. In one way this emphasis is not surprising. Dickens, after all, was a writer and his life was full of papers: the papers he wrote on, the paper labels he stuck on blacking pots, the papers he submitted to newspapers and journals, the written notes, memoranda, and letters of a writing life, and the paper money and bills of exchange that circulated around it. Pickwick too is a writer, an investigator who attempts to depict the world in his notebook and who consistently fails to recognize the problems and difficulties it creates. He encounters a stone inscribed '+BILST/UM/PSHI/S.M./ARK' and produces a pamphlet of ninety-six pages containing twenty-seven different interpretations of it. Key scenes in the book centre on writing and its absurd and uncontrollable consequences. Even the briefest list is a lengthy one: in chapter 2, Pickwick, making notes on a cabman's horse, finds himself, as a result, in the middle of a fight; Snodgrass, reporting the cricket match at Muggleton, 'took a great mass of notes . . . his writing almost unintelligible, and his style wholly so' (86); the trial of Bardell versus Pickwick turns the most innocent letters into the most sinister evidence; Pott and Slurk, the Eatanswill editors, quarrel endlessly in print; Sam Weller writes an exceptionally funny valentine and his father a very moving letter on the death of his wife. Writing in most of these scenes is a futile affair, as in the erased inscription on Prince Bladud's public baths (455), Bill Stumps's stone, that 'illegible monument of Mr Pickwick's greatness' (137), Serjeant Stubbins's illegible writing (384), and Bob Sawyer's servant's devotion to 'writing his name on the counter, and rubbing it out again' (483).

Early in the novel, Pickwick describes himself as 'an observer of human nature' (11), one who wishes to see things for himself directly, with no intermediary. Yet he is forced to depend on mechanical and other aids, such as spectacles, a telescope, and a notebook, in his quest. What was intended to be a journey directly to observe and describe the world is always being delayed or frustrated by this equipment, and often what enables Pickwick to see or record something equally prevents him from doing so. At first it seems as if the novel is opposing the pleasures and virtues of simplicity and speech to the perils of writing and artifice: Pickwick writes everything down and understands nothing; Sam Weller, by contrast, has no equipment, writes little, and understands almost everything. In Pickwick's trial for breach of promise, it is his writing that provides the crucial evidence for his conviction, as his two innocent letters to Mrs Bardell—'"Dear Mrs. B.—Chops and Tomata sauce. Yours, PICKWICK"' and '"Dear Mrs. B., I shall not be at home till to-morrow. Slow coach . . . Dont trouble yourself about the warming-pan"' (426)—become the subject of Buzfuz's destructive hermeneutics. There could be no more graphic illustration of the perils of writing. But speech is an equally problematic affair in the book, as dangerous in its own way as writing, and as disconcerting as Sam Weller's 'alphabet of winks' (699) or Jingle's ability to speak in 'stenography' (82). In the trial, the climactic scene of linguistic deviation and misdirection in the book, even the simple repetition of phonemes, on which all writing and speech depend, breaks down: Elizabeth Cluppins becomes Tuppins becomes Juppins becomes Muffins (427); Nathaniel Winkle becomes Daniel Winkle becomes Nathaniel Daniel or Daniel Nathaniel (429); Phunky becomes Monkey (421).

If the very fact of writing and speech causes problems, so too does their transmission. The novel is very interested in the apparatus by which acts and exchanges of writing take place: the paper, marks, traces, messengers, and vehicles of circulation. When Sam Weller receives an invitation from John Smauker to his 'swarry', he

did what a great many people do when they are uncertain about the writer of a note,—looked at the seal, and then at the front, and then at the back, and then at the sides, and then at the superscription; and, as a last resource, thought he might as well look inside, and try to find out from that. (464)

This is well observed, but it also points to a more general concern of the book. Sam is right to watch the post so carefully, for writing in this book almost invariably doesn't do what it is supposed to, or go where it is intended. Language either gets in the way of what one wants to do, as when the pike-keeper keeps the Pickwickians talking for no reason and prevents their pursuit of Jingle, or has no effect on its listeners at all, as when Winkle falls asleep over Pott's editorials (160). Messages continually get delayed, returned, lost, mislaid, diverted, or misappropriated, as when Dr Slammer of the Fourth, attempting to challenge Jingle who has insulted him, writes to Winkle by mistake and causes the whole sorry mess of the aborted duel.

It may thus be better to think of *Pickwick* as a novel not so much about language as about the post. The novel is a very mobile one, as the characters travel and post themselves all over the place. Indeed, Dickens seems to find the pre-Rowland Hill postal service intrinsically comical: Lord Mutanhed's main topic of conversation is his new mail-cart (451); a knock on the door sounds like that of 'an insane post boy' (18); the Pickwickians' coat is 'like a general postman's' (18). The post, however, is not simply a theme. Jacques Derrida's *The Post Card from Socrates to Freud* is one of the most rigorous (and playful) explorations of the topic of the post (which is so much more than a topic), and an exhaustive compendium of the figures, addresses, puns, and practices of the postal system and principle.[25] Derrida's work explores this mainly in relation to 'autobiographical' material, and to various theoretical and philosophical texts, but the book also has implications for the history of the novel and for novel criticism, which have mutual and intimate relations with almost everything that can arrive or be despatched under the headings of the post, the postal system, and the postal principle.

Dickens throughout his career is interested in the post, and often reaches for analogies and allusions to it in his writing. Remarking on the smallness of the cabin in which he and his wife Kate were to travel to America in 1842, he wrote: 'Any one of the beds, with pillows, sheets and blankets complete, might be sent from one place to another through the post office, with only a double stamp.'[26] He described a bad hotel in *The Uncommercial Traveller* as a place 'where we have no individuality but put ourselves into the general post, as it were, and are sorted and disposed of according to our division'.[27] 'Putting into the general post' is something Dickens is always doing, or having done to him, or doing or having done to other people

[25] Jacques Derrida, *The Post Card from Socrates to Freud and Beyond* (Chicago: University of Chicago Press, 1987).

[26] Pilgrim, III, 7.

[27] Charles Dickens, *The Uncommercial Traveller and Reprinted Pieces* (Oxford: Oxford University Press, 1958), 60.

and things, and this is often a strange or worrying affair for
the senders, receivers, and bearers of such letters and posts:
Dickens, his characters, and his readers. In the late 1830s, for
example, Dickens was widely rumoured to have gone mad.
Reporting the story in the preface to *The Old Curiosity Shop*,
and recalling Sheridan's *The School for Scandal*, Dickens
remarks that the supporting evidence for his insanity was 'of the
same excellent nature as that brought to bear by Sir Benjamin
Backbite on the pistol shot, which struck against the fire, grazed
out of the window at a right angle, and wounded the postman,
who was coming to the door with a double letter from
Northamptonshire'.[28] Evidence, like the pistol shot, has an
uncertain destiny in Dickens, and not only when it deals with
the border between sanity and madness. Like Derrida, Dickens
is interested in the mistakings, doublenesses, and potential fatality associated with the post, as this anecdote and citation about
an author's madness, a wounded postman, a ricochet, and a
double letter from Northamptonshire suggest, and *Pickwick
Papers* often confirms.[29]

The characters in *Pickwick* are constantly travelling and
posting themselves and others and things in a novel full of
postmen, coachmen, post-coaches, post-horses, mails, and posts
of all kinds. Much of its action occurs in transit, post-haste, a
matter of farce and comic sketches, as in Bob Sawyer's ride on
the outside of Pickwick's coach, or Pickwick on his way to court.
In chapter 1, Mr Pickwick's first speech to the Club is troubled
by 'stage coaches . . . upsetting in all directions, horses . . .
bolting, boats . . . overturning and boilers . . . bursting' (71); in
chapter 2, Pickwick catches a cab from St Martin's le Grand,
the site from 1829 of the General Post Office, and the Pickwickians set off by coach to Rochester; much of chapter 4 takes

[28] Charles Dickens, *The Old Curiosity Shop*, ed. Paul Schlicke (London: Everyman, London, 1995), xxxviii–xxxix.
[29] Jacques Lacan analyses a fiction about the post by a contemporary (and correspondent) of Dickens—Edgar Allan Poe's *The Purloined Letter*—to reach the
conclusion that 'a letter always reaches its destination': 'Seminar on "The Purloined
Letter"', *Yale French Studies*, 48 (1972), 38–72. See also Barbara Johnson, 'The
Frame of Reference: Poe, Lacan, Derrida', *Yale French Studies*, 55–6 (1977),
457–505. Derrida's treatment of Lacan in *The Post Card* is concerned among other
things to have some fun at the expense of this claim by demonstrating the vagaries
and misdirections of things that put themselves or get put into the post.

place in a barouche, and chapter 5 in a chaise. And then there follow more coaches, posts, perambulations, travels, and adventures—a whole geography of journeys back and forth—to Muggleton, Great Winglebury, Ipswich, Rochester, Bath, and Birmingham.[30] Appropriately enough, Pickwick himself is accused at his trial of being 'a criminally slow coach . . . whose speed will now be very unexpectedly accelerated, and whose wheels . . . will very soon be greased' (426).

Tony Weller is a coachman and he and his son Sam are deeply involved in the post. Tony, for example, writes a tender and affecting letter on the death of his wife and Sam is the writer of a celebrated valentine, a form of writing that both requires and refuses a recognizable signature and which Sam writes with the assistance of his father and signs in the name of Pickwick. The scene takes place on the day that Pickwick's trial begins, when the novel goes to law to discuss the rights and wrongs of Mrs Bardell's suit. The chapter works in the classic form of the double-plot, reworking and transcoding the subject-matter of the trial—the nature of promises, the fears and hopes of sexual desire and its legitimation in marriage, the interpretation of written documents, the role of chance and choice in human life, the nature of figurative language—in comic form.[31] At one point in the chapter, Sam and Tony disagree whether to use the word 'circumscribed' or 'circumwented' to describe Sam's feelings as he writes to Mary (407). Sam seems to have first written 'circumscribed', if we believe that he can successfully decipher his own handwriting, but his father prefers 'circumwented'. The two words offer an interesting choice. To be circumscribed is to have a line drawn round one, to be placed within bounds or a limit, literally to be 'written around' or held in place by writing. To be circumvented, by contrast, is to be evaded or gone round; more sinisterly, it means to be entrapped in conduct or speech, to be over-reached or deceived, or to be beset with evil.

---

[30] See Robert L. Patten, 'Introduction' to *The Pickwick Papers* (Harmondsworth: Penguin, 1972), 29.

[31] On this chapter, see Hillis Miller, *Topographies*, 105–33, and Maria H. Fein, 'The Politics of Family in *The Pickwick Papers*', *ELH: English Literary History*, 61 (1994), 363–79. On the double plot, see William Empson, *Some Versions of Pastoral* (London: Hogarth, 1986), 27–86, and on transcoding, Peter Stallybrass and Allon White, *The Politics and Poetics of Transgression* (London: Routledge, 1986), 9.

Language, writing, and the declaration of passion here seem to be either a restriction or an entrapment, a circumscription or a circumvention. In the following chapters, Pickwick and Mrs Bardell will find themselves both circumscribed and circumvented by the law and their lawyers. But valentines are also a form of confession—of passion, desire, or love—and we see through this chapter Sam Weller's deft ability both to use and outwit the conventions of his chosen form. His valentine is, to borrow a term from Derrida, more of a 'circumfession' than a confession, a text that both declares his passion and evades the constraints and demands of confessional writing.[32] Sam may disagree with his father, but what they share—that mobile, circulating prefix 'circum'—is greater than their difference, the sign of a postal freedom that simultaneously circumvents and circumscribes the disciplines of a genre—that of the valentine card—and the force of a law.

III

Much of *Pickwick Papers* is about imposture. It is a novel full of humbugs: Pickwick is a humbug antiquarian or scientist; Winkle is neither the sportsman nor the skater he claims to be; Tupman is a failed lover; Snodgrass and Mrs Leo Hunter are terrible poets; Jingle is a con-man, a humbug actor, and captain, Stiggins a humbug preacher. At times, the whole world seems to be a matter of hoaxes and impositions, impostures and deceptions.[33] What often opposes this humbug and fraud is the power and force of friendship, particularly male friendship. There are many friendships in the book: of the Pickwick Club itself, which, like the Last Supper, has (in Phiz's illustration at least) thirteen members, one of whom is dissatisfied and treacherous;

[32] Jacques Derrida, 'Circumfession', in Bennington and Derrida, *Jacques Derrida*, 3–315. See Richard Rorty's generously grudging response to this text in 'Derrida and the Philosophical Tradition', in *Truth and Progress: Philosophical Papers Volume Three* (Cambridge: Cambridge University Press, 1998), 327–50. For an influential account of discourses of confession, see Michel Foucault, *The History of Sexuality: Volume One* (Harmondsworth: Penguin, 1981).

[33] Malcolm Andrews notes its 'pastiche-oriented, self-reflexive modes' in his introduction to Charles Dickens, *The Pickwick Papers* (London: Everyman, 1998), xxxii.

of the travelling companions—Pickwick, Snodgrass, Tupman, Winkle; of Sam Weller and Mr Pickwick and Sam Weller and his father; beyond the novel lies the friendship that Dickens so often invokes, between himself and his readers; and beyond that, the friendship among readers, in the many Pickwick Clubs that followed the non-existent original. All of these are for the most part male friendships, a fraternal democracy whose solidarity stretches even to the undertakers who usher away our friends:

"Vell," said Sam, venturing to offer a little homely consolation after the lapse of three or four minutes, consumed by the old gentleman in slowly shaking his head from side to side, and solemnly smoking; "vell, gov'ner, ve must all come to it, one day or another."

"So we must, Sammy," said Mr. Weller the elder.

"There's a Providence in it all," said Sam.

"O' course there is," replied his father with a nod of grave approval. "Wot 'ud become of the undertakers vithout it, Sammy?" (658)

These friendships and the virtues which they embody and sustain—solidarity, equality, fraternization, trust—are often under threat in the book. Jingle, most clearly, does not obey the rules of friendship—he assumes other people's names, borrows their clothes, and betrays them. He threatens the sociability of disinterested friendship by feigning its affability and frankness.

The most important friendship of the book, upon which the whole novel eventually comes to depend, is that between Pickwick and Sam Weller. It begins at first not as a relationship of equals but of opposites, a relation of service between a bourgeois and a worker, a rich man and a poor one who has slept under the 'arches of Waterloo Bridge' (189). Chesterton allegorized it as a relationship in which 'knowledge . . . [is] the servant and innocence the master'.[34] The two Samuels can also be described as the meeting and partnership of Age and Youth, Chastity and Desire, Simplicity and Cunning, or the enquiring mind and native wit. As early as 1837, the *Metropolitan Magazine* had compared them to Don Quixote and Sancho Panza, and they also resemble a doubly inverted Falstaff and Hal.[35] In

---

[34] Chesterton, *Chesterton on Dickens*, 22.

[35] Anonymous review of *Pickwick Papers*, IX, *Metropolitan Magazine* (January 1837), xviii, 6, reprinted in Philip Collins (ed.), *Charles Dickens: The Critical Heritage* (London: Routledge and Kegan Paul, 1971), 31.

semantic terms, Pickwick seems to represent literal meaning and Sam the figurative and metaphoric. As the novel proceeds, each of these oppositions seems an increasingly inadequate characterization of their partnership, as the two figures more and more take on each other's qualities. The relation of Pickwick and Weller cannot be reduced to any pair of such oppositions, although their friendship seems to hold out the possibility of a stable and certain structure of differences behind their partnership, a structure that permits an easy, effortless commerce and exchange between old and young, and rich and poor.

It is sometimes argued that the 'affectionate communion' of Weller and Pickwick has a particularly Christian colouring and that this is evidence that a 'Christian vision was native to Dickens's temperament'.[36] For W. H. Auden, for example, Pickwick's self-imposed incarceration in the Fleet is his first step towards the recognition that 'there is a difference between Law and Grace, the Righteous man and the Holy man'. Auden attempts to give the novel the shape and purpose of an explicitly Christian allegory, whose main theme is the Fall of Man.[37] It is true that the book is concerned with the need for charity, philanthropy, and forgiveness, but it is too simple to assimilate the ethical obligations of care and compassion to this pattern. There are strong anti-clerical elements in the book, most notably the treatment of Reverend Stiggins, whose expulsion from the family pub by Tony and Sam is important enough to become one of the title-pages of the book. Although many acts of charity and forgiveness in the novel can be described in Christian terms, most notably Pickwick's charitable relief of Jingle and Trotter and his release of Mrs Bardell from the Fleet, Pickwick turns on his heel (587) when he first sees Mrs Bardell in prison, and there is no scene of forgiveness or reconciliation between them. His last action with Dodson and Fogg is, perfectly justifiably, to abuse them roundly as 'mean, rascally, pettifogging robbers' (674): no forgiveness there either. Sam Weller might believe Pickwick to be 'a reg'lar thorough-bred angel' (575), but he is no saint and when he releases himself from the Fleet, he goes not to Heaven but to Birmingham. He re-enters the world almost as daft as he left it, haring off to the dirtiest city in

[36] Marcus, *Dickens: From Pickwick to Dombey*, 31, 51.
[37] Auden, 'Dingley Dell and the Fleet', 408, 428.

England in order to try to gain Ben Allen's father's approval for his son's clandestine marriage, with Bob Sawyer drunk on the roof of the coach. If *Pickwick* is the novel in Dickens's oeuvre that, in the Fleet at least, comes closest to a humble, forgiving, and redemptive faith, it is also, in its festive, celebratory cheer, the most secular of his works, a pagan, catholic book about friendship in this world.

Sam Weller's relationship with his father is the other important friendship of the book. Although critics have sometimes tried to fit their reciprocal and ironic affection into an Oedipal pattern, it resists such a characterization as strongly as the novel resists an overly Christian reading. For Steven Marcus, Dickens tells in *Pickwick* the first of his many Oedipal tales, and works through his own ambivalent hostility to his father in a complex set of displacements and identifications.[38] Pickwick, for Marcus, is a substitute father for Sam's inadequate natural one. But this is to misrecognize their relationship, which is not that of 'ideal parent' and child, but of employer and master.[39] This continues until Sam transforms their relationship in the Fleet and thus allows or creates the moral elevation of their companionship, which is such a surprise and strength of the book's later chapters. The scene in which Sam returns to Pickwick as a voluntary fellow-prisoner is the moment of this change, signalled by Sam's refusal to respond to Pickwick's call. As 'serious and resolved' as his master (539), Sam defies Pickwick, Weller defies Samuel. At the end of the next chapter, he returns to the Fleet but on quite another footing, as a fellow-prisoner who, 'folding his arms, looked fixedly and firmly in his master's face' (551). It is a silent gaze of simultaneous defiance, equality, and mutuality, and an act of liberation in a prison. Pickwick has just called Sam a 'good lad' and 'my faithful fellow' (550), but he will not do so again, having met the radical challenge of his self-asserting, self-incarcerating stare.

Just before this moment, Sam's father, in conversation with Solomon Pell the lawyer, has called Sam 'a reg'lar prodigy son!'. Corrected by Pell to 'Prodigal-prodigal son', Tony replies ' "Never mind, sir . . . I know wot's o'clock, Sir . . . Ven I don't, I'll ask you, Sir." ' (550). A prodigy is of course an amazing or

---

[38] Marcus, *Dickens: From Pickwick to Dombey*, 33.   [39] Ibid., 35.

marvellous thing, especially a child of precocious gifts. Sam is a prodigy son, and in this brief, utterly polite exchange between bourgeois professional and working man, all the wit, dignity, and insight are with the latter. The preceding passage, in which Sam and Tony debate their plot to imprison Sam, is as revealing as it is funny:

"The officer will be here at four o'clock," said Mr Pell. "I suppose you won't run away meanwhile—eh? Ha! ha!"

"P'raps my cruel pa 'ull relent afore that," replied Sam, with a broad grin.

"Not I," said the elder Mr Weller.

"Do," said Sam.

"Not on no account," replied the inexorable creditor.

"I'll give bills for the amount at sixpence a month," said Sam.

"I won't take 'em," said Mr Weller. (549)

At such moments, Sam is filial without piety, his father paternal without authority.[40] And just as Tony recognizes his son as a prodigy, beyond or outside nature, monstrous in some way, so Sam recognizes the prodigious qualities of Pickwick, 'an angel' (575) in tights and gaiters whose heart is twenty-five years younger than his body (499), a happy monster.

Friendship is not solely the property of Pickwick and the Wellers, but of a much wider imagined community, between Dickens, his readers, and characters, a friendship that will grow over later decades and many novels. Indeed at times, the writing and reading of fiction is seen wholly as a matter of friendship. On the final pages of the book, for example, Dickens writes the first of many scenes of farewell to his own characters:

Let us leave our old friend in one of those moments of unmixed happiness, of which, if we seek them, there are ever some to cheer our transitory existence here. There are dark shadows on the earth, but its lights are stronger in the contrast . . . It is the fate of most men who mingle with the world and attain even the prime of life, to make many real friends, and lose them in the course of nature. It is the fate of all authors or chroniclers to create imaginary friends, and lose them in the course of art. (717)

---

[40] For the phrase 'filial without piety', see Jacques Derrida, 'Dialanguages', in *Points . . . Interviews, 1974–1994* (Stanford: Stanford University Press, 1995), 150–1.

Fiction and the creation of fiction is here seen as a matter of friendship and companionship, a friendship that is close to mourning. It is also worth noting the word 'cheer' in the passage, for it is a word that tolls through the book, appearing at one point five times on a single page. 'Cheer' and 'cheerfulness' derive from the Greek for 'head', which becomes the late Latin for 'face' and comes, in our tongue, to mean disposition, or mood, reception or entertainment, fare, viands, food, solace, encouragement, welcome, approbation, congratulations, and, above all, gladness, mirth, and gaiety. The face of Pickwick, that great sun, is at the centre of the book, as are welcome, food, and approbation; as are entertainment, gladness, and mirth.[41] All of these are commemorated in Dickens's farewell to his readers, friends, and characters: in the head, the face, the solace, the disposition, the cheer of *Pickwick* and of Pickwick, a cheer not inseparable from loss.

IV

Women are almost entirely excluded from the friendships of the novel, and are often the occasion for dissension between men: Slammer and Winkle nearly fight over Mrs Budger; Tupman and Jingle quarrel over Rachael Wardle; Peter Magnus challenges Pickwick to a duel over Miss Witherfield; Winkle is pursued by the irate husband of Mrs Dowler. Such events both underpin and undermine the binding-together of men in the book, which at times comes close to endorsing the dirty-faced man's assertion in chapter 14 that 'Rum creeters is women' (160).[42] The women of *Pickwick Papers* are stereotyped, probably more so than in any other Dickens work, as predatory spinsters, husband-hating wives, bluestockings, or conventional young women. This stereotyping seems part of a deep anxiety about sexuality that many of the male characters in the book share, together with a fear of the loss of sexual power and potency in women's company. This is most clear in the comedy of Tony Weller's fear of 'widders' (244), those predatory and sexually

---

[41] Hillis Miller, *Illustration* 97.

[42] '[T]he major plot-lines of the novel are overtly . . . anti-erotic': Margaret Anne Doody, *The True Story of the Novel* (London: Fontana, 1998), 382.

knowledgeable beings who contrived to destroy his widowed bliss, but also in Pickwick's sexlessness and 'grossly epicene' appearance.[43] Vulnerable parts of the body are often liable to be lopped off, as the Pickwickians learn in the second chapter, when they nearly lose their heads as they leave the Golden Cross. Losing one's head is a deeply resonant image—for Freud it is a sign of castration; for Derrida, of dissemination[44]—and Dickens immediately reinforces this disseminating or castrating opening to the Pickwick Club's adventures by Jingle's instant subsequent reference to the decapitation of Charles I on the Banqueting House balcony.

Sam Weller, who starts off well and gets better and better, is the exception to this rather fearful and uncertain relation to women and sex. He never loses his head, which is quite firmly screwed on. Indeed, he is, in many ways, the name and power of desire in the book, Mr Pickwick's phallus, and in his wooing of Mary one of the few plausible young lovers in Dickens's work. In that favourite adjective of the novel, he is also its most 'singular' character, and its most important one. Dickens throughout his career creates figures who suffer a lot and yet survive, like Dick Swiveller in *The Old Curiosity Shop*, who, under the weight of all the staggerers that he is prey to, remains unsnubbably optimistic, bobbing like a cork on the seas of his poverty; Micawber is another version, and Montague Tigg and the Artful Dodger are criminal variations. These characters share the capacity to withstand events and changes of fortune that under normal circumstances would be devastating or fatal, and yet come up capable of smiling and of making us smile. They are charming and morally ambiguous, possessing qualities that subvert or suspend normal ethical considerations.[45] Sam Weller, with his resilience and relish for the world, is the first and purest version of this type.

Indeed, *Pickwick Papers* had sold badly until the moment in

---

[43] Hillis Miller, *Illustration*, 104.

[44] Sigmund Freud, *The Interpretation of Dreams* (Harmondsworth: Penguin, 1976), 485. 'To lose one's head, no longer to know where one's head is, such is perhaps the effect of dissemination': Jacques Derrida, *Dissemination* (London: Athlone, 1981), 20.

[45] The distinctions that Barbara Hardy makes in her *The Moral Art of Dickens* (London: Oxford University Press, 1970) are acute about certain kinds of moral life, but there are other principles at work in Dickens's novels, as here.

chapter 10 when Dickens hit on the idea of creating Sam Weller, who simultaneously rescued Mr Pickwick and the novel, and became in the process the most famous working man of the nineteenth century. Like his job, Sam is 'a sort of compo' (142) of many things, who introduces into the novel new ways of behaviour, different criteria of judgement, and, above all, forms of speech and discourse which are distinct from those of most of the other characters. Sam's ways of speaking, of conceiving time, and of representing the world to himself and others both easily inhabit the novel and greatly extend it. He does not disrupt or subvert *Pickwick Papers*, but seems able to free and unbind it, to move it to a more ample sense of what human life may be and what language can do. We see this, for example, in the book's figuring of time and space. Whereas Mr Pickwick uses prosthetic aids—telescope, spectacles—in order to see things properly, Sam, by contrast, seems to have everything in perspective, a perspective that combines the sharpest of street-wise chaff with a gaze *sub specie aeternitatis*. He gives the sense of great leisure and space, the space almost of infinity, the time almost of eternity. His rarely hurried equanimity often incites readers to think of immortal beings, but the book has severe doubts about the use of such language to describe human affairs, from Tupman's distaste at being called 'Bacchus' (16) to Tony Weller's advice to his son to avoid terms such as 'angel' or 'Wenus' to describe the woman he loves (407). Frank Kermode makes a distinction between the fictional times of *chronos* and *kairos* on the one hand and of *aevum* on the other.[46] *Aevum* is an 'intermediate order', the time of the angels and of novelists, of creatures who live in time but who are nevertheless eternal. This 'second-best eternity' is Weller's time, just as his sense of space seems more than human without ever being divine, a strange ether in which he and the novel move.[47]

Much of Sam's power seems to come from his awareness of other and simultaneous actions. The simple words 'as' and 'like' do much of the good work of the novel, from the moment when Pickwick bursts 'like another sun from his slumbers' (6) at the beginning of the novel, but they are most effective in Sam

[46] Frank Kermode, *The Sense of an Ending* (London: Oxford University Press, 1967), 71–4.
[47] Ibid., 71, 74.

Weller's mouth. The characteristic form of his sayings is 'As
... said ... ven he ...'—as in ' "reg'lar rotation, as Jack Ketch
said, ven he tied the men up" ' (109), ' "out vith it, as the father
said to the child, ven he swallowed a farden" ' (141), ' "Business
first, pleasure arterwards, as King Richard the Third said ven
he stabbed the t'other king in the Tower, afore he smothered the
babbies" ' (304), or ' "Werry glad to see you, indeed, and hope
our acquaintance may be a long 'un, as the gen'l'm'n said to
the fi' pun' note" ' (314). A proverb or cliché is supplemented
or twisted to give a sense of the singularity of the event (the
comparisons are comic and ridiculous) and the sense that
somehow, obscurely, it is part of some wider pattern and order;
that everything is both just what it is and a part of a larger
whole. For Sam, there seems to be no contradiction between
respecting the particularity of something and considering the
possibility of a wider order or pattern: 'exactly the same thing',
he seems to be saying, but in a different place and time, and so
completely different too.

These sayings became so famous in the nineteenth century
that they became popularly known as 'Wellerisms'.[48] Although
for the most part they are figurative elaborations of everyday
speech—' "There; now ve look compact and comfortable, as the
father said ven he cut his little boy's head off, to cure him o'
squintin' " ' (344)—they seem to invite further interpretation,
which neither the novel nor Sam is willing to give us. Much of
the prose of *Pickwick Papers* is long-winded, a quality both satirized by the novel and part of its own style and tone. Sam's language both contrasts with and resembles what surrounds it, for
his speech is simultaneously leisured and epigrammatic, both

---

[48] Engel, *Pickwick Papers: An Annotated Bibliography*, 73–4, lists a number of
Joke Books, including *Sam Weller: A Journal of Wit and Humour*, *Sam Weller's
Pickwick Jest Book* (published in twenty-five numbers), and *Sam Weller's Budget
of Recitations*. Wellerisms appear both in full-length fiction such as Reynolds, *Pickwick Abroad*: ' "You may laugh, Sir, as the Eel said to the 'Oman when she was a
skining on him" ' (5), and such publications as *The Pickwick Comic Almanac for
1838*: ' "Why, Sir, for the matter o' that, Missus Glitter ain't none of the brightest
pieces of haminated matter; as the Mussel said to the Oyster, when they quarrelled
about beauty; therefor it warn't to be wondered at, Sir, if anything as I did should
astonish her weak nerves, as the Doctor said when he 'lectrified his patient' "(5).
For Bruce Robbins, *The Servant's Hand: Fiction from Below* (Durham: Duke University Press, 1993), 83, 'the Wellerism ... is closer to ... a momentary collaboration of servant with narrator than to the realistic grappling of dialogue'.

narrative and aphorism. Sam often takes his time, but he can also puncture the surrounding diffuseness with a terse wit that is both proverbial and his own:

"You may order your officers to do whatever you please, Sir," said Mr Pickwick, "and I have no doubt, from the specimen I have had of the subordination preserved among them, that whatever you order, they will execute, but I shall take the liberty, Sir, of claiming my right to be heard by force."

"Pickvick and principle," exclaimed Mr Weller, in a very audible voice.

"Sam, be quiet," said Mr Pickwick.

"Dumb as a drum with a hole in it," replied Sam. (306)[49]

Sam often uses metaphor and simile, in contrast to Pickwick's literal-mindedness. Metaphor is commonly defined as a 'transaction between contexts', which also defines Sam's function in the novel. Like his father's description of a coachman, Sam acts as 'a sort o' con-nectin' link' (660), translating across and between the different contexts of the book. Like metaphor, he 'speaks obliquely, exploits lateral connections, insinuates things without really saying them, suggests ideas without making them explicit' and so becomes the book's metaphor of metaphor, a simile of simile.[50] Through this power, Pickwick is able to find himself at ease, if not at home, in the most surprising contexts, and to transact himself there.

Sam also has a fertile gift of renaming those whom he meets: the Fat Boy is, at various times, 'young dropsy' (340), a 'young boa constructer' (349), and 'young brockiley sprout' (403), Master Bardell 'young townskip' and an 'infant fernomenon' (321), and Tony Weller 'my Prooshan Blue' (405) and 'corpilence' (410). But it is not simply proper names that Sam plays with. Like his father, he is a master punster (itself a word that Tony puns on). Tony insists that Pickwick needs an 'alleybi' (408) in court, a bye-way or alley and a word (like 'properiator' (443), which dispossesses the proprieties of property) that can evade and escape the law. Tony invents the ludic delusions of the 'dilluded' (405) and the different little jests just there in 'adjestin' our little differences' (690). An 'audit' becomes the more material and yet more figurative 'hordit' (701), the

---

[49] On the servant's right to speak, see Robbins, *The Servant's Hand*, 74.
[50] Bennington and Derrida, *Jacques Derrida*, 119.

probate becomes a 'probe it' (694), legatees 'leg-at-ease' (694), and a chair a 'cheer' (703). The rhetorical name for this linguistic creativity is catachresis, the term for the abuse of words, as when 'habeas corpus' becomes 'have-his-carcase' (510) or a five pound note a 'fi' pun' note' (314). All of these puns are no doubt invested in the funds that Tony deftly turns into the 'funs' (661). It is often said that Dickens brings a certain kind of popular speech and culture into the bourgeois novel, the sort of street-wise banter that the Wellers do so well. But it is important to see how many of these jokes depend on their written nature, and how much of their effect comes from the gap and passage between speech and writing. Almost all these examples—leg-at-ease, fi' pun' note, probe-it—are difficult, if not impossible, to make funny in speech. They stem from the play between the different demands and possibilities of speech and writing, and cannot be reduced to one or the other without loss, unless we follow Derrida's suggestion of a much more ample and extended concept of writing, which would both include and precede speech.[51] If Derrida is right, it is from this strange and uncertain position in language that the disseminating force of this paronomasia stems, from a speech and writing beside, near, by, along, past, and beyond the proper name, in by-names and alleybis that comprise so much of the book's investment in the funs.

Sam and Tony are more than a set of linguistic or rhetorical principles, however much their wit rests on an unconscious mastery of tropes and figures. Sam's character has roots in the portrayal of witty servants in eighteenth-century and earlier drama, and he shares his precursors' sceptical relativism and ability to 'slip censored or contradictory ideas past the reason's defences'.[52] Like that of earlier servants, his voice tends to 'project itself out of dialogue and into monologue'.[53] But if in one way Sam is at the end of a line of comic servants, a last gasp of Regency England before such cheek is stifled by

[51] '[T]he concept of writing exceeds and comprehends that of language ... And thus we say "writing" for all that gives rise to an inscription in general.' Jacques Derrida, *Of Grammatology* (Baltimore: Johns Hopkins University Press, 1976), 8–9. See also Bennington and Derrida, *Jacques Derrida*, 49–50.

[52] Robbins, *The Servant's Hand*, 75.

[53] Robbins notes that Sam and Pickwick are 'the last of the novel-length couples': *The Servant's Hand*, 80.

Victorian constraint, he is also more than this, with a self-possession akin to that of both a good actor and a sincere man. This is clear in such scenes as John Smauker's soirée, where Dickens takes one of the most familiar, not to say clichéd, scenes and settings of the English novel—Bath society—and transcodes its conventions of gentility and fashion into a footman's swarry. This popular imitation and parody of the genteel world is itself imitated and parodied by Sam Weller, to create what Smauker, footman and dandy, calls, in a rich pun, the very 'vortext of society' (465), a simultaneous foretaste, vortex, and foretext of all that Bath is and represents in fiction.

Freud makes a distinction in his essay on humour between jokes ('*witz*') and humour ('*humor*'). As an example of humour, Freud tells the story of a criminal who is led out to the gallows on a Monday and who remarks 'well, the week's beginning nicely'.[54] Such humour, writes Freud, 'is a way of sparing oneself the affect to which a situation would naturally give rise'—here fear, horror, anger—'and dismissing the possibility of such emotions with a jest'.[55] For Freud, this kind of humour 'has something liberating about it', 'something of grandeur and elevation', which comes from 'the victorious assertion of the ego's invulnerability'.[56] The ego refuses to be distressed by the provocations of reality and takes the impending trauma simply as an occasion to gain pleasure. This triumph of the pleasure principle, argues Freud, 'shows a magnificent superiority over the real situation', which gives the humour a 'dignity wholly lacking in jokes'.[57] Much of Sam Weller's humour is like that in Freud's examples. Before any threat or danger—Buzfuz's cross-

[54] Sigmund Freud, 'Humour', in *The Pelican Freud Library Volume 14: Art and Literature* (Harmondsworth: Penguin, 1985), 427.

[55] Ibid., 428.

[56] Ibid., 427–8.

[57] Ibid., 429. Freud goes on to say that this kind of humour is one in which 'the subject is behaving towards them [other people] as an adult does towards a child when he recognises and smiles at the triviality of interests and sufferings which seems so great to it'. The humorist identifies himself to some extent with his father: 'is there any sense', asks Freud, 'in saying that someone is treating himself like a child and is at the same time playing the part of a superior adult towards that child?' (ibid., 430). In *Master Humphrey's Clock*, Sam has a son whose great gift is to imitate and take on the identity of his grandfather: Charles Dickens, *Master Humphrey's Clock and Other Stories*, ed. Peter Mudford (London: Everyman, 1997), 105.

examination, Nupkins the magistrate, the Fleet itself—Sam refuses to be disturbed, is certain that he cannot be harmed, and takes the event simply as an occasion for taking pleasure. He demonstrates his own superiority over situations, like the insouciant man of his own story who remarks on the way to execution: ' "If you walley my precious life don't upset me" ' (230).

Apart from telling jokes and Wellerisms, Sam also tells stories, quite lengthy ones at times, such as the one about the man who ran a sausage shop and 'rashly converted his-self into sausages' (380). In his essay on the art of the storyteller, Walter Benjamin argues that the art of Nikolai Leskov's narration is to leave the story 'free of explanation as one reproduces it'.[58] This is precisely what Sam does. He is always aware that there is another story, other stories to be told, like doors perpetually opening to a place and time in which Living Skeletons talk (187), Blue Beard is a 'wictim o' connubiality' (246), and polar bears practise their skating (363). Benjamin uses the example of Leskov to make a contrast between the world of the novel and that of the story, which rests on the novel's essential dependence on the book: the novel, he argues, 'neither comes from oral tradition nor goes into it'.[59] But Wellerisms, which are such a necessary part of this, 'the most important single novel of the Victorian era', both stem from and feed into oral tradition, not that of a timeless folk, but of the working and lower-middle classes of pre-Victorian London.[60]

Sam Weller also resembles Leskov's characters in that he seems to possess the ability, as Benjamin puts it, to 'move up and down the rungs of . . . experience as on a ladder. A ladder extending downwards to the interior of the earth and disappearing into the clouds.'[61] Dr Faustus and the Devil, Richard III and the man going to Tyburn: all are harnessed easily to the banter of everyday life: ' "He wants you particklar; and no one else'll do, as the Devil's private secretary said ven he fetched avay Doctor Faustus" ' (175). Weller's stories have that 'chaste

---

[58] Walter Benjamin, 'The Storyteller: Reflections on the Work of Nikolai Leskov', in *Illuminations* (London: Fontana, 1973), 87.
[59] Ibid.
[60] John Sutherland, *The Longman Companion to Victorian Fiction* (Harlow: Longman, 1988), 506.
[61] Benjamin, 'The Storyteller', 102.

compactness which precludes psychological analysis' which Benjamin calls an 'artisan form of communication', marked by the handprints of its creation.[62] Sam's hands leave their prints on his stories and sayings in the form of misplaced 'v's and 'w's, which are both peculiarly his and shared with his father and other Cockneys. When he is asked in the Pickwick and Bardell trial whether his name is spelled with a 'v' or a 'w', a voice from the gallery, that of his father, shouts out ' "Put it down a we, my Lord, put it down a we" ' (434). There is, of course, no such letter as 'we', but there is a pronoun, that of the first person-plural. Tony's and Sam's 'we's are all over the novel, substituting for the letter which should be there in 'vurks' and 'vells' (572), 'varm vater at vunce' (570), 'veels within veels' (512), and 'vite-vash on vun's clothes' (506). Their vaggery is marked by singular, plural letters which are no letters, and are neither part of speech nor writing, but the signs of an irreducible and collective plurality and play beyond them both.

In one of his richest aphorisms, Benjamin asserts that 'the storyteller is the figure in which the righteous man encounters himself'.[63] Sam Weller is a righteous man who usually knows (except with Job Trotter) how to judge justly, and the difference between the law and justice. Like Benjamin's righteous man, he offers counsel to Pickwick and the reader, and does so by telling stories and making jokes. Sam has counsel for Pickwick 'not for a few situations but for many, like a sage', even if his advice can be as riddling as an oracle's and his expression 'somewhat homely and occasionally incomprehensible' (195).[64] The ironic and pragmatic reason of his stories and sayings exemplifies the 'cunning and high spirits' that Benjamin found and commended in the folk-tale.[65] The storyteller, writes Benjamin, is the figure in which the righteous man encounters himself, but here the righteous man encounters not himself but his other self: Samuel Pickwick encounters Samuel Weller.

---

[62] Benjamin, 'The Storyteller', 91.   [63] Ibid., 109.

[64] Ibid., 108. Compare also Walter Benjamin, 'Franz Kafka: on the Tenth Anniversary of his Death', in *Illuminations* (London: Fontana, 1973); like Kafka's parables, Wellerisms 'unfold . . . the way a bud turns into a blossom . . . lend themselves to quotation and can be told for purposes of clarification' (122).

[65] Benjamin, 'The Storyteller', 102.

V

If we wanted a contrast with the insouciance of Weller, his sanity and sense, we need only look at the hasty, fevered, and mortal 'interpolated' tales, which, like their characters, burn for a few pages on the edge of death and then die. These stories resemble Wellerisms insofar as they introduce into the novel different subject-matters, temporalities, and forms of narration from those of the 'main' story, subjects and forms that can only with difficulty be assimilated into the novel proper. But whereas Sam can move with ease between different places and contexts in the novel, the stories relate only with difficulty to contexts other than the ones they create themselves. Their listeners in the novel take little notice of them, or fall asleep like Mr Pickwick listening to Mr Potts's editorials (150). Critics have the choice of attempting either to assimilate them to the rest of the text, or to ignore them on the grounds of their incompetence and tedium.[66] Neither of these approaches wholly works and so these additional and supplementary stories remain both part of the novel and nothing at all to do with it. It is as if Dickens had tried, as Garrett Stewart remarks, 'to *cement* the separateness of the two worlds' that nevertheless must be made to co-exist.[67]

Nicolas Abraham and Maria Torok have written about certain aspects of a person or text that seem to make their presence felt but cannot readily be explained by conventional ideas of presence or absence. These they call 'cryptic', in testament to the fact that they are often expressed in coded or cryptic forms of language, and are caused by deeply buried traumatic material, often belonging to an earlier generation. Crypts, in their sense, are places (which are not strictly places) where things that are both dead and alive continue to exist, as both part of a psyche or a text and not part of it, buried and locked away, inaccessible to most forms of analysis, but still making their

[66] Edmund Wilson, 'Dickens: The Two Scrooges', in *The Wound and the Bow* (Cambridge: Houghton Mifflin, 1941), 1–104. The most important discussions of the tales are Robert L. Patten's articles, 'The Art of *Pickwick*'s Interpolated Tales', *ELH: English Literary History*, 34 (1967), 349–66, and 'The Unpropitious Muse: Pickwick's "Interpolated" Tales', *Dickens Studies Newsletter* (March 1970), 7–10.
[67] Stewart, *Dickens and the Trial of Imagination*, 35.

presence felt.[68] The interpolated tales of *Pickwick Papers* are very like crypts. They are full of violent and traumatic material, which often seems to defy sense and reason. The dead come alive in these stories, and bloody conflicts take place between the generations, but their relationship to the main story that enfolds and tries to contain them is never clear. They do not have settled causal, biographical, or narrative connections to each other or the rest of the novel. Pain, violence, murder, and talking furniture simultaneously appear and disappear within them and are contained and not contained by them. These crypts resemble Wellerisms in their impropriety and inability to be assimilated to the main story, but it is a traumatic impropriety, not its comic analogue.

Many of the interpolated tales are about ghosts, spirits, or the dead returning to life. They share Sam Weller's interest in death, and, like him, often link writing and mortality. Indeed, Sam often acts as a kind of death's head or *memento mori* of *The Posthumous Papers*, revelling in an intimate and obsessive concern with death. At his first appearance in the novel, for example, he asks Pickwick: ' "what the devil do you want with me, as the man said ven he seed the ghost?" ' (115). Sam greets his father as a 'corpilence' and 'old ghost' (410) and even an apology from him brings death and violence in its wake: ' "Wery sorry to 'casion any personal inconwenience, Ma'am, as the housebreaker said to the old lady vhen he put her on the fire" ' (322). The tales are troubled by ghosts and spectres: John Edwards in 'The Convict's Return' is thought to be dead but comes back alive; the madman in 'A Madman's Manuscript' is haunted by his dead wife 'fresh from the grave; and . . . so very death-like' (130); Heyling in 'The Old Man's Tale about the Queer Client' returns like an 'apparition' to condemn his enemy to a 'living death' (265); Gabriel Grub, like Scrooge after him, sees spirits of the living and the dead. The text finds itself troubled, even on its most hasty and hackneyed pages, by questions and spectres of the hope and possibility of life beyond life, a life that we need not hasten to call immortal life.

It would be easy to dismiss this side of the book as a

---

[68] Nicolas Abraham and Maria Torok, *The Shell and the Kernel* (Chicago: University of Chicago Press, 1994), 16.

residual and adolescent Gothicism. But it is important to note how closely the novel and the interpolated tales weave together their concern with the apparatuses of writing—what we called the 'postal principle'—with their interest in the interpenetration of 'life' and 'death'. The dedication of the book, for example, is interested in what happens to writing after the death of an author, and what can or should return in copyright to 'the widowed mother and the orphan child' (xxii). The concern with what lives on in writing and what can return from it to the living and the dead continues throughout the book. The 1847 preface begins by bequeathing a legacy to Posterity ('who will come into an immense fortune'), continues with a discussion of what should or should not return in credit to Robert Seymour, the book's first illustrator, and ends with that figure of the animate dead, the 'Dance of Death'.[69]

This interest in the strange doublings of ghosts and posts comes together most strongly in 'The Tale of the Bagman's Uncle', one of only two interpolated stories in the latter half of the novel and the only one after Pickwick's release from the Fleet. It appears in chapter 49, well after the plot is wrapping itself up, and tells a ghost story. The bagman's uncle falls asleep after a heavy night's drinking in Edinburgh in a yard where they keep 'the decaying skeletons of departed mails' (615). He wakes to find the coaches restored and the yard full of figures who 'seemed to start up in some strange manner from the ground or the air, and to disappear in the same way' (616). A voice tells him ' "You're booked for one inside" ' (615), whereupon he boards the mail and is called 'Jack Martin' by the mail guard, which is 'a liberty which the Post-office wouldn't have sanctioned' (616). After a fight in which he stabs his opponent's hat with a sword, he is driven off in the post-coach with two men and a woman into an enigmatic and mysterious adventure of sexual desire and violence. They are all taken to a house, where the bagman's uncle rescues the woman from the men, one of whom (the son of the Marquis of Filletoville) she kills by pinning him to the wall 'in cockchaffer fashion'. ' "You have cut off the entail" ', says the bagman's uncle to her, and the two of

[69] Charles Dickens, 'Preface to the Cheap Edition, 1847', reprinted in *The Pickwick Papers*, ed. Robert L. Patten (Harmondsworth: Penguin, 1972), 47.

them speedily board the mail again to escape (622). They fall in love and he promises to love her for ever, but then wakes in the yard again, devoted to a life of bachelorhood. Refusing several offers of marriage in his later life, he 'always said what a curious thing it was . . . that the ghosts of mail coaches . . . were in the habit of making journeys every night'. The landlord of the inn asks: ' "I wonder what these ghosts of mail coaches carry in their bags" ', to which the bagman replies: ' "The dead letters, of course." ' (625).

It is a puzzling story. The bagman's uncle is booked on the coach (and by the book) onto the Edinburgh and London Mail and into an enigmatic narrative of male possession, the threat of death, desire for a ghost, lifelong bachelorhood, the delivery of the mail, the power of spirits, the fate of dead letters, and the sense of dreams. It is simultaneously a comic anecdote, a ghost story and a vision, told by the forerunner of today's commercial traveller, an identity that Dickens both takes on and refuses in his own later uncommercial travels.[70] To catch the mail in this story is to enter into a relationship with the spirits of the dead, who become objects both of mortal threat—the men try to kill him—and of overwhelming desire. The bagman's uncle is solicited or interpellated in a dream or memory which stands outside normal temporal sequence and possesses and transforms him, a story and event concerned with both writing and romance.[71] In his story, the uncle is the archetypal romantic hero who rescues a woman in distress and loves her for ever. In his waking life he is, like Pickwick, a celibate bachelor. His relation to writing is similarly double: in the course of his adventures he resolves to write to both the post office and the papers (618, 620), but in fact leaves his story to be told by another and written by a third. In this way, 'The Tale of the Bagman's Uncle' can be seen as an allegory of writing and male desire, a deeply literary story which the bagman suspects his uncle may have made up 'out of some book afterwards' (615) about a dead

[70] Dickens, *The Uncommercial Traveller*, 1–2.

[71] 'We are in ourselves only as *Andenken*, as a dead letter come from the other; before any living act . . . we are solicited or interpellated by a dead letter that is addressed to us—whether it be by preceding generations, by the ancientness of language, or the opacity of history': Maurizio Ferraris interviewing Jacques Derrida, 'Istrice 2: Ick bünn all hier', in Derrida, *Points*, 320.

man's desire for a woman who is simultaneously absent, imagined, and dead.

Derrida has written about the relationship between writing and death. In Geoffrey Bennington's paraphrase:

Writing communicates my thoughts to far distances, during my absence, even after my death. At the moment of reading my letter, the addressee knows that I might have died during the time, however minimal it may be, between the moment at which the letter was finished and the moment of its reception ... What is here called 'death' is the generic name we shall give to my absence in general with respect to what I write—whether this absence be real or an absence of intention or sincerity or conviction ... When you read me, not only do you not know whether or not I am dead, but whether what I write is really what I meant, fully *compos mentis*, at the moment of writing, etc. That there be this fundamental and irreducible uncertainty is part of the essential structure of writing.[72]

It is not so surprising that the bagman, his uncle, and their tale are so enigmatic. For they repeat in miniature the same impossibilities and contradictions that permeate *Pickwick* and perhaps all writing. We will never know whose story this is, whether it rightly belongs to the bagman, his uncle, or the editor of the Pickwick Club papers, nor whether it has a stable or proper relationship to what surrounds it in the book. Nor can we know whether what it narrates occurred or did not occur; whether the bagman, his uncle, or the editor was drunk or sober, alive or dead, awake or dreaming when it happened or did not; whether he or they met or imagined they met living, dead, fictional, or real characters; whether the story is about desire or the absence of desire; or whether it is part of literature or not. Nor is it clear whether we should treat the story as a profound allegory about the implication of desire, subjectivity, and what is called 'human life' within structures of writing, repetition, and death, or as a shaggy-dog story made up from old books, or as both and neither.

Like deconstruction and the bagman's coach, *Pickwick Papers* happens more in the journey than in the arrival.[73] This final interpolated tale can be seen as a form of conjuration, an

---

[72] Bennington and Derrida, *Jacques Derrida*, 51.
[73] '[D]econstruction happens more in the journey than the arrival': ibid., 169.

attempt to conjure up and conjure away ghosts, ceding a place where ghosts, posts, and various symbols of castration can be separated and detached (but not quite detached) from the text of which they will always be a part. And yet these forces, ghosts and posts, often escape, walking the corridors of the books, popping up in Sam Weller's stories, and everywhere else in which writing and repetition figure. 'The Tale of the Bagman's Uncle' is a bad story for literature, and one in which Dickens, like the bagman's uncle, resolves to memorialize the post office, to write a memo to it, through the post, and to enact a work of remembrance, particularly of the dead, as I do now too.

VI

Pickwick Papers appeared in the middle of many political, literary, and cultural transitions and one of the most turbulent decades of the century. Although the Swing Riots are mentioned by Pickwick in his first address to the Club (5) and Dickens's experience as a parliamentary reporter is put to use in the Eatanswill election episode, the book seems for the most part to be indifferent to politics, concerned to create a discursive space above and beyond them.[74] Indeed, *Pickwick* may be the least politically or socially focused of Dickens's novels, with none of the ambition of *Little Dorrit* or *Bleak House* to characterize an entire social system, none of the dramatic scenes of insurrection of *A Tale of Two Cities* and *Barnaby Rudge*, and none of the reforming zeal and raw social anger that animates its successor, *Oliver Twist*. The Eatanswill chapters, the most direct representation of politics in the book, simply satirize the excesses of early nineteenth-century electoral bribery and drunkenness, and when there are two mobs, Pickwick counsels Snodgrass to shout with the largest (239). 'The praise of mankind was his Swing', it is reported of our hero: bourgeois benevolence substitutes for popular struggle (5).

[74] Contrast Dickens on the Northampton by-election of December 1835: 'No artifice has been left untried, no influence has been withheld, no chicanery neglected by the Tory party: and the glorious result is, that Mr Maunsell is placed at the head of the poll by the most ignorant, drunken and brutal electors in these kingdoms, who have been treated and fed, and driven up to the polls the whole day like herds of swine': *'The Amusements of the People' and Other Papers: Reports, Essays and Reviews*, ed. Michael Slater (London: J. M. Dent, 1996), 28.

In the second chapter of the book, Jingle tells the Pickwickians that he was at the July events in Paris in 1830 and there composed a ten-thousand-line epic on the spot, in which the fall of the Bourbons passed directly into verse: 'Mars by day, Apollo by night,—bang the field-piece, twang the lyre' (11). The possibility of such a poem on the subject of political insurrection appears briefly in the mouth of a failed actor and confidence trickster, troubles the surface of the text, and then disappears.[75] Shortly afterwards, as they pass by the window of the Banqueting House, Jingle reminds them of another violent political upheaval, by pointing out the window from which Charles I walked to his execution. William Wordsworth, who remade the epic for English letters, confessed himself baffled by the affection in which the young men of the time seemed to hold the prospect of 'Bozzy's next No.' and worried how the young Dickens's success would affect the sale of the classics.[76] It is tempting to allegorize this moment: the English epic makes its final absurd comic bow in the mouth of Jingle, and leaves the field (along with revolution, romanticism, and politics) to the victorious Bozzy and his contemporary novel, full of low matter and absurd puns, illustrated, undignified, comic, and vulgar. Forgetting the July events and the death of Charles I, Mr Pickwick and his friends bowl along the streets of London into the timeless world of an eternal England, seemingly free of politics for ever.

The possibility of political change haunts the fringes of the novel, however, and the novel shares with its Romantic precursors an interest in radical social change. It figures this through the use of what are essentially pastoral conventions, if we use that term in William Empson's extended sense.[77] To think of

[75] On the awkwardness of the July revolution for English liberal opinion at the time, see Dror Wahrman, *Imagining the Middle Class: The Political Representation of Class in Britain, c. 1780–1840* (Cambridge: Cambridge University Press, 1995), 309–12.

[76] William Wordsworth, from a letter to Edward Moxon, 1 April 1842, *The Letters of William and Dorothy Wordsworth Vol. VII The Later Years: Part IV: 1840–1853,* ed. Ernest de Selincourt, rev. Alan G. Hill (2nd edition, Oxford: Clarendon, 1988), 314.

[77] 'From seeing the two sorts of people combined like this you thought better of both . . . The effect was in some degree to combine in the reader or author the merits of the two sorts; he was made to mirror in himself more completely the effective elements of the society he lived in': Empson, *Some Versions of Pastoral,* 11–12. See also pp. 20–3.

Pickwick as a pastoral work might seem a strange idea. The natural world is full of unpleasant surprises in the book: the Bower at Dingley Dell is a sanctuary for spiders, Pickwick is carried off by a runaway horse, and his shooting expedition ends in a wheelbarrow in the pound. Nature often trips up the Cockney sportsmen, and Pickwick's praise of country life— 'Who could live to gaze from day to day on bricks and slates, who had once felt the influence of a scene like this? Who could continue to exist where there are no cows but the cows on the chimney pots; nothing redolent of Pan but pantiles; no crop but stone-crop?' (75)—is the prelude to Winkle shooting Tupman in the arm. But the novel shares the ambition of pastoral to create a form which can counter or bypass the social distinctions and aesthetic segregations imposed by class-divided societies. In its multiple plots and actions, which complexly parallel and allude to each other; in its sense of human waste and limitation even in the midst of achievement and happiness; in the centrality it gives to the wit of Sam and Tony Weller—in these the novel marks its affinity to the ironic pastoralism 'that not merely evades but breaks through' the class conventions of the society in which it appears.[78]

There are, though, other forces at work in the book, as pastoral and politics become subject to the vagaries and absurdities of writing and repetition. Jingle, for example, tells the Pickwickians that his poem is about the July events of 1830. The novel takes place, however, in 1827, so that Jingle's imaginary poem precedes the event it is said to describe. And the text, far from glossing over or eliding this strange anomaly, draws attention to it with a footnote praising 'the prophetic force of Mr Jingle's imagination' (727). A little later, at Mrs Leo Hunter's literary lunch, Pickwick meets Count Smorltork, a Russian Count who, like a foreign double of Pickwick himself, is researching English life and taking notes on what he sees. Pickwick begins to address him on the topic of politics:

---

[78] Empson writes of pastoral that 'it is important for a nation with a strong class-system to have an art-form that not merely evades but breaks through it, that makes the classes feel part of a larger unity or simply at home with each other. This may be done in odd ways, and as well by mockery as admiration': Empson, *Some Versions of Pastoral*, 199.

"The word politics, Sir," said Mr Pickwick, "comprises, in itself, a difficult study of no inconsiderable magnitude."
"Ah!" said the Count, drawing out the tablets again, "ver good— fine words to begin a chapter. Chapter forty-seven. Poltics. The word poltics surprises by himself—" And down went Mr Pickwick's remark, in Count Smorltork's tablets, with such variations and additions as the Count's exuberant fancy suggested, or his imperfect knowledge of the language occasioned. (184)

Beneath and through the satire of small talk and political theory, Pickwick meets his double, who repeats but does not double his words, which come back to him displaced, varied, and supplemented. The Count, in a scene of speech and writing, translation, transcription, catachresis, and reappropriation, re-introduces into a serious conversation about politics some of the absurdity and misdirection inseparable from language and its translation. And in doing so, Pickwick, who has already found himself transformed into Pig Vig, Big Vig, and Peek Weeks, comprises and surprises himself, itself, and ourselves (184).

Pickwick Papers has rightly been praised for containing in its pages a vision of the good life. It also, in a century of in-creasing economic and fictional rationalization, creates a very different fictional economy, one of impulse, excess, and misdi-rection. The novel is concerned to create, in a political culture that identifies festivity and celebration with Tory politics and the corruption of the democratic process, a very different festive culture.[79] Many of the spaces of the novel, like the inn-yard in which Sam meets Pickwick for the first time, have the qualities of the marketplace or agora, where we find 'a commingling of categories usually kept opposed: centre and periphery, inside and outside, stranger and local, commerce and festivity, high and low'.[80] There is a similar transgressional mingling in the book's excessive and exorbitant plotting and characterization, its impure and distended fictional body, its generous and casual inclusiveness, its odd protuberances and strange holes. It is not a Lenten book, not closed, monumental, centred, parsimonious,

---

[79] Patrick Joyce notes that in this period 'The Tories were associated with . . . what may be termed the politics of bonhomie': *Visions of the People: Industrial England and the Question of Class, 1848–1914* (Cambridge: Cambridge University Press, 1991), 35–6.
[80] Stallybrass and White, *Politics and Poetics of Transgression*, 27.

or economical, nor does it believe that the good life depends on these qualities.[81] Dickens's later novels are in many ways more politically focused than *Pickwick* but they are also more restricted fictional economies, better organized but more tightly bound. Although *Pickwick* may have given, of all the novels of the nineteenth century, the greatest happiness to the greatest number, there could not be a less Benthamite book.

These concerns of the book gather together with the characters of the novel at Christmas at Dingley Dell. Christmas is a season and festivity that fascinates Dickens throughout his writing career, not least because of its ability to intermingle the qualities of life and death.[82] Christmas occurs almost at the death of one year and just before the birth of a new one and commemorates the birth of a divinity who is born to die and is then reborn, and whose teaching often plays on the paradoxes of death-in-life and life-in-death. Christmas in Dickens is often thought to be a sentimental utopia, but *Pickwick* does not allow such a reading. For death punctuates *Pickwick Papers*'s Christmas 'with the same regularity as the Reaper does in the processions that pass around the cathedral clock at noon':[83] Manor Farm is where dead English yeomen would have feasted (347); Bob Sawyer and Ben Allen relish the similarity of feasting and cannibalism (365–6); Gabriel Grub's Christmas Box is a coffin (356). Christmas thus becomes the occasion for a festive mourning and affirmation which can never be reduced to an ideal or utopia. This counter-sentimental affirmation is most clear in chapter 28, 'A good-humoured Christmas Chapter . . .', at the turning-point and centre of the book, which portrays for a brief moment a happy and just society, and we are asked to remember, of all people, Socrates: 'the old year was preparing, like an ancient philosopher, to call his friends around him, and amidst the sound of feasting and revelry to pass gently and calmly away' (334). It is a significant moment, one that binds together pleasure, festivity, and death in the figure of a philosopher at the beginning of the epoch of writing, who lives on in the words of others. Socrates was condemned to die, we remember, for cor-

---

[81] Stallybrass and White, *Politics and Poetics of Transgression*, 22–3.
[82] See Catherine Waters, *Dickens and the Politics of the Family* (Cambridge: Cambridge University Press, 1997), 58–88.
[83] Benjamin, *Illuminations*, 95.

rupting the young and being a threat to the security and happiness of the polis. Dickens remembers him at the beginning of the novel's most assured depiction of the friendship and cheer of the good society, not long before Pickwick will go to prison, with his friends around him. Pickwick, like Sam Weller (189), has already been called a 'philosopher' in the novel (110), although when offered the costumes of 'Plato, Zeno, Epicurus, Pythagoras—all founders of clubs' at Mrs Leo Hunter's, he modestly refuses them, being unwilling to 'put himself in comparison with those great men' (177). Later, we will fear for his death in prison. Emrys Jones has praised the 'freedom and casualness and audacity' with which Shakespeare used elements of Plato's description of the death of Socrates in the Hostess's description of Falstaff's end in *Henry V*.[84] They are equally appropriate nouns for Dickens's writing here.

As the novel evokes the possibility of happiness, it also invokes a very different logic and force which suspends or subverts many of the differences on which the novel and its criticism rest: between the comic and the tragic, the human and the inhuman, between life and death, philosophy and fiction, Pickwick's Club and Plato's Academy. To speak of the good life in *Pickwick* is also to speak of the good society, which is also to speak, as the novel does here, of the beginning of writing and the after-life, of ghosts and puns and Plato. It is also to remember the speech and writing of Sam Weller who comes after Pickwick in rank and status, but who so often comes before him in knowledge and insight, Plato to his Socrates, Socrates to his Plato, the same with the names transposed.[85]

---

[84] Emrys Jones, *The Origins of Shakespeare* (Oxford: Clarendon, 1977), 21.
[85] Derrida, *The Post Card*, 178.

CHAPTER THREE

Nancy's Truth: *Oliver Twist*
and the 'Stray Chapters'

I

THE PREFACE TO *Oliver Twist*, Dickens's longest, is one of
the most interesting documents of nineteenth-century fiction,
although most critics pass it by or find it absurd.[1] Nancy's love
for Sikes, it says, is 'a contradiction, an anomaly, an apparent
impossibility, but it is a truth'.[2] It is an interesting assertion,
this binding together of anomaly, contradiction, and truth. Like
the unconscious, it appears, the truth embraces contradiction.
It seems very different from the first use of the word 'truth' in
the same preface, which says that the statement that 'a lesson
of the purest good may . . . be drawn from the vilest evil' is a
'recognised and established truth' (xxv). Here there is no contradiction or anomaly; in drawing the lesson, the novelist and
reader refine social evil into good. Any material 'festering in St
Giles' or 'flaunting in St James' can be 'materials towards the
truth' (xxv). But it is unclear whether Nancy's love for Sikes,
the figure of a desiring and transgressive woman, can be such
material towards the truth, or whether it does not in some way
undo Dickens's and the reader's pursuit of truth. As the second
passage implies, it is not that truth can be found anywhere, or
that bad things can be made good and true, but that truth and
anomaly, impossibility and contradiction are of necessity linked,
and in this case through the question of Nancy's desire or
(perhaps better and more disturbingly for us) love for Sikes.

---

[1] 'These defensive tactics are sometimes foolish . . . The most flagrant example of
such an error is his lame reply to Thackeray and other reviewers defending the
reality of Nancy in *Oliver Twist*': George H. Ford, *Dickens and his Readers: Aspects
of Novel-Criticism since 1836* (New York: Norton, 1965), 133.

[2] Charles Dickens, *Oliver Twist*, ed. Kathleen Tillotson (Oxford: World's Classics, 1982), xxviii. All references will be to this edition and placed in the text.

Truth, for Dickens, is an important word in the preface. 'It is useless', he writes, 'to discuss whether the conduct and character of the girl seems natural or unnatural, probable or improbable, right or wrong. IT IS TRUE' (xxviii). This is the only capitalized statement in the whole book, from an author who usually eschews such emphasis. Truth, it seems, is not a matter of probability or inference, but stands above them, 'God's truth' (xxviii), the meeting of apparently irreconcilable forces or ideas in a knowledge beyond the claims or judgement of reason or nature.

This epistemological dimension to the book, which asks what truth in fiction is, and binds the question to the truth of desire and a woman, is not merely a matter for the preface. The novel itself contains a clear polemical edge turned against 'philosophers', among whom Dickens includes Benthamite utilitarians, but which also cuts wider. There is a constant distrust of philosophical reasoning's complicity with social and familial exploitation; against this, the book sets the contradictory and anomalous truths of fiction. *Oliver Twist* begins with this resistance. Dickens will not tell us the time or place of Oliver's birth, and tells us that he won't tell us. It is clearly a process of typification and Oliver is a representative character. Yet if he is typical, he is also anomalous and transgressive—transgressive, not just because he is illegitimate, but also because he is curiously privileged. If he had not been born in a workhouse but in a prosperous home, he would have died, the novel tells us, of over-attention. The workhouse 'is the best thing . . . that could by possibility have occurred', for 'if . . . Oliver had been surrounded by careful grandmothers, anxious aunts, experienced nurses, and doctors of profound wisdom, he would most inevitably and indubitably have been killed in no time' (1). It is a difficult, if characteristic, effect, and I am unclear how much we should simply call it a rather black joke, a piece of irony, or a grotesque inversion. In one sense it simply sets off a train of questioning in the reader (as good jokes often do) through the reversal or interruption of expected judgements, hierarchies, or narratives, in this case a questioning of family love and the reader's likely sense that he or she is better off than Oliver. Is Oliver privileged or unprivileged? Fortunate or unfortunate? Typical or untypical? There are clear answers in the discourses of political economy and the bourgeois novel on the one hand, and in the idiom of the grotesque on the other: unfortunate and fortunate respectively. But the novel makes us hesitate, as it does later with Nancy's love for Sikes, and our own feelings for Fagin, Sikes, and the Artful Dodger, troubling us where truth might find a home or lie.

Oliver Twist is quite a theoretical novel, in a way, although it distrusts the effects of theorizing in the world.[3] A lot of this theorizing (or anti-theorizing) concerns itself with 'Nature', sometimes capitalized. It is a contentious word, then as now, 'perhaps', as Raymond Williams says, 'the most complex word in the language'.[4] Oliver, we are told immediately after the robbery of Mr Brownlow, 'was not theoretically acquainted with the beautiful axiom that self-preservation is the first law of nature' (60). 'Nature' is here a term in political-economical discourse, as it is on other occasions in the book, and is distrusted as a rationalization of self-interest or oppression. But 'Nature' is also a central feature of anti-utilitarian arguments, particularly within its main ideological opponent, Romantic humanism.[5] When Oliver is safely captured by the domestic bliss of the Maylies, the novel has a brief paean to nature, that 'foretaste of heaven' (201). But more often its uses are ironic or satiric and it is not clear that the book believes that there is such a thing as nature or human nature in the way that Romantic and post-Romantic writers are often thought to; or if there is, that we can know what it is like. Later on the same page the narrator speaks of the 'passion *for hunting something* deeply implanted in the human breast' (61). This implies that there is a human nature or soil, and that it requires an agency to plant it. The properties of the soil and planter are left unclear—God, nature, and society are all possible candidates for the planter, but Dickens has no interest in taking either part of the figure any further. In a way, he is just playing fast and loose with the received ideas of his day, but he does so with great skill, and to some purpose, allowing himself to condemn some things as

---

[3] Steven Marcus notes 'the genius of abstraction which presides over this novel'; *Dickens: from Pickwick to Dombey* (London: Chatto and Windus, 1965), 74. See also pp. 63–4.

[4] Raymond Williams, *Keywords* (London: Fontana, 1976), 184.

[5] Raymond Williams, *Culture and Society 1780–1950* (Harmondsworth: Penguin, 1963).

unnatural while at the same time refusing any coercive sense to the idea of nature. Bad philosophy no doubt, but an effective rhetorical stance, caught well in Noah Claypole's taunting of Oliver which shows 'what a beautiful thing human nature may be made to be', a manufacturing as untrustworthy as the Dodger's manufacturing of handkerchiefs.[6]

The preface begins with a quotation from Fielding's *Tom Jones*: 'Some of the author's friends cried "Lookee, gentlemen, the man is a villain; but it is nature for all that;" and the young critics of the age, the clerks, apprentices &c., called it low, and fell a groaning' (xxv). This implies that only low people will think that the portrayal of nature in the book is 'low', which cunningly puts the reader's snobbery on the defensive. After this the preface studiously avoids the term 'nature', except when paraphrasing others, and prefers to claim the portrayal not of nature but of 'truth'. It seems to be an important distinction, as the truth in Dickens's usage is clearly something made, mobile, complex, and ambivalent, not discovered, single, and simple. Oliver opens up the question of nature through his presence. What is it natural for him to do? What happens when all the forces that surround a child are brutal, violent, exploitative? The novel is deeply suspicious of the ideological uses of the idea of an intrinsic human or personal nature, but also wants to create a space for identity that is not reductively or brutally behaviourist, which believes that brutality makes brutes. Oliver is a natural child but not a wild one, and his intolerable, necessary demand, is perfectly polite—' "Please, sir, I want some more" ' (10). Innocence and corruption, nature and nurture, are pushed to extremes in the book, starkly posed against each other, and Dickens then gives the reductive accounts of such differences a hard time, to leave a space, a gap—the space of Oliver—to emerge. Oliver has been called a Rousseau-like Child of Nature, but this is too simple; Oliver and Nature in the first chapter 'fought out the point between them' (1), but in the next chapter we find that 'nature or inheritance had implanted a good strong spirit in Oliver's breast' (4).[7] The behaviour of the

---

[6] This phrase first appears in the 1850 edition of this much-revised novel. See Charles Dickens, *Oliver Twist*, ed. Kathleen Tillotson (Oxford: Clarendon, 1966), 28.

[7] John Lucas, *The Melancholy Man: A Study of Dickens's Novels* (London: Methuen, 1970), 32.

board of workhouse guardians is 'very natural' (23), Nancy's assumed timidity is 'natural' (79), as is Oliver's unassumed hunger and thirst (69). These uses cannot be reconciled or reduced to the stable operations of fictional irony. The great junction-point and twist in Oliver's tale is his meeting with the Artful Dodger, but we cannot simply oppose artful Dodger and artless Twist, for the Dodger follows 'the first law of nature' (60) in letting Oliver take the rap for the theft, and his mentor Fagin, like his creator Dickens, has an art, of performance, which is both 'very funny and natural' (57).

What the book most seems to distrust is not philosophy, but the claim of discursive reason to be able to stand outside human society. This it does very neatly by transcoding the heights of utilitarian philosophy to describe the philosophical escape of the Artful Dodger and Master Bates after the Brownlow theft:

That when the Dodger, and his accomplished friend Master Bates, joined in the hue-and-cry . . . they were actuated by a very laudable and becoming regard for themselves; and forasmuch as the freedom of the subject and the liberty of the individual are among the first and proudest boasts of a true-hearted Englishman . . . [t]his strong proof of their anxiety for their own preservation and safety, goes to cor-roborate and confirm the little code of laws which certain profound and sound-judging philosophers have laid down as the mainsprings of all Nature's deeds and actions . . . Thus, to do a great right, you may do a little wrong; and you make take any means which the end to be attained will justify; the amount of right, or the amount of the wrong, or indeed the distinction between the two, being left entirely to the philosopher concerned: to be settled and determined by his clear, com-prehensive and impartial view of his own particular case. (73)

This passage manages to have a pretty comprehensive smack at legal, political, 'philosophical', polite, and patriotic cant in a way that reminds us of Swift. It would be possible to speak here of Dickens's critique of the lack of self-consciousness in utili-tarian reasoning, and perhaps connect it with a point about Hegel, or its abstract idealism and speak of Marx, or to link such writing with more recent theoretical interest in the his-torical and material situatedness of philosophical reason; but the point is made quite clearly by the book itself, which makes the pursuit of self-interest identical with the pursuit of the bleed-ing and terrified Oliver through the streets of London. The 'truth' of this philosophy rests on its claim and wish to invoke and master the figure of nature, 'a female', it is remarked, 'acknowledged by universal admission to be far above the numerous little foibles and weaknesses of her sex' (73), weaknesses such as 'heart', 'impulse and feeling'. Oliver is later rescued from Fagin's and Sikes's pursuit of self-interest by a woman, Nancy, whose action in terms of 'self-interest', that theory of the subject, is incomprehensible, a matter of heart and impulse, but also, I shall argue, something beyond that too, through which she dies, and dies again, and again.

Oliver Twist is first born in Mudfog, and then nowhere at all. Dickens became editor of Bentley's Miscellany, originally to be called The Wit's Miscellany, in December 1836. The first number promised its readers that 'our path will be single and distinct . . . we have nothing to do with politics', and contained Dickens's story, 'The Private Life of Mr Tulrumble', a tale of the Mayor of Mudfog.[8] The following and subsequent months carry instalments of Oliver Twist, or The Parish Boy's Progress, with two significant exceptions: October 1837 when Oliver's path is prevented by 'The First Report of the Mudfog Association for the Advancement of Everything' and September 1838 which carries 'The Second Report on the Mudfog Association for the Advancement of Everything'. These two papers, together with 'The Private Life of Mr Tulrumble' and some others, are later collected as The Mudfog Papers, but are known as 'Stray Chapters' in the index to the Miscellany, and provide a sort of hors d'œuvre to, and outwork of, the novel. Oliver Twist is very concerned with those who stray, Nancy and Oliver in particular, so it is worth asking where these chapters

---

[8] Bentley's Miscellany, January 1837. Bentley later collected 'The Private Life of Mr Tulrumble', 'The Full Report of the First Meeting of the Mudfog Association for the Advancement of Everything' (first published October 1837), and 'The Full Report of the Second Meeting of the Mudfog Association for the Advancement of Everything' (first published September 1838), in Charles Dickens, The Mudfog Papers (London: Bentley, 1880), with three other papers from the period, one ('Mr Robert Bolton') not by Dickens. They are usually collected in later editions of Sketches by Boz. Charles Dickens, Sketches by Boz and Other Early Papers 1833–39, ed. Michael Slater (London: Dent, 1994), reprints 'Full Report of the First Meeting of the Mudfog Association for the Advancement of Everything' and 'Full Report of the Second Meeting of the Mudfog Association for the Advancement of Everything', as well as 'The Pantomime of Life' and 'Some Particulars Concerning a Lion'. All page references are to this edition and placed in the text.

might have strayed from, and where they might be going. Oliver and Nancy find homes in the course of the novel, a grave and a home without father, mother, or proper name, respectively. I do not want to find these chapters a home, but nor can we bury them.

Mudfog is one of the select place-names of Dickens's imagination: Mudfog, Mugby, Muggleton, Blunderstone, Borioboola Gha, Dullborough, Eatanswill, Eden, Great Winglebury—mainly found in the early work. Usually (like Fielding but unlike George Eliot), he places 'imaginary' characters in 'real' places. Naming, real and imaginary names, proper and improper uses, are matters of great importance in the novel from the moment Oliver is placed in the sequence 'Swubble', 'Twist', 'Unwin', by that 'literary character' (6) Mr Bumble and renamed as the imaginary Tom White by the nameless court usher before Fang at the Old Bailey. Mudfog is a good name, wet air and wet earth. For Chesterton, in one of the essential passages of Dickens criticism, fogs are the author's damp, essential, ungraspable, ungrounded, ground. Dickens, he writes, is:

> their only poet . . . Just as every lamp is a warm human moon, so every fog is a rich human nightfall . . . Fog for us is the chief form of that outward pressure which compresses mere luxury into real comfort . . . the first man that emerges out of the mist with a light, is for us Prometheus, a saviour bringing fire to men . . . every rumble of a cart, every cry in the distance, marks the heart of humanity beating undaunted in the distance. It is wholly human: man toiling in his own cloud.[9]

The apotheosis of Mud is perhaps a less easy task, although Dickens comes close in his introduction to Mudfog in the Tulrumble paper, an aqueous and fluid place, the elements dribbling together, the town and its atmosphere moist and fluid, the narrator in a wonderfully mobile passage triumphantly carrying the celebration of that 'perverse sort of element' water through false inference and sublime non sequiturs to the 'indisputable and veracious conclusion' that 'admitting Mudfog to be damp, we distinctly state that it is salubrious'.[10] Perversity is a great concern of the novel too, as Oliver's surname seems obscurely

---

[9] G. K. Chesterton, *Charles Dickens* (London: Methuen, 1906), 167.
[10] Charles Dickens, *Sketches by Boz* (Oxford: Oxford Illustrated Dickens, 1957), 607–8.

to hint, and Sikes's characterization of him as a 'perwerse imp'
(a perverted perverse, and worse (135)) confirms.

The papers, or stray chapters, at first appear to have almost
nothing to do with the story of *Oliver Twist*. They are linked
by a single word—'Mudfog'—excised in later editions. None of
the characters reappears and the name of the town is never cited
again after the first page. Yet we cannot safely bury the stray
chapters, for they are straying still, into and around this other,
better-known story, which, like them, is troubled by the diet of
paupers, the injustice of the law, by hunger, starvation, and
need, and the need to find an appropriate, urgent language to
speak and represent them. 'The Private Life of Mr Tulrumble'
is a story, like *Oliver Twist*, and later *Great Expectations*, of
someone born in provincial poverty, who travels to London, and
returns wealthy. It is also a story of representation, of the representation of a representation, the provincial repeating of a
metropolitan staging of the symbols of political power, and a
small carnivalesque inversion of the dignity and honour of that
staging. The accounts of the Mudfog Association for the
Advancement of Everything are concerned, like the preface and
text of *Oliver*, with nature and truth, and the claims of certain
discourses—science and 'philosophy', journalism and the law—
to know and possess such truth.

The correspondent who relates the Association events is
one absurd pursuer of the truth, alternately badly fanciful ('the
sun . . . shed a refulgent lustre' (*MF* 520)) and baldly literal:

Half past nine. "Some dark object has just appeared upon the wharf.
I think it is a travelling carriage."
 A quarter to ten. "No, it isn't." (*MF* 533)

Scientists do even worse, and the folly of their speculations is
revealed through the brute materialism of animals, food, and
money; the first account begins with Professors Muff and Nogo
sending for 'a live dog . . . a knife and fork, and a clean plate'
(*MF* 516) and the closing pun of the second transforms the
spread of science into a spread of food 'and a glorious spread it
is' (*MF* 550). Animals are like humans: the dissected dog was
'much and deservedly respected by the whole of his acquaintance' (*MF* 518). The Zoology and Botany section is troubled by
the condition of performing fleas (some of whom are female),

and wishes to set up infant schools, an almshouse, and houses of industry for them to place them 'upon a level with the rest of mankind' (*MF* 522). Humans are like animals: discovering the loss of her dog, his mistress bites the learned professors. Mr Blunderum gives a paper on the tragic death of the learned pig, whereupon a questioner enquires if the pig-faced lady 'who was reported to have worn a black velvet mask, and to have taken her meals from a golden trough' (*MF* 524) was a relative. A member replied 'that the pigfaced lady was his mother-in-law and that he trusted the President would not violate the sanctity of private life' (*MF* 524). The lack of performing bears is put down to the prevalence of bear's grease, which may infuse itself into young men's heads, and affect their behaviour for the worse.

When Oliver is first caught by Sikes and Nancy, he is taken past Smithfield meat market. In one of many repeated journeys in the book, he passes the market again on the way to rob the Maylies. He is called a 'kid' (127) by Sikes, whom he follows 'Like a lamb' (127) while walking with 'a kind of trot' (130). His mother's name, Agnes, means 'lamb', and she is called one too (150). The Artful Dodger's friend is called Chitling, and Oliver earlier encounters Mr Limbkins, a jointed lambkin. There is a repeated undercurrent or fear of cannibalism in the story, as Dickens, the great humanist, worries at the limits of the human, and Mr Grimwig knows only 'Mealy' and 'beef-faced' boys (86). Noah Claypole changes his name to Morris Bolter, one who eats too fast, and just before the pursuit of Nancy that will lead to Sikes's fatal assault, he begins 'a voracious assault' on a 'monstrous' (288) piece of bread.[11] A monster is partly brute and partly human, and we are left to wonder what other humans—Fagin, Fang, Bumble—are also capable of the monstrous, or indeed whether we can readily or ever distinguish the two.[12] If

[11] Dickens's later reading of the final section of *Oliver Twist* begins at this point. See Charles Dickens, *Sikes and Nancy and other Public Readings*, ed. Philip Collins (Oxford: World's Classics, 1983), 232.

[12] '[T]heir monstrosity luxuriates without depth or concealment': John Bayley, '*Oliver Twist*: "Things as they really are" ', in Martin Price (ed.), *Dickens: Twentieth Century Views* (New Jersey: Prentice Hall, 1967), 84. On monstrosity in general, see Jacques Derrida, *Of Grammatology* (Baltimore: Johns Hopkins University Press, 1976), 5; *Writing and Difference* (London: Routledge, 1978), 293; Geoffrey Bennington and Jacques Derrida, *Jacques Derrida* (Chicago: Chicago University Press, 1993), 22.

humans are liable to turn into animals, animals into humans, or both into something monstrous, neither human nor animal, they cannot be saved by reason, detachment, or submission to the law. Both *Oliver Twist* and the 'Stray Chapters' show the production of monstrous and absurd confusions of human and mechanical, human and animal, rational and irrational, through simultaneous obedience to and transgression of the claims of law and reason. Mr Crinkle invents a pickpocketing machine which he hopes Parliament will take up, and Mr Coppernose proposes an entirely new police force and magistracy, composed of automaton figures, half-human, half-machine, with realistic groans and wooden heads for the leisure and entertainment of the aristocracy, who may knock them down and insult them at will (*MF* 544–5). Paupers from the local workhouses will be provided for similar pleasures, and in the 'pantomimic investigation' and simulacrum trial that follows, horses may be brought as witnesses (*MF* 545). Fang is a magistrate, and reaches a monstrous judgement on Oliver, as monstrous as Professor Muff's willingness to stake his professional reputation on the small amount of food necessary to sustain human life: 'the twentieth part of a grain of bread and cheese' together with a fifteenth part of a grain of pudding twice a week makes a 'high diet' 'in workhouses (*MF* 526). Pipkin's interesting paper on homeopathy tells the story of a man who is shot. If his servant had immediately dosed him with 'an infinitesimal dose of lead and gunpowder', he would have recovered immediately. Unfortunately, 'the woman did not possess the power of reasoning by analogy, or carrying out a principle' (*MF* 547).

Intoxicated and disturbed by the powers and dangers of analogy and principle, metaphor and concept, the science of Mudfog is also troubled by dreams (a man swallows a key and dreams of being a wine-cellar door) and crime (on his death, a medical student takes an impress of the dead man's stomach, copies the key imprinted on it, and robs his house) (*MF* 525). *Oliver Twist* contains at least two important dreams, a robbery of a house, a body starved in a workhouse, and humans who might be animals or machines. Stories about the cause of dreams and the fact of desire, where truth is found only in a copy, in death, and in a breach of law, absurd and monstrous stories, invoking interpretation and a convulsive laughter which science cannot know.

II

When Oliver is first taken by Mr Brownlow to his home after his court appearance, he wakes from a 'long and troubled dream' (68) to see over his bed a picture. It looks 'as if it was alive, and wanted to speak' (71) until it is turned to the wall by Mrs Bedwin, that 'motherly old lady' (68), although Oliver continues to see it in his mind's eye. Mr Brownlow has already been reminded of 'a vast amphitheatre' (63) of dead faces when he sees Oliver at court, and he is once more struck 'by the resemblance between his features and some familiar face' (72). Suddenly he points to the picture and then to Oliver: 'There was its living copy. The eyes, the head, the mouth; every feature was the same. The expression was, for the instant, so precisely alike that the minutest line seemed copied with a startling accuracy' (72). Oliver is, it seems, a living copy of a lost original, and he is reinserted through that resemblance into a family and a home. Mrs Bedwin has earlier spoken to Oliver of the machine for taking likenesses, and it appears as if its promise is fulfilled and the travails of the boy ended in the likeness of his mother returning as living copy. As so often in Dickens, we appear to have an ethic and aesthetic of presence, figured through a return to origins and the mother, a purity of presence and identity found in the 'truth' of Oliver's face. Oliver's wanderings, it appears, are about to come to an end in this scene of naming and resemblance, about a child and its mother, and the return to a safe and secure home and origin; this promise for the rest of the book.

Yet it is not as simple as this. This is not a family scene. Brownlow is not his father, nor Mrs Bedwin his mother, and neither is a blood relative. Nor is naming a secure thing: Mr Brownlow at first calls Oliver 'Tom White', the name the usher has given him in court. When Oliver tells him his 'true' name, he wonders if the child is lying, as he will wonder again when he fails to return from the bookshop. Later we will learn the apparently impossible fact that Monks knows Oliver because of his resemblance, not to Agnes but to his father, a contradiction and anomaly (like Nancy's love for Sikes) that we are also asked to think true. Nor is the promise of return fulfilled: the home with which the novel ends will not be this one; Oliver will have new relations, and Agnes will be represented by an empty tomb, not a portrait. A scene about repetition and representation, naming and identity, a story about kinship and home, a promise unfulfilled.

Oliver Twist is all homes and journeys, a pattern of repetitions and attempted repetitions, of substitutions and displacements, where each figure, place, or journey seems to echo and invoke a double. Oliver takes seven days to walk to London, and Nancy seven days to tell Brownlow and the Maylies where he is, and both events parody the time of Creation. Brownlow is a 'respectable-looking . . . old gentleman' (59–60) and Fagin a 'pleasant old gentleman' (53). Mr Bumble is 'quite a literary character' (6) and Brownlow wonders if Oliver will become one too (83). Oliver travels from home to home in the novel—baby-farm, workhouse, Sowerberry's, Fagin's, Brownlow's, Fagin's, the Maylies—repeating the steps he has taken with Bumble to see little Dick, once more passing Smithfield on the way to the Maylies, to whom he will later return. He is taken home to Fagin's twice, the first freely, the second under duress, is then forced to go the Maylies, and then returns to them of his own free will (except that, as so often in the book, his free will is constrained by sickness and the fear of death). The figures he meets repeat similar functions and roles—Fagin, Brownlow, Losberne, Bumble, Sikes, Sowerberry are all fathers to him (and not fathers), and Mrs Mann, Mrs Sowerberry, Mrs Bedwin, Mrs Maylie are all mothers (and not mothers). The uncanny pursuit of Sikes by the presence of the dead Nancy ('If he stopped, it did the same. If he ran, it followed' (368)) is the clearest of these doublings, and itself doubles the earlier pursuit by Morris Bolter of Nancy ('stopping when she stopped: and, as she moved again, creeping stealthily on' (291)), the Bolter who is (and is not) also Noah Claypole. Nancy's pursuit of Sikes, which at times and fatally at his death becomes 'a vision before him' of 'widely staring eyes . . . light in themselves, but giving light to nothing' (308), is a doubling (of Nancy, and her eyes) which is then redoubled by Sikes's dog, a dog that is called 'Bullseye', which means both a single eye and something to aim at, a target, and then redoubled by Sikes, who haunts himself as 'the very ghost of Sikes' (324). The 'semblance' that follows Sikes is 'like a corpse endowed with the mere machinery of life' (308), an uncanny mechanical policeman, following and leading (as do all these doublings and repetitions) to death.

None of these is a successful or identical repetition, and each points to a difference. The most striking of these is when Oliver, having recovered from the shooting at the Maylies, sees the house where he was held by Sikes. Losberne rushes to the door, to be greeted by an ugly hump-backed man, a 'ridiculous old vampire' and 'mis-shapen little demon' (198). The house bears no resemblance to Oliver's description of it. It is a repeated motif in the story, this seeking for repetition to reveal a home and a truth, only to find something quite different and other there, not simply an absence or a change but something quite radically in excess, something that in this case simply cannot be assimilated to the narrative, and which makes you wonder if you are where you think you are at all. And to say that it is a repeated motif is also to recognize that there can be no repetition of such motifs.[13]

Journeys, especially Oliver's, are always being detoured, delayed, or broken in the story, sending him to entirely different, or other, places from where he is intended to go. Mr Bumble tries to send Oliver off, and offers to pay the postage of 'three pound ten' (16) to Gamfield the sweep 'whose face was a regular stamped receipt for cruelty' (18) and five pounds to the Sowerberries, who will in turn pack Oliver off as a mute behind the hearse. He is destined several times for the gallows when young, and is about to be sent to Australia by Fang, when the bookstall-keeper arrives late and intervenes. The book is full of messengers, messages, transmissions, scenes of sending and writing. Oliver twice becomes a little postman, taking Mr Brownlow's book back to the shop and Mrs Maylie's letter to Harry.[14] Both times he is interrupted, first by Nancy and Sikes who take him back to Fagin's parcel office, and then by Monks, who instantly recognizes him as the copy of his father, and falls violently on the ground, writhing and foaming. Even Oliver's most famous moment—' "Please, sir, I want some more" ' (10)— is a message he carries for others, a task for which he is chosen

---

[13] J. Hillis Miller, *Fiction and Repetition* (Oxford: Oxford University Press, 1982), 6; Jacques Derrida, *The Post Card from Socrates to Freud and Beyond* (Chicago: Chicago University Press), 351.

[14] Derrida, *The Post Card*, 7–256.

(or which he chooses) by lot. Once or twice he even sends himself off, like a parcel with no destination, to be found by Jack Dawkins at the side of the road and bundled off to Fagin's, a little message, a fold or twist of paper, passed on and read by Agnes, Bumble, Sowerberry, Brownlow, Fang, Fagin, Sikes, Monks, the Maylies, and many others, to say nothing of Dickens and his readers.[15] And finally, but not finally, in some kind of fatal closure, a message concerning Oliver is passed on by Nancy, a message to which Dickens will return again and again, to provide another (but the same) fatal closure.

The Adventures of Oliver Twist; or, The Parish Boy's Progress. What is at stake in that title? A choice to begin with, of name and identity—Oliver Twist or the Parish Boy, individual or type? But also a narrative question: a Progress or a Twist, something that goes forward or that tropes and turns? What or who is 'Oliver Twist', as character, as novel, as name? It is a question raised many times in the book. The list of characters at the beginning of some editions names Oliver Twist, but also names him as 'a nameless' boy, which means among other things 'one without proper title, illegitimate'.[16] There are other scenes of naming-which-is-not-naming in the novel, as in Dickens's willingness (and then unwillingness) to name 'Mudfog' as the place of his orphan's birth. Oliver is an 'item of mortality' (1) in the first chapter and then 'an excellent example of the power of dress' (3) before Bumble enters him

---

[15] For Steven Marcus, Oliver is a 'vessel of Grace', an angel, a *'lusus naturae* the Christian boy', Christian in *The Pilgrim's Progress*, and the young Dickens: *Dickens: From Pickwick to Dombey*, 80–4.

[16] 'Oliver Twist, a poor nameless orphan boy', Charles Dickens, *Oliver Twist*, ed. Peter Fairclough (Harmondsworth: Penguin, 1966), 43. 'Nameless' means 'obscure or inglorious, or bearing no legitimate name . . . inexpressible or indefinable'. Oliver never gains a legitimate name, retaining Bumble's first inscription. Nancy has only a Christian name; Fagin and Monks surnames without title; Agnes Fleming is 'Agnes' on her tombstone in Cruikshank's illustration. Oliver, Agnes, Nancy: nameless names. There is something distinctly anal about the names of Oliver's father-figures, Brownlow and Bumble. Bumble taps Oliver on his back with his stick, and Brownlow is bending over when the Dodger's hand goes in and out. A 'bum-bailiff' (which may be behind Bumble's name) was a 'beadle of the meanest kind', 'so called because he attacks from the rear'. Gary Wills has argued that Fagin has pederastic intentions towards Oliver (Gary Wills, 'The Loves of *Oliver Twist*', in Charles Dickens, *Oliver Twist*, ed. Fred Kaplan (New York: Norton, 1993), 593–608), but the textual evidence is slight. We are supposed to think of Mrs Mann as unwomanly, and Mrs Bedwin spends a good deal of time over Oliver's bed.

into the immortal signifying chain 'Swubble... Twist...
Unwin... Vilkins' (6), another naming by Oliver's second or
third father. In the Old Bailey, before the law, he is Tom White,
a name that blanches him out, an anonymous, nameless name.
Dickens never places Oliver unequivocally or simply within the
law, never seeks to remove the mark of illegitimacy from him—
indeed insists on it in the final lines of the book. But if Oliver
has no legitimate or proper name, he has plenty of illegitimate,
improper ones—Tom White, Oliver White, Nolly, young Green,
young gallows, Workus, lazy legs, Ned.

Why 'Twist' though? Cruikshank wanted to call him 'Frank
Foundling' or 'Frank Steadfast', which keeps things simple, and
promises an identity of identity and name.[17] 'Oliver' is of course
a republican hero's name, the Lord Protector and one of the few
unequivocal heroes of Dickens's *A Child's History of England*,
the man who cuts off King Charles's head, an item that keeps
getting into the head of a character called Mr Dick in a later
book about a brutalized boy, the 'autobiographical' *David
Copperfield*.[18] 'Twist', if not quite 'Swubble', is pretty unheroic,
leaving readers to wonder whether they are reading about a hero
or a victim, one who comes to the good or goes to the bad, or
who perhaps awkwardly twists the two together.[19] The question
of the name raises a wider question of Twist's identity, which
often seems to leave readers and critics rather nonplussed. In
part this is because the novel is concerned to show how the
things the reader takes for granted in the forming of identity—
a name, a home, a family, the destinations and institutions that
allow a message or person to be safely parcelled up and sent on
its way, to arrive more or less complete at a true home or self—

[17] Robert L. Patten, *George Cruikshank's Life, Times and Art* (Cambridge:
Lutterworth, 1996), II, 50–94.
[18] Oliver may have been an unpopular name in England in the earlier nineteenth
century because of its republican associations. See Barry Westburg, ' "His Allegorical way of Putting It": Civil War and Psychic Conflict in *Oliver Twist* and *A Child's
History*', *Studies in the Novel*, VI (Spring 1974), 27–3. See also Patricia Ingham,
'The Name of the Hero in *Oliver Twist*', *Review of English Studies*, XXXIII (1982),
188–9.
[19] 'It is two novels which Dickens... attempts but fails to join together by a preposterous plot... The first part lies nearer to his journalism... the second—the
strange evil world... These two parts *are* joined; not by the plot, but by the figure
of little Oliver.' Angus Wilson, *The World of Charles Dickens* (London: The Book
Society, 1970), 128–9.

are different for the abject poor, in a way that puts many conceptions of character and identity in novels into doubt. Nor does the novel move to assuage those doubts, as *Tom Jones* does, to provide the lost and brutalized infant with the requirements of identity he has (temporarily) mislaid. Oliver is often only a little parcel, one that frequently loses itself in swoons, faintings, mislayings, beatings, misnamings, and collapses, abused by the dense material and signifying practices by which we distinguish humans and animals, living and dead, ghosts and machines, selves and others, swerving aside into absences, robberies, kidnaps, coalholes, and funerals. Dickens often makes Oliver a kind of limit-case of the human, where almost anywhere he goes or is sent—the baby-farm, up chimneys, to get some more, to funerals, to rob, to court—is a mortal threat to him, a little hunger artist of a peculiarly vulnerable and representative sort.

In a sense, then, Oliver Twist is only a name, but what a name! Twist is quite a complicated word, but a brief list can give us a good range of its senses and meanings as both verb and noun: the action of dividing and separating; the action of uniting or joining; the part of something where it divides, especially at the junction of the thighs; part of a hinge; a combination of two elements; a turn or a twist; a strain or a wrench; a turning aside; a deviation; a vicissitude; a healthy appetite. So it is a very good name for him: he is divided from his family, and eventually joins them; his life is a series of twists and turns; he is a combination of the lowest of the low and a young gentleman, a criminal and a wronged innocent, a hero and a victim, and so on. He joins together the parts of the story and the parts of his family, although they remain divided too. He is constantly turning or being turned aside in a story full of vicissitudes and deviations. There is also the bonus of the 'hearty appetite' sense, which ties up with all the scenes of eating and starvation in the book, and Oliver's role as a hunger artist. A 'twister' is also a thief or swindler and slightly later in the century it means a perversion or a distortion. A twist of language is a trope, and the book is full of perversions and distortions, tropes, twists, and catachreses, of which the Artful Dodger's 'japanning his trotter-cases' (111) is only the most sublime. Dodging of course is similar to twisting except perhaps more artfully evasive, and the Dodger, whose final appearance before the law in the Old Bailey dodges an unjust justice through multiple catachreses (' "That's a case of deformation of character . . . Did you redress yourself to me, my man?" ' (281–2)), twisting roles and characters (' "I won't show you no mercy" ', he tells the bench). He also dodges the novel's desire for justice and the reader's wish for certainty, for we never learn whether he is one of 'the chief remaining members of . . . Fagin's gang' who are transported (348).

Transportation is a form of monstrous state violence, but it is also another way of saying 'metaphor', which is a trope, or twist of language which carries things about and bears them off. In the final chapter of the book, in one of very few italicized passages in the narrative, Mr Grimwig 'remarks that Oliver *did not come back*, after all' (349). It is just a silly joke between friends, this last-but-one use of Oliver's name in the story, because of course Oliver has come back from all the transports, twists, and turns of the story. Unless nothing comes back, after all.

III

The figure of the hysterical woman and its relation to the male pursuit of knowledge is important in the writing of the nineteenth century, both in fiction and in scientific and medical discourses, most notably the work of Freud.[20] Indeed, for Freud, it has been argued, the problem of knowledge is itself hysterical. In many of these texts, as Jacqueline Rose has argued in relation to George Eliot's *Middlemarch*, 'the woman stands . . . for a corruption of the visible and a degradation of the scientific pursuit of truth'.[21] In the preface to *Oliver Twist*, by contrast, Nancy is identified with truth itself: true to Oliver and her

---

[20] Claire Kahane, *Passions of the Voice: Hysteria, Narrative, and the Figure of the Speaking Woman, 1850–1915* (Baltimore: Johns Hopkins University Press, 1995).

[21] Jacqueline Rose, 'George Eliot and the Spectacle of the Woman', in *Sexuality in the Field of Vision* (London: Verso, 1986), 110. Rose argues that Gwendolen in George Eliot's *Daniel Deronda* 'could perhaps be defined as the original literary hysteric' (116), but it is unclear what could support such a claim to knowledge, definition or priority. See Jenny Bourne Taylor and Sally Shuttleworth (eds), *Embodied Selves: An Anthology of Psychological Texts 1830–1890* (Oxford: Clarendon, 1998), 184–98.

love for Sikes, a contradictory and impossible love, but nevertheless 'TRUE', and part of her wider truth, which is not scientific, but literary, paradoxical, and contradictory. Dickens, like George Eliot, sees 'the link between male truth and a woman's failing' in Agnes's love for Oliver's father, and Nancy's love for Sikes, but it is a very different truth, which does not displace but focuses 'questions about social inequality and misery'.[22] This pursuit of truth, of Nancy, and of Nancy's truth is also a complex and potentially fatal business—fatal to her, to Sikes, to Fagin, and perhaps to Dickens too. One of Cruikshank's illustrations will be called 'Recovering Nancy', a scene that has more than a passing resemblance to Charcot's hysterical demonstrations at the Salpêtrière; but it is not clear that Nancy can be recovered in this, or in any other, way.[23]

Readers have disagreed sharply about the portrayal of Nancy in the novel. For Dickens's later collaborator Wilkie Collins, she was 'the finest thing he ever did. He never afterwards saw all the sides of a woman's character.'[24] For Thackeray, by contrast, she was 'the most unreal fantastical personage possible; no more like a thief's mistress than one of Gessner's shepherdesses resembles a real country wench'.[25] For Angus Wilson, she is an 'oleograph madonna' with 'only the shadowiest existence', but to Michael Slater, 'the only character in whose portrayal Dickens seems to be seeking to explore a conception of female nature itself'.[26] These disagreements between men about Nancy, disagreements about real wenches and 'female nature', about shadows, existence, and all sides of a woman's character, begin not in criticism but in the novel itself, whose characters, narrator, and readers often ask what she means and what she is doing, whether she is speaking truthfully or not, whether she is acting

---

[22] Rose, *Sexuality in the Field of Vision*, 111, 113.

[23] Georges Didi-Huberman, *Invention de l'hystérie: Charcot et l'iconographie photographique de la Salpêtrière* (Paris: Macula, 1982), 255.

[24] Wilkie Collins, marginalia to John Forster's *The Life of Charles Dickens*, in Philip Collins (ed.), *Dickens: The Critical Heritage* (London: Routledge and Kegan Paul, 1971), 587.

[25] W. M. Thackeray, from 'Going to see a Man Hanged', *Fraser's Magazine*, xxii (August 1840), 154–5, in Collins (ed.), *Dickens: The Critical Heritage*, 46.

[26] Wilson, *The World of Charles Dickens*, 96, 129. Michael Slater, *Dickens and Women* (London: Dent, 1983), 221. Perhaps the most surprising judgement on Nancy is that she is 'very genteel and self-abasing': S. S. Prawer, *Karl Marx and World Literature* (Oxford: Oxford University Press, 1978), 91.

or sincere, innocent or guilty, alive or dead, questions that return to the fact or question of her desire (or love, or sexuality), figured through a body described as hysterical and a battle of interrogating glances in scenes that will end with her death and the fatal haunting or fantasy of Sikes in the apparition of a shadow and a pair of sightless eyes.

In many of Nancy's appearances in the novel, she is described as 'hysterical'. When she and Sikes find Oliver in the street she 'got . . . dreadfully hysterical' (93) but almost instantly recovers. We are meant to think she is acting, but there will be more hysteria and recoveries that cannot be so safely assigned. Passing Newgate, Nancy thinks of the young men about to die, 'such fine young chaps', to which Sikes replies ' "Yes; that's all you women think of" ' (95). If Sikes were going to be hanged, she tells him, she would walk round and round the prison and when Sikes asks ' "what good would that do?" ', Nancy 'burst into a laugh', and Oliver notices that her hand trembles and her face looks 'deadly white' (99). Among Smithfield and its butchery, Newgate and its executions, the awful majesty of the law and Sikes's festive memory of 'Bartlemy time' (95), we find questions of Nancy's truth and goodness, the question of her ability to dissimulate and to dissemble hysteria, the question of her desire or compassion or something else entirely for those about to die, and the question or knowledge of 'what all women think of', questions for the reader but also for the man who will kill her (the men who will kill her, Sikes and Dickens), and for an observing, bewildered child who sees a white face, a laugh, a tremble: the glimpse of the body as ambiguous, hysterical sign.

When Nancy intervenes to save Oliver from Bullseye, Sikes says ' "The girl's gone mad, I think" ' and then asks her: ' "Do you know who you are and what you are?" ' (100), a question about male knowledge of female identity, and of male power over female sexuality. ' "Oh, yes, I know all about it," [Nancy replies] laughing hysterically; and shaking her head from side to side' and then, in a 'passion . . . frightful to see . . . not speaking but pouring out the words in one continuous and vehement scream' (100–1), she defends Oliver and herself until, in a final spasm, within language but beyond it altogether, 'tearing her hair and dress in a transport of frenzy' (101), she darts at Fagin and faints. Later, sent to fetch Oliver for the Chertsey robbery, Nancy has what appears to be a full-blown hysterical attack.

She rocked herself to and fro; caught her throat; and, uttering a gur-gling sound, struggled and gasped for breath . . . The girl beat her hands upon her knees, and her feet upon the ground; and suddenly stopping, drew her shawl close round her, and shivered with cold . . . "I don't know what comes over me sometimes," said she. (125)

Oliver has just had something come over him too, through a book, *The Lives of Great Criminals*, given him by Fagin in one of many scenes of reading and writing in the book, often used (as in the extraordinary scene of Monks and Fagin at the window in chapter 34) as a way of making the realism of the book touch other forces—unconscious, uncanny, supernat-ural—and then move on. The stories in the book are about the return of repressed material to consciousness and the world. The earth throws up well-buried corpses to drive their killers mad; sleepers are tempted and led on by their own thoughts to dread-ful bloodshed; the words of the book itself seem to Oliver as if they 'were whispered, in hollow murmurs, by the spirits of the dead' (124). As when Mr Brownlow 'contemplated running away himself' (61) when Oliver is caught by the mob, and later is threatened with arrest by Fang for taking the stolen book, the boundaries of innocence and guilt, self and other, shudder and bend. The simple directness of Nancy's and Oliver's language—' "Who's there?" "Me. Only me" ' (125)—distances the uncanny stories that Oliver reads but also brings them uncannily close in the consciousness of a small terrified boy and a hysterical woman, or girl. The reader moves from the knowledge of crimes to the consciousness of crimes in the minds of the criminals and then to the consciousness of that consciousness in Oliver, and then our own consciousness of all that, in a process that multi-plies the terrors and hauntings, in return upon return, the crime distanced and brought closer at each step and visitation.

Nancy later spies on Fagin, seeking the truth about Oliver and his parentage. In chapter 39, there is a simple paragraph divi-sion at the moment when Nancy takes her fateful decision to try and save him by revealing what she knows. Now scanned in a fraction of a second, there was a two-month interval here for the first readers of the *Miscellany*, where Nancy and Dickens decided what to do next. In the gap, Dickens placed the 'Full Report of the Second Meeting of the Mudfog Association for the Advancement of Everything', a report that satirized the claims and pretension of male science and reason, whose medical section, among other things, investigates a case of 'monomania' in a woman, who wants to have a 'full set of pearls'. 'Finding her wishes ungratified', she is sullen and peevish, refusing 'to perform domestic duties', becoming tearful and incoherent and wishing herself dead. The doctor prescribes a dose of calomel, a workhouse diet of 'weak gruel', and threatens to shave her head, whereupon she recovers and becomes 'cheerful and good-humoured' (MF547). It is another tale, in very different idiom, of female behaviour and the male pursuit of truth and knowledge of a woman, the distinction of truth and falsehood, and the relation between need and desire. A joke at the expense of the woman certainly, but it is also at the expense of a male narrator and an absurd male reason, which, like hysteria and the figure of irony, says what it says but does not know that it says it.[27]

After this interruption, hesitation, or detour into a story about male knowledge and female madness, domesticity and the threat of death, Nancy returns home to Sikes, who likens her to 'a corpse come to life again' (251), linking her to Rose Maylie, who has been on the edge of death, to Oliver who has been reborn, to the corpses in the stories that Oliver is given to read, to Sikes who will become 'the very ghost of Sikes' (324), and

---

[27] The whole passage is worth quoting:

'Finding her wishes ungratified, she fell sick . . . the prominent tokens of the disorder were sullenness, a total unwillingness to perform domestic duties, great peevishness and extreme languor, except when pearls were mentioned, at which times the pulse quickened, the eyes grew brighter, the pupils dilated, and the patient, after various incoherent exclamations, burst into a passion of tears and exclaimed that nobody cared for her, and she wished herself dead'. (MF547)

It is a story about starvation, domesticity, and the threat of death, about the distinction between truth and feigning and the relation between need and desire. The discourses of hysteria in *Oliver Twist*, of Nancy's hysteria, move between acting and madness, feigning and truth, the sincere inscription of the body and its dissimulation. Six decades later, Freud will make another search for truth through the questioning of female hysterics, telling stories that bear uncanny resemblances to this one. See, for example, the use of the figure of the 'blindness of the seeing eye' in Sigmund Freud and Joseph Breuer, *Studies on Hysteria* (Harmondsworth: Penguin, 1974), 181, and of 'eyes . . . light in themselves, but giving light to nothing' in *Oliver Twist*, 327–8.

indeed to the future Nancy who will come to life (and death) in
Dickens's public readings. She gives Sikes a 'wild and rigid' look
(251) and puts her hands over her eyes, the eyes that will pursue
him to death and which have 'fire' in them, occasioning from
Sikes the oath 'Burn my body' (251), something he will try to
do to himself after he has killed her. Running to see Rose, the
people in the street shout out 'The woman is mad' (252) and
Rose tells her that it is 'madness' (258) to return to Sikes in
an interview which had 'more the semblance of a rapid dream
than an actual occurrence' (289). When she returns, laughing
'without merriment . . . noisy without cause or meaning' (283),
Sikes and Fagin do not know what to make of her, saying that
she is 'out of her senses' and 'stark raving mad' (285); when she
speaks, she 'places both hands upon her breast, as though to
keep down by force some violent outbreak' (285); overpowered
by Sikes, she 'rocked herself to and fro; tossed her head; and
after a little time, burst out laughing' (286). A woman placed
between the familial bourgeois care of the Maylies and Brownlow, which asks her to be purified, domesticated, and transported to a new life, and a brutal male violence, which will
bludgeon her to death. Both of which want to know her, both
of which think her mad.

Nancy will of course die, after seeing an imaginary coffin in
the street, feeling 'a fear that has made me burn as if I was on
fire' and seeing the word ' "coffin" written in every page' of a
book she is reading (293), but the pursuit of her truth continues. It has recently been suggested that Nancy's 'mutilated
body expresses intense hostility to the working classes' because
of her 'mixing of illicit sexual features with the attributes of the
good mother', but it is hard to think of Nancy as a mother figure
to Oliver, unless she gave birth at the age of six.[28] She is only a
little older than the boy, and in a novel full of scenes of eating
and nurturing, Nancy does not feed him. Indeed the two hardly
meet, scarcely speak. It is the critic here who is determined that
young women should be mothers, not the author or text.
Nancy's life and death in the book are a good deal more
complex and disturbing than a reading which so readily assigns
a class position and a family romance to a text that both

[28] Nancy Armstrong, *Desire and Domestic Fiction: A Political History of the
Novel* (Oxford: Oxford University Press, 1987), 182–3.

multiplies and resists such identities. Contemporary popular stage adaptations of the book and her death roused such emotions in their audiences that they were banned by the Lord Chancellor.[29] Thirty years later, the sick and dying Dickens staged her death once more, again and again, through a reading, 'Sikes and Nancy', which became the awesome highlight of his last tours. Dickens will fear arrest as he leaves the theatre after murdering her one more time, pursuing Nancy and then the pursuer of Nancy, seeking the truth of her woman's nature in her death and the deaths which follow.[30]

IV

Let me end with two illustrations, both by George Cruikshank, both executed in 1838, both intended to illustrate the final episode of *Oliver Twist*. The first, the 'Fireside' plate, shows a family scene framing a large mirror over a fireplace, with a portrait, presumably of Oliver's mother, next to it. The second, two figures—Oliver and Rose—contemplating a church wall, on which is a plaque inscribed 'Agnes'.[31] It was clear to the artist

---

[29] Angus Wilson, Introduction to *Oliver Twist* (Harmondsworth: Penguin, 1965), 15.

[30] Edgar Johnson, *Charles Dickens: His Tragedy and Triumph* (1952, revised and abridged, Harmondsworth: Penguin, 1986), 552–3, 555. Peter Ackroyd, *Dickens: A Life* (London: Sinclair-Stevenson, 1990), provides an anthology of the complex identifications made in Dickens's letters of this period: 'I am murdering Nancy . . . My preparations for a certain murder . . . The crime being completely off my mind and the blood spilled . . . I commit the murder again . . . imbue my hands in innocent blood . . . I have a great deal of murdering before me' (1098). Ackroyd also reports Dickens saying at one point that he was 'at present nightly murdered by Mr W. Sikes' (1090), but the source for this remark is not clear. On the trial reading before friends, 'A doctor said, ". . . if only one woman cries out when you murder the girl, there will be a contagion of hysteria all over the place" ': Fred Kaplan, *Dickens: A Biography* (London: Hodder and Stoughton, 1988), 532. See also Dickens, *Sikes and Nancy*, 229–31. Dickens also had 'a vague sensation of being "wanted" as I walk about the streets': Ackroyd, *Dickens*, 1098. For Johnson, 'in deciding to add the murder of Nancy to his repertoire, he was sentencing himself to death': *Charles Dickens*, 553. On the subject of 'criminals from a sense of guilt', see Sigmund Freud, 'Some Character-Types met with in Psychoanalytic Work', in *The Pelican Freud Library Volume 14: Art and Literature* (Harmondsworth: Penguin, 1985), 317–19. Freud identifies such feelings with Oedipal desires. Dickens, like Oedipus, was often lame when he read 'Sikes and Nancy'.

[31] Both are reproduced in the Clarendon edition, facing pages xxiv and 368 respectively. See also Patten, *George Cruikshank's Life, Times, and Art*, II, 84–7.

that the former was more successful, and ended a story of a lost child in the safe destination of hearth, home, and looking-glass. Dickens, however, disagreed and demanded its replacement. His friend and confidant, John Forster, wrote to the book's publisher Bentley calling the picture 'a vile and disgusting interpolation on the sense and bearing of the tale' and 'a Rowland Macassar frontispiece to a sixpenny book of forfeits'.[32] It is an interesting dissension between Dickens and one of his first readers, for Cruikshank was right to recognize the strong forces in the book moving forward to create a bourgeois and domestic order at the end of this tale of crime and violence, a future that is also a recovery of a lost home and family. But there are other forces at work in the text which know that nothing in the book comes back, nothing can come back, just the possible building of the future. The penultimate paragraph of the book is, significantly, written in the subjunctive mood:

I would fain linger yet with a few of those among whom I have so long lived and move, and share their happiness by trying to depict it. I would show Rose Maylie ... I would paint her ... I would follow her ... I would watch her ... I would paint her ... I would summon before me ... I would recall the tones and conjure up the sympathising tear ... I would fain recall them every one. (349–50)

Few endings of novels speak so much of desire as this one, the desire of the author to linger and watch and follow his creation, as Noah Claypole did Nancy. The wish to picture, and to picture your pictures picturing ('I would paint her, and her dead sister's child ... passing whole hours together in picturing the friends whom they had so sadly lost' (350)) is strong in this passage, the desire to achieve the stasis, identity, and recovery of the past that picturing seems to offer. But it is written subjunctively and, we are told, by a 'hand' that as it 'traces these words, falters' (349). These faltering traces mark both loss and gain, as the passage mediates between desire and memory, future and past, moving from painting and summoning, mimesis and apostrophe, to recall and then to the wish to recall. Graham Greene speaks of the 'music of memory' in Proust and in the Dickens Proust learned from.[33] This is the music of memory, but

[32] Pilgrim, I, 451.
[33] Graham Greene, 'The Young Dickens', in The Lost Childhood and Other Essays (Harmondsworth: Penguin, 1979), 101–10.

the sound also of desire and need, both subjective desire—to be loved, to be cared for—but also the need and desire for social justice and the end of the workhouse. These two are profoundly dependent, as the book shows. There is not then a return to origins at the end of the book, but an arrival: at traces, a faltering hand, and an empty tomb inscribed 'Agnes', the material signifier of another sexual and transgressive woman, the sign of the impossibility of Oliver's return to family and home, and the commemoration of the many who were suffering and dying through the brutality of the New Poor Law, one of whose major provisions was to make the responsibility of illegitimacy, and therefore the punishment, devolve upon women and children.[34]

[34] Relevant passages from *The Annual Register* of 1834 and 1835 are conveniently gathered in Charles Dickens, *Oliver Twist*, ed. Fred Kaplan (New York: Norton, 1993), 365–74.

CHAPTER FOUR

Performing Business, Training Ghosts: *Nicholas Nickleby*

IN AUGUST 1860, Dickens wrote to a friend:

My mother, who was also left to me when my father died (I never had anything left to me but relations), is in the strangest state of mind from senile decay: and the impossibility of getting her to understand what is the matter, combined with her desire to be got up in sables like a female Hamlet, illumines the dreary scene with a ghastly absurdity that is the chief relief I can find in it.[1]

A passage about domestic irritability and high tragedy, about inheritance of wealth and obligation, about desire and forbidden desires in families and fictions; about Shakespeare and Dickens, parent and child, darkness and death; the costuming of revenge in the apparition of a figure which implicates and undoes theatricality and domesticity, tragedy and comedy, sexuality and madness; which is male and female, mother and son, author and character; a spectacle of horror and despair, the melancholy site of a grotesque, black laughter. In November, Dickens reports that his mother is 'much better than I supposed', as 'the instant she saw me, she plucked up a spirit, and asked for a pound'.[2] The next five lines of the letter have been removed, probably by Georgina Hogarth, Dickens's sister-in-law, executor and first editor of the letters. Plucking up spirit and money in writing and excision; the strangest state of mind, and the impossibility of getting him to understand what is the matter; family business.

---

[1] Pilgrim IX, 287. See also Michael Slater, *Dickens and Women* (London: Dent, 1983), 14–15.
[2] Pilgrim, IX, 342.

I

Nancy Armstrong in her *Desire and Domestic Fiction* has argued that a profound shift occurs in the history of the novel in the course of the nineteenth century, which grants an unprecedented centrality to the figure of the domestic woman. Through the elaboration of a set of norms and fictional understandings of desire and the self, a deeply depoliticized conception of middle-class life emerges. Novels, particularly from the 1830s, she argues, enclose political conflict within the domestic sphere and detach the household from politics to provide the 'complement and antidote to it'. The household thus becomes 'the "counter-image" of the modern marketplace, an apolitical realm of culture within the culture as a whole'.[3] At first, *Nicholas Nickleby* seems a useful illustration of the main lines of Armstrong's argument. It values the domestic virtues to excess, and its central characters move through difficulties and dangers to a happy resolution of multiple marriages and the return to the family home. Women in the book are valued for their virtue, domesticity, and silence, condemned for interference and excessive talk. Against male aristocratic immorality, the virtues of the industrious, home-loving bourgeoisie are victorious.

Yet such an account abstracts the domestic issues both from the dense economic and political forces within which Dickens embeds them and from the specific fictional form and strengths of the novel. Characters are often impelled by economic motives in the book, but Dickens is not concerned simply with the depiction of a multiplicity of human agents whose economic situation and motives are in play; he also attempts to depict economic forces that are not reducible to individual intentions. Families in the book—the Mantalinis, the Cheerybles, the Crummleses, the Squeerses, the Nicklebys—are also family businesses, where the claims of the domestic and economic are intimately bound together. They have the force of institutions—a school, a mercantile house, an acting troupe—which extend and transform the social relations of both their members and those for and upon whom they work. A lot of the comedy stems from

---

[3] Nancy Armstrong, *Desire and Domestic Fiction: A Political History of the Novel* (Oxford: Oxford University Press, 1987), 48.

this, as in the mixture of domestic affection and economic self-interest in Vincent Crummles's fostering of the Infant Phenomenon or the older Wackford's feeding of the younger, but the serious point is made too: that the family is not, cannot be, free of economic determinants, or the violence and conflict of the wider society. Indeed it often provides a particular focus for it, tragically in the brutalization and death of Smike, comically in the Kenwigses and Mantalinis.

The novel at the level of its explicit ideology celebrates the domestic virtues in the closures of Nicholas's marriage to Madeline, Kate's to Frank Cheeryble, and Miss La Creevy to Tim Linkinwater. It moves towards the birth of children and the return to the father's home, a new beginning that is also a return to origins, where the errors and crimes of the past are redeemed in the renewing of generations and regained possession. Women are safely subordinated in domestic affection, silence, and family life. Yet the peculiarly ambivalent transformational energies of Dickens's writing undercut the domestic ideology of early Victorian capitalism through the frankness of its recognition of the economic forces beneath it (Mr Lillyvick won't marry because of the expense; Nicholas and Kate at first feel obliged to renounce their respective partners); through its recognition or half-recognition of incestuous and murderous desires within families (Smike and his father Ralph; Mrs Nickleby and her son; Mr Bray and his daughter Madeline); and through the hysterical and carnivalesque laughter and inversion that permeate the novel, mischievously and promiscuously intermixing and confusing distinctions, identities, places, families. Marriage is highly valued in the book, but it is also, as the first page of the novel tells us, 'like a sparring-match . . . set to for the mere pleasure of the buffeting'.[4] It is Dotheboys that promises 'every comfort of home that a boy could wish for' (33) and Squeers ('Squeery' to Mrs Squeers) who is the most affectionate husband in the book. In the Mantalinis' marriage, which like so many others in the novel is also a business arrangement, Mrs Mantalini owns and runs the business, and her husband is expressly excluded from it, restricted to the domestic sphere, subsisting eventually

[4] Charles Dickens, *Nicholas Nickleby*, ed. Paul Schlicke (Oxford: World's Classics, 1990), 1. All further references will be to this edition and placed in the text.

on an allowance of pocket-money. His career is one of sexual self-commodification and public display, his dominant idiom semi-hysterical manipulation and prostration. When he bank-rupts the firm through his silliness, Mrs Mantalini successfully abandons him and creates a new partnership with Miss Knag. In the penultimate chapter of the book, Kate and Nicholas encounter Mantalini in the cellar doing the washing, the female domestic labour on which his self-display has always rested: reversal upon reversal, economic, sexual, domestic.

It has been said that *Nicholas Nickleby* creates 'a purely comic space', but it is better to see it as an impurely economic one, for few novels in the language are as interested in money.[5] In the course of the book we find out, in great detail, what economic survival in the 1830s entailed. Dickens is extremely specific, both about the larger sums of money in the book—Godfrey Nickleby's £1,000, Mr Bray's debts of £1,700 and £975 4s. 3d., Mr Mantalini's debt of £1,527 4s. 9½d.—and about wages and salaries. Nicholas is offered £5 a year at Dotheboys, his sister between 5s. and 7s. a week at the Mantalinis. A cook earns between 12 and 18 guineas a year, with tea and sugar provided. Nicholas is offered 15s. a week by Gregsbury and £1 (with literary adaptations and Smike) by Crummles. Miss Block-son, Kenwigs's domestic, earns 9s. a week, and the apotheosis of the Infant Phenomenon in the Fairy Porcupine raises a remarkable house of £4 12s.[6] Most of these examples (and there are many more) come from the first third of the book, and the economic specificity continues at equal density throughout, as characters insistently reach for economic metaphors and modes of financial self-dramatization: Squeers tells Mrs Sliderskew that she looks ' "twenty pound ten better than you did" ' (752) and promises ' "an arrear of flogging" ' when he returns home (749);

[5] J. Hillis Miller, *Charles Dickens: The World of his Novels* (Cambridge: Harvard University Press, 1958), 87.
[6] There is a great deal more of such detailed economic information: Ralph inher-its £3,000, the elder Nicholas £1,000 and the farm; Nicholas earns 5s. a week for teaching French to the Kenwigses; his benefit makes £20 and the Cheerybles pay him £120 a year, the same amount as Mr Mantalini's allowance; Ralph has earned at least £2,000 from Verisopht; Mr Folair's notoriety on stabbing Nicholas might have earned him 8s. or 10s. a week; Gride's debt is £1,300. It costs 18d. to white-wash a ceiling; Kenwigs buys the cheapest white kid gloves for 14d.; a haircut is 6d. and a drawing-room chair £2 15s.

Mr Mantalini, failing to subsist on his 'property' of whiskers, threatens to kill himself by changing a sovereign, filling his pockets with halfpence and drowning himself (430).

This is not merely a characteristic Dickensian superfluity, or Orwell's 'unnecessary detail'.[7] The opposite in fact, because the economic concerns, obsessions indeed, are at the centre of the novel, and almost every significant relationship (with the important exception of Kate and Nicholas) is at some point challenged, mediated, or enabled by economic demands or needs. The opening chapter, 'which introduces all the rest', recounts the history of the Nickleby family and is almost entirely a matter of the possibilities created by money, or the difficulties and limitations by its lack. The tone is set in the first paragraph, indeed in the first sentence, where we are told that Godfrey Nickleby, 'not being young enough or rich enough to aspire to the hand of a lady of fortune, had wedded an old flame out of mere attachment . . . Thus two people who cannot afford to play cards for money, sometimes sit down to a quiet game for love' (1). The relationship established here between the claims of feeling and those of money and speculation for money echo through the book and bind it together. From the naming of Lillyvick Kenwigs to Nicholas's and Kate's renunciation of their prospective partners, the novel consistently recognizes the significance of economic claims and their conflict or (more rarely) collaboration with human desires. This is perhaps most clear in the novel's concern with inheritance: Godfrey, Ralph I, Ralph II, Nicholas I, Nicholas II, Kate, Miss La Creevy, Madeline Bray, Frank Cheeryble, and the small boy whom Miss La Creevy paints with a family nose are all heirs or potential heirs to wealth, and much of the novel is designed to ensure the steering of inheritance into the right, if initially implausible, hands. But the contrast between Dickens's world and that of Austen, for example, is very clear. For *Nickleby* presents a highly mobile economic system, in which wealth can be directly obtained through entrepreneurial activity by the Crummleses, the Mantalinis, the Cheerybles, and Ralph Nickleby, and where the fear of destitution is ever-present. This is most directly presented in

[7] George Orwell, 'Charles Dickens', in Sonia Orwell and Ian Angus (eds), *The Collected Essays, Journalism and Letters Volume One: An Age Like This 1920–1940* (London: Secker and Warburg, 1968), 450.

Crummles's daily battle for an audience, but also in Squeers's struggle for pupils (' "I'm afraid of one of them boys falling off, and then there's twenty pound a year gone" ' (47), he tells Nicholas on the coach to Greta Bridge), in Miss Knag's jealousy of Kate, Nicholas's scene with Gregsbury, and Miss La Creevy's sad search for subjects.

   Nicholas Nickleby has often been seen as a rather crude and flawed story, but what critics have usually objected to is its resistance to precisely those forces in the history of the novel that Armstrong identifies.[8] Through a variety of formal means and innovations (typification, moral exhortation, the punctuation of representation with formulation, retropings and transcodings between scenes and genres of discourse) and the use of disturbing or transgressive material (violence, insanity, hysteria, haunting), Dickens tells a very different story of domesticity in the novel. It may seem that by saying that the book has a centre is also to mark a difference from the belief that the Dickens of this period was an essentially improvisatory writer, whose improvident strength lies in particular scenes and characters, not in overarching design or thematic coherence. These oppositions between academic and popular, the plan against the moment, the story against the 'turn', which have so troubled criticism of Dickens, are thematized in Mr Curdle's hope that Nicholas's compositions will obey the Unities. They seem sterile pairings, and I hope to offer a better way of putting it, neither John Lucas's 'incoherent muddle' nor Curdle's 'universal dovedtailedness' and 'general oneness' (311).[9] There is a group of problems which permeate the book, are reinforced and retroped within it, and which are presented and resolved in formally radical and innovative ways.

---

   [8] For Gissing 'the faulty construction . . . becomes a meanness, a limitation': *Charles Dickens: A Critical Study* (London: Gresham, 1902), 50; for John Lucas, the book is 'an incoherent muddle' in which 'much of the plot and narrative are mismanaged', the 'flabbiest and least dramatic of the novels', full of 'serious irrelevancies, discrepancies and plain inconsistencies of tone': *The Melancholy Man: A Study of Dickens's Novels* (London: Methuen, 1970), 55, 61; for Philip Collins, 'the novel has no theme . . . the plot is meaningless': *Dickens and Education* (London: Macmillan, 1963), 110. Steven Marcus, by contrast, has warm praise for the book, which 'seems to consolidate the most impressive qualities of the two novels that preceded it—the vitality and materiality of his first novel, the seriousness and moral intention of his second': *Dickens: From Pickwick to Dombey* (London: Chatto, 1965), 92.
   [9] Lucas, *The Melancholy Man*, 55.

The first chapter tells the story of the Nickleby family over four generations through their economic life. It produces a pattern of repetition, both of names—Nicholas and Ralph—and of economic fates. The first Ralph intended to leave his money to the Royal Humane Society until it saved the life of a poor dependant (we are told his cost: 3s. 6d. a week) and the will is changed. The second Ralph is equally cold-blooded, as the second Nicholas is as virtuous as his benevolent and guileless father. At a certain historical and comic distance, we see a pattern of family inheritance, akin to the story we are about to be told, in which the pursuit of wealth and virtue is divided and opposed, in which the contingencies and injustices of the pursuit and inheritance of wealth are central and troubling facts, and in which the ideologies of public profession are undercut by economic reality. But what appears at first a safely pleasurable, known, and repetitive historical and narrative structure of virtue and vice, poverty and wealth, of identity of name and character, is immediately undone by the threat of poverty and the desire of speculation. Just before he is saved by old Uncle Ralph's legacy of £5,000, Godfrey 'was seriously revolving in his mind a little commercial speculation of insuring his life next quarter day and then falling from the top of the Monument by accident' (2). It is done lightly enough, but the link between the demands of domestic preservation, violent death, and 'commercial speculation' is made early. There is other speculation in the chapter. Ralph is christened after his uncle in a 'desperate speculation' (2), and we are left to speculate the effects on his character. The most significant speculation is Nicholas's, the hero's father, who, in speculating, loses his patrimony, breaks his heart, and impels the action of the novel. It is not, in Dickens's account, a matter of mere personal folly, but the consequence of a whole financial system. Speculation, we are told:

is a round game; the players see little or nothing of their cards at first starting; gain may be great—and so may losses. The run of luck went against Mr Nickleby. A mania prevailed, a bubble burst, four stockbrokers took villa residences in Florence, four hundred nobodies were ruined, and among them Mr Nickleby. (5)

With the swiftness of farce and the clarity of theory, the first Nicholas Nickleby is dispatched. The novel's remaining eight hundred or so pages tell the story of his son's and daughter's attempt to survive in a world that so lightly balances the needs of four hundred against the pleasure and power of 'four stockbrokers'.

There is of course a direct historical context for this in the speculative mania of the early 1830s.[10] But it is equally important to note the general terms in which Dickens tells the story. The whole chapter is designed to, as he would later put it, 'Strike the Key-note'. Nicholas's foolish speculation and Ralph's precocious usury, 'in which he speculated to considerable advantage' (7), define a rapacious and precarious financial world within which the later action of the novel has to find its way. With heavy irony, Dickens recommends Ralph's methods to 'capitalists . . . money-brokers and bill-discounters' (3) and reinforces this link in the second chapter of the book, which punctuates the *representation* of the novel with a more abstract *formulation* of the economic forces within and through which the domestic, moral, and familial struggles of the book occur. The story does not begin with Nicholas and Kate grieving at their father's death, but with the spectacle of Ralph at business, part of a syndicate that uses drunken aristocrats and corrupt legislators to raise the share price of a paper company. The establishment of the United Metropolitan Improved Hot Muffin and Crumpet Baking and Punctual Delivery Company is in one way strictly inorganic to the story. The muffins, aristocrats, and Honourable Members disappear, never to return. Yet their force and significance for the story are immense. We are presented with capitalist and entrepreneurial activity in its purest, most speculative and exploitative form. The Company has no intention of trading, not even in the conditions of monopoly it claims to want to establish. Its task is, through the strategic manipulation of opinion, to enable a quick profit to be made without risk for Nickleby and his fellow-puffers. Ralph is, even today, described by critics as a 'miser', but Dickens expressly gives us the opposite impression.[11] Ralph is not a hoarder of loot, counting his pots of gold in squalor (as later Gride will do), but

---

[10] Norman Russell, '*Nicholas Nickleby* and the Commercial Crisis of 1825', *Dickensian*, 77 (1981), 144–50.

[11] Paul Schlicke, 'Introduction' to *Nicholas Nickleby* (Oxford: World's Classics, 1990), xxv.

an entirely contemporary figure, a master-manipulator of the new complexities of publicity, monopoly, and speculation. The source of his wealth is presented at first as a puzzle: 'Mr Ralph Nickleby was not, strictly speaking, what you would call a merchant, neither was he a banker, nor an attorney, nor a special pleader, nor a notary. He was certainly not a tradesman, and still less could he lay any claim to the title of a professional gentleman' (6). But the puzzle is only an apparent one. He is first described as a 'man of business' and then in his most revealing and explicit nomenclature as 'the capitalist' (10). Should we miss the point of Dickens's attack, the public meeting is furnished with 'a business-looking table and several business-looking people' (11). Mr Squeers, Dickens tells us in the 1848 preface, 'is the representative of a class' (xlv). So too, it is clear, is Ralph.

Dickens, then, is portraying, in the most specific and yet general way, the particular exploitative dynamics of which Ralph is a type, embodiment, and manipulator. Much of the energy of this and later scenes comes from their wish to show the gap between so many central Victorian ideologies and their material and economic reality. Dickens does this through dramatic and novelistic techniques that can be usefully parallelled to those of Brecht, who was also willing to ignore or break conventions of realism for the sake of depicting deeper economic forces and needs, to risk charges of crudity in the frank and cheerful depiction of the gap between ideological justifications and economic practice, and to unsettle and punctuate narrative continuity and character identification through what I want to call *formulation*.[12] A good example of this technique occurs at Nicholas's first meeting with Squeers:

" 'Never postpone business,' is the very first lesson we instil into our commercial pupils. Master Belling, my dear, always remember that; do you hear?"

"Yes, sir," repeated Master Belling.

"He recollects what it is, does he?" said Ralph.

"Tell the gentleman," said Squeers.

" 'Never', " repeated Master Belling.

[12] I take the term from Brecht's 'The Literarization of the Theatre', in Bertolt Brecht, *Brecht on Theatre: the Development of an Aesthetic*, ed. John Willett (London: Methuen, 1964), 43.

"Very good," said Squeers; "go on."

" 'Never,' " repeated Master Belling again.

"Very good indeed," said Squeers. "Yes."

"P," suggested Nicholas, good-naturedly.

"Perform—business!" said Master Belling. "Never—perform—business!" (37)

Squeers is here doing a performance as part of his business, as later Crummles and others will do. It is also a scene of education as repetition. Like so many of Dickens's great characters, Squeers is an inveterate repeater, here inscribing memory through labour, beating, and fear: 'W-i-n, win, d-e-r, der, a casement. When the boy knows this out of the book, he goes and does it' (90). There are other formulaic scenes in the book, such as the appearance of the Old Lord and the Young Lady at the Mantalinis and Nicholas's interview with the MP Gregsbury. It is easy to dismiss them as crude 'prentice work, yet like speculation and Belling's failure to repeat, they punctuate the safe continuities and pleasures of narrative representation and identification with the facts of poverty and exploitation and the claims of radical social and political critique. Criticism of nineteenth-century fiction has often valued its rich sensuous concreteness against the dry abstractions of calculating reason. Yet such fiction can have difficulty in transcribing those processes, particularly economic ones, that treat human agents and actions as abstract and commensurable equivalents. In this passage Dickens uses what have often been seen as residual survivals of older traditions—parable, fairy story, moral typification—as abstraction in fiction in the service of a radical critique of abstraction in society, to analyse not old morals but new social and economic forces.

Critics have rightly pointed to the immediate scandals of the Yorkshire schools in the portrayal of Squeers, but Dickens is determined to generalize out from this, to understand the economic conditions within which such schools arise, and to see Squeers's affinity to the capitalist Ralph Nickleby as a structural one. Squeers, like Ralph, is adept at speculation and publicity in the service of profit. He becomes his own walking advertisement:

"My dear child," said Mr Squeers, "All people have their trials . . . You are leaving your friends but you will have a father in me, my dear, and a mother in Mrs Squeers. At the delightful village of Dotheboys, near Greta Bridge in Yorkshire, where youth are boarded, clothed, booked, washed, furnished with pocket-money, provided with all necessaries—" (32)

He is interrupted in this particular 'rehearsal of his advertisement' but takes many other opportunities in the book to repeat it, and continues to call the school a 'shop' (87), or 'the business'. Ralph comes to see him 'on a matter of business' (36). Chapter 8 ('Of the Internal Economy of Dotheboys Hall') shows the 'business' (95) of beating the boys because 'Bolder's father was two pound ten short' (93). The boys are simply so much working capital: 'There's youth to the amount of eight hundred pound a-year, at Dotheboys Hall at the present time. I'd take sixteen hundred pound worth, if I could get 'em, and be as fond of every individual twenty pound among 'em as nothing should equal it!' (437). Critics often see in the book's concern with gentility either the insecurity of the parvenu Dickens or simple vulgarity.[13] Yet if we trace the term 'lady' and 'gentleman' through the novel, we see a more subversive use of the terms. It is not that Dickens is attempting to make the classical bourgeois claim of essential equality with the aristocracy through gentility. His irony is a good deal less stable than this, as a brief list of characters who are described as 'lady' or 'gentleman' in the book makes clear: Mr Bonney and all his fellow-speculators (10); the whole Squeers family (98); Miss La Creevy (115); Newman Noggs (133); everyone at the Kenwigses (168); Gregsbury and all his constituents (192–3); Mr Mantalini (211); all the members of Ralph's dinner-party (231); the Crummles's audience (280); Smike (282–3); Crummles's acting company (293–5); the Gentleman in Small Clothes (528); Mulberry Hawk (662–3). It is an utterly promiscuous use of the terms, from which almost no significant or insignificant character escapes inclusion. Radically levelling, consistently witty, we have here not the uncertainty of the young Dickens but his courage to push one of the central social distinctions of early Victorian England—genteel/non-genteel—to the point of meaninglessness.

The gap between public profession and economic power is also there, perhaps most importantly, in the description of

---

[13] Lucas, *The Melancholy Man*, 58.

sexual and romantic relations in the book, precisely situated between the first and second halves of Mr Mantalini's immortally seductive 'What about the cash, my existence's jewel?' (207). It is there in Fanny Squeers's rage and wounded pride at being 'refused by a teacher, picked up by advertisement, at an annual salary of five pounds, payable at indefinite interval' (141–2). Most importantly, it occurs in the treatment of Kate Nickleby and Madeline Bray (whose Christian name invokes Mary Magdalen, just as Nicholas is named after the patron saint of poor scholars). The description of the dinner-party which Ralph arranges for Verisopht to meet Kate is saturated with economic terms. Kate is made to perform for Verisopht 'as a matter of business' (231) and when they are introduced he precisely estimates its economic value: 'An unexpected playsure, Nickleby . . . and one that would warrant the addition of an extra two-and-a-half per cent' (237), later complaining that Hawk is 'monopolising your niece' (236). Two particular humiliations for Kate are also economic matters. At first she is the subject of a wager, a mere speculative game for the rich aristocrats but a mortal threat to her: ' "Capital!" said Sir Mulberry Hawk, putting the stake in his pocket. . . . Pyke and Co. responded . . . the toast was drunk with very little trouble from the firm relative to the completeness of Sir Mulberry's conquest' (240). Hawk's friends—Pyke, Pluck, and Snobb—are a limited company, a firm, acting corporately for economic ends. The novel has often been seen as anti-aristocratic, posing a bourgeois hero against aristocratic decadence, but it is clear here both that the peer Verisopht is the best of a bad bunch and that the criticism of their conduct is made in explicitly anti-capitalist terms: 'monopoly', 'capital', 'the firm', 'and Co'.

Kate's second great trial occurs when Hawk attempts to rape, and Ralph fails to protect, her. His subsequent confrontation with Hawk is extremely revealing both of the terms of their relationship, and the forces that threaten Kate:

"You would sell your flesh and blood for money, you . . . Do you mean to tell me that your pretty niece was not brought here as a decoy for the drunken boy downstairs?" . . .

"I tell you this," replied Ralph, "that if I brought her here, as a matter of business—"

"Aye, that's the word," interrupted Sir Mulberry, with a laugh. (242)

The fear and threat of prostitution—of the commodification of sexuality—is present through the book, in comic idiom in Mrs Nickleby's fear that she will go to 'the Magdalen hospital' (253), in the effective selling of Madeline Bray to Gride—'You are betrayed and sold for money', Nicholas tells her (698)—and in the threats to Kate by Mantalini, Hawk, and Verisopht: ' "Selling a girl—throwing her in the way of temptation, and insult and coarse speech. Nearly two thousand pounds profit from him already though. Pshaw! match-making mothers do the same every day . . . She must take her chance. She must take her chance" ' (341). It is a speculative economy governed by exploitative and ruthless exchange under the threat of male force, constantly entwining domestic and familial relations with those of economic success and failure.

II

I want now to show how these forces—the gap between ideological justification and economic reality, the pervasiveness and destructiveness of economic relationships, the speculative instability of economic life, and the particular threat to women posed by this system of sexual commodification—are transformed and set to work in the course of the novel in the portrayal of familial and domestic life. Criticism of Dickens is usually founded on differently valorized but familiar oppositions: learned and popular traditions, high and low materials, serious and trivial intentions. These oppositions too often stand outside novels concerned precisely with their relationship. The Wititterlys' Cadogan Place, 'the one slight bond between the aristocratic pavements of Belgrave Square and the barbarism of Chelsea' (264), is 'like the ligament which unites the Siamese twins' (265) and there is a huge repertoire of effects in the novel, designed, ligament-like, to bring high and low, rich and poor, 'Cheers, Tears, and Laughter!' (626) into complex, overdetermined relations. Unlike Miss La Creevy, Dickens has no wish to keep the serious and smirking apart, but through symbolic inversion and ambivalent dependence, the use of transgressive material and grotesque effects, to push antitheses to their limits while at the same time uniting them. Clerks become soldiers in Miss La

Creevy's hands as readily as Muntle can become Mantalini, 'l'eau' be the sign of a dismal or a cheerful language, or Mrs Mantalini can transmute from a goblin to a fairy. Smike wears 'a skeleton suit', the vestment and anatomy of an animate corpse, child and man together. When Fanny Squeers and Miss Knag move in an instant from conduct-book politesse or sisterly solidarity to the frankness of '"'Tilda I hate you"' (112), Dickens appears to be making a moral point, but the structure of feeling exists both above and below the level of the active moral agent. Much of the power of the writing comes from sudden juxtaposition, rapid mobility, and ambivalent ligature within and between hierarchies of social and linguistic order and disorder, as the struggle between class positions and discourses, gentility and vulgarity, high and low, rich and poor is fought out through the symbolically rich, often materially poor, cultural resources and contradictory class locations of the urban lower-middle class, deracinated bourgeoisie, and abject poor.

Families are not exempt from these processes, but frequently their most densely determined place of transition and displacement, the most richly comic and symbolically ambivalent spaces and structures in the book. Whereas Dickens often seeks for simpler, if not wholly unambiguous, emotional effects in his portrayal of economic life, as in the virtuous poverty of Kate and Noggs or callousness of Ralph, the home life of the novel among the Squeerses, Nicklebys, and Kenwigses achieves particularly complex and ambivalent effects. In Squeers's grotesque paternal care—'my son as is the young Norval of private life, and the pride and ornament of a doting willage' (780)—or Mrs Nickleby's protean somatic and social heterodoxy, we find not the 'subordination of all social differences to those based on gender',[14] but a restless and mobile transcoding of them in multiple, aleatory relations of parent and child, desire and courtship, death and inheritance.[15] In Fanny's strong feelings for Nicholas's legs, Miss Knag's for Mantalini's whiskers, Mrs Nickleby's for Frank Cheeryble's nose (' "Do you call it a Roman or a Grecian?" '(727)), the aerial cucumbers of the Gentleman in Small Clothes and the umbrella that Squeers takes to bed with

---

[14] Armstrong, *Desire and Domestic Fiction*, 4.

[15] On transcoding, see Peter Stallybrass and Allon White, *The Politics and Poetics of Transgression* (London: Routledge, 1986), 9.

him, we find a cathected universe, freighted with desire, where the mere mention of paternity can send John Browdie into hysterical spasm. This is not always for comic or grotesque effect, as Hawk's amorous persecution of the disgusted Kate shows. Indeed the book works nearly as hard as Mr ('"I will be a body"' (431)) Mantalini to link desire to death, as the conversion of Mrs Nickleby's mourning garments into the romantic 'signals of very slaughterous and killing designs upon the living' (528) shows. Children are particularly ambivalent figures here, the sign both of new-created life and of real and difficult emotional and economic demands. '"Let him die!"' exclaims Mr Kenwigs on learning that the newborn Lillyvick is not to inherit, '"He has no expectations, no property to come into. We want no babies here!"' (465).

One of the more celebrated chapters of the novel is the appearance of Nicholas, having fled Dotheboys, at the Kenwigs's dinner-table. Dickens is clearly engaged here: witness the blacking-bottles (161) and the pugnacious chapter heading: 'Having the misfortune to treat of none but Common People, is necessarily of a Mean and Vulgar Character'. J. Hillis Miller uses this chapter as an example of a fault in Dickens's work in which 'the individual scene swells out of all proportion to its significance in the whole'.[16] My sense is that the opposite is the case: that its strength derives from its ability to reprise and transcode material from earlier scenes in a way that makes every detail work more forcefully. The card game they play is 'Speculation', invoking again the concern with wealth and speculation for wealth which opens the novel.[17] The whole social event is in a sense a speculative one in which the Kenwigses hope to stay in the good books (and therefore the will) of the collector Lillyvick. But it is Lillyvick who 'appropriated the property of his neighbours', so much so that 'he deserved to be Chancellor of the Exchequer at least' (166); the fundamental social relations are unchanged and it is only the (comparatively) rich Lillyvick who profits. Like Ralph's meal for Verisopht, it is a quite blatant use of hospitality for financial gain, but it also transforms the violence of the preceding Dotheboys chapter

---

[16] Miller, *Charles Dickens: the World of his Novels*, 87.
[17] See Tatiana M. Holway, 'The Game of Speculation: Economics and Representation', *Dickens Quarterly*, 9 (1992), 103–14.

into 'slaps on the head' for the infant Kenwigses, and the rebellion of Nicholas and Smike against Squeers becomes the
summary banishment of 'two of the most rebellious' (166) children from the table. Shortly after, Mrs Kenwigs bursts into tears
at the sight of her children: ' "oh! they're too beautiful to live,
much too beautiful!" ' (167), a performance 'with attitudes',
Dickens remarks, 'which Miss Petowker herself might have
copied' (167). Affectingly sentimental and absurd at the same
time, the passage like the chapter transcodes the material of
the novel—performance, murderous and affectionate impulses
towards children, rebellion and family order, festive and speculative sociability—into complexly overdetermined and mobile
effects. Allon White has argued that 'the most valuable, endur-
ing thing in Dickens's work [is] the mutual solidarity of kinship
which finds its central expression in the bond between parent
and child', an ethic of a truthful, loving, detached, and protected
hearth and home.[18] But the Kenwigses do not separate festivity
from speculation or the pursuit of domestic goals from economic ones, nor is it easy or necessary to distinguish truthful
feelings from feigned ones or murderous impulses from parental
affection. On the contrary, the scene demonstrates, like the
book itself, the constant mutual implication of apparently
contradictory activities and emotions. It is damage to Squeers's
legs, Fanny tells Nicholas, that prevents him from holding a
pen.

There are many such instances, in which Dickens moves with
astonishing facility between plots and genres of discourse or
creates complexly hybrid scenes and idioms to bring them
together. This can consist of parallel plotting, as in Fanny
Squeers's attempted seduction of Nicholas which, in its assumption of sexual disposability by the economically more powerful,
anticipates Mulberry Hawk's more deadly threatening of Kate.
Crummles's troupe straddles discursive and generic boundaries
with aplomb, well captured by Crummles's greeting of Nicholas
'with an inclination of the head, something between the cour-
tesy of a Roman Emperor and the nod of a pot companion'

[18] Allon White, 'Language and Location in Bleak House', in Carnival, Hysteria
and Writing (Oxford: Oxford University Press, 1993), 93.

(278). Dignified and familiar, sincere and feigned, his gesture is as hybrid as his playbills. London is the central force and instance of these transformations, as in the famous description in chapter 32, which moves from 'Emporiums of splendid dresses' and 'vessels of burnished gold' through 'clothes for the newly-born, drugs for the sick, coffins for the dead' and then out of the shop window to the 'half-naked shivering figures' who 'stopped to gaze at Chinese shawls and golden stuffs of India' within. There is 'a christening party at the largest under-takers' as 'Life and death went hand in hand; wealth and poverty stood side by side; repletion and starvation laid them down together' (408–9). Writing here is a process of mediation and transcription across boundaries and between oppositions, like the consumption that kills Smike 'in which death and life are so strangely blended, that death takes the glow and hue of life and life the gaunt and grisly form of death' (637). The whole process is a dance of death, a metaphor that is later literalized in the dancing drunkard whom Ralph encounters in the church-yard on the way to his own suicide.

One of the most interesting of these transcodings is Dickens's use of the story of *Hamlet* whose themes and associations—revenge, inheritance, the relation of parent and child, obligation to the dead—are echoed and put to work in the novel. Nicholas, like Hamlet, has a dead father whose name he shares and a wicked uncle who will send him away on a plausible errand hoping he will never return. Nicholas's uncle has not killed his father or married his mother, but the economic system Ralph embodies has ended the first Nicholas Nickleby's life and Mrs Nickleby is foolish enough to be complicit with his plots. Nicholas spends time with actors, is knowledgeable and sym-pathetic to them, writes for them, and then curses himself for delaying from his real task. There is no *The Mousetrap* but the Crummles's play hints obscurely at incest: 'after a good deal of groping in the dark, everybody got hold of everybody else, and took them for somebody besides . . . after which the patriarch came forward, and observing, with a knowing look, that he knew all about his children now' (304–5). There are many verbal echoes too: when Mrs Nickleby is talking to Kate about her late husband, she says ' "I think I see him now" ' (481), and her justification of her designs on the Gentleman in Small Clothes is that ' "there's a great deal too much method in *his* madness, depend upon that, my dear" ' (540). Crummles, characteristically, gets in on the act too with his invocation of 'that bourne from which no traveller returns' (390).

But when Nicholas and Smike tour with Crummles's troupe, it is not *Hamlet* but Act Five, Scene One of *Romeo and Juliet* that they play, with Nicholas as Romeo and Smike the Apothecary. Here, as with Belling and Squeers at The Saracen's Head, there is a scene of instruction by repetition. Smike is unable to read and Nicholas by dint of repetition helps Smike to memorize his lines from 'Who calls so loud?' This time the message returns as it was sent in a scene of speech and sentiment, piety and patience, between Shakespeare and Dickens, Nicholas and Smike, through which the dead word becomes living spirit. In the scene, Smike as the poor and starving Apothecary sells Nicholas as Romeo a poison, sold under duress to unite him with Juliet and end the narrative, a poison intended as a cure. Slightly later, Mr Mantalini too will stage a scene in which poison is intended as a cure: by threatening to take his life, he preserves both it and the flow of Mrs Mantalini's wealth that supports its excesses. Both scenes are full of ambivalences and ambiguities: the poison is not a poison, but nor is it a cure; Smike is not an apothecary; Nicholas is not Romeo; neither is an actor; Juliet and the actress playing Juliet are just playing dead, as is Mantalini; both are tragic scenes played as comedy, sentimental and farcical respectively. These ambivalences extend to the portrayal of romantic love: the reciprocity and chastity of Nicholas's love for Smike seems a good deal more interesting to Dickens than his perfunctory passion for Madeline Bray, and this in turn is supported only by the sexless bachelor business of the brothers Cheeryble.

Hamlet is of course 'the great model in earlier English literature for the haunting of ancestral presences',[19] and there are a great many hauntings and visitations in the book, some of which are derived from stock situations in popular melodrama, as for example when Nicholas pursues Gride to his lair and, in a scene

[19] Jonathan Arac, '*Hamlet, Little Dorrit* and the History of Character', in Michael Hays (ed.), *Critical Conditions: Regarding the Historical Moment* (Minneapolis: University of Minnesota Press, 1992), 90.

that anticipates Marley's visitation on Scrooge, is described in turn as a 'form' and 'spirit' before his identity is made clear (703–4). Ralph Nickleby is described as like 'a man who had seen a spirit from some world beyond the grave' (244). The windows, like the embroidery, in *The Five Sisters of York* 'raise up the ghosts of earlier years' (63). Mrs Nickleby recounts an extraordinary anecdote of being haunted by Shakespeare during her pregnancy with Nicholas, concluding that ' "it was quite a mercy ma'am . . . that my son didn't turn out to be a Shakespeare, and what a dreadful thing that would have been" ' (353).[20] Squeers, in one of his most remarkable, rather Derridean, passages of philosophy, tells Nicholas that: ' "A wisitation, sir, is the lot of mortality. Mortality itself, sir, is a wisitation. The world is chock full of wisitations; and if a boy repines at a wisitation and makes you uncomfortable with his noise, he must have his head punched. That's going according to scripter, that is" ' (740). Nicholas believes that Smike is haunted when Brooker appears to him near the end of his life, but the most disturbing haunting of the book is Ralph's by Smike, not a dead father who haunts his son, but a living son who haunts his father. There is a strange, multiple set of identifications and

---

[20] The whole passage is worth quoting:

' "After we had seen Shakespeare's tomb and birthplace, we went back to the inn there, where we slept that night, and I recollect that all night long I dreamt of nothing but a black gentleman, at full length, in plaster-of-Paris, with a lay-down collar tied with two tassels, leaning against a post and thinking; and when I woke in the morning and described him to Mr Nickleby, he said it was Shakespeare just as he was when he was alive, which was very curious indeed. I recollect I was in the family way with my son Nicholas at the time and I had been very much frightened by an Italian image boy. In fact it was quite a mercy, ma'am," added Mrs Nickleby, in a whisper to Mrs Wititterly, "that my son didn't turn out to be a Shakespeare, and what a dreadful thing that would have been!" ' (353)

It is a remarkable piece of discourse, linking as it does questions of death and authorship, images and effigies, the power of writers over their readers and mothers over their sons, through figures of dreaming and haunting, birth and death. There is a long tradition, dating from the publication of the novel, identifying Mrs Nickleby and Dickens's mother, an identification made at times by Dickens himself. The best account is in Slater, *Dickens and Women*, 16–17. Dickens had visited Stratford in October 1838, not long before Mrs Nickleby's nocturnal visitation, and had suffered 'an ecstacy of pain' in his side, akin to the ones he suffered as a boy in the blacking factory. His biographers often identify such attacks with moments of deep emotional or psychological stress. *Oliver Twist* had already caused Dickens to be compared to Shakespeare, as in the anonymous review from *The Literary Gazette, and Journal of the Belles Lettres* (24 November 1838), reprinted in Charles Dickens, *Oliver Twist*, ed. Fred Kaplan (New York: Norton, 1993), 402.

slippages here: Ralph and Smike, Dickens and Shakespeare, haunting and doubling, visitations according to scripter.[21]

' "Train up a Ghost—child, I mean—" ' (642), says Mrs Nickleby, who is often thought of as someone who cannot remember, but of whom it is truer to say that she cannot forget. Like Mr Mantalini and Mrs Wititterly, she is haunted in what Chesterton calls 'her beautiful mazes of memory' by memories of an often imagined past.[22] She remembers others' memories, and is haunted by others' hauntings—such as her great-great-grandfather's (possible) haunting by the Cock Lane Ghost (or Thirsty Woman of Tutbury).[23] Her symptoms, as Freud says of his hys-

[21] The hauntings continue in Dickens's letters of this period, in particular those written during or about his trip to Greta Bridge to investigate the Yorkshire schools. He writes to Mrs S. C. Hall on 29 December 1838 about the 'origin' of Smike:

'There is an old Church near the school, and the first grave-stone I stumbled on that dreary winter afternoon was placed above the grave of a boy, eighteen long years old, who had died—suddenly, the inscription said; I suppose his heart broke—the Camel falls down "suddenly" when they heap the last load upon his back—died at that wretched place. I think his ghost put Smike into my head, upon the spot.' (Pilgrim, I, 482)

Throughout the period before the writing of *Nicholas Nickleby*, Dickens was 'haunted' nightly by the presence of Mary Hogarth, his dead sister-in-law. He wrote to his wife about the visitations during the trip to Greta Bridge in February 1838:

'Is it not extraordinary that the same dreams which have constantly visited me since poor Mary died, follow me everywhere? . . . I have dreamt of her ever since leaving home . . . I should be sorry to lose such visions for they are very happy ones—if it be only the seeing her in one's sleep—I would fain believe too, sometimes, that her spirit may have some influence over them, but their perpetual repetition is extraordinary.' (Pilgrim, I, 366)

The dreams or visions then ceased, for a period of several years. The same year he told W. B. Archer that 'our spirits commonly hold intercourse with those of the beloved dead in waking thoughts and dreams in which we see them (knowing them to be no longer in this world), without fear or pain' (Pilgrim, I, 486). This is very close in sentiment to a passage in chapter 43 in *Nicholas Nickleby*:

'It is an exquisite and beautiful thing in our nature, that when the heart is touched and softened by some tranquil happiness or affectionate feeling, the memory of the dead comes over it most powerfully and irresistibly. It would almost seem as if our better thoughts and sympathies were charms, in virtue of which the soul is enabled to hold some vague and mysterious intercourse with the spirits of those whom we dearly loved in life.' (564)

See also the passage extracted from Walter Scott's diary in Dickens's diary for 14 January 1838 (Pilgrim, I, 632).

[22] G. K. Chesterton, *Charles Dickens* (London: Methuen, 1906), 115.

[23] The Cock Lane Ghost also appears in *A Tale of Two Cities* and *Dombey and Son*. It is perhaps the archetypal meeting of literary celebrity and the returning dead. See E. J. Clery, *The Rise of Supernatural Fiction 1762–1800* (Cambridge: Cambridge University Press, 1995), 13–32. Mr Mortimer Knag, a 'literary' character, the author of much unpublished work, is described as 'ghostly' (221), and Nicholas works as a ghost-writer for Crummles.

terical patients, insist on joining in the conversation.[24] Against thepurity, order, and submissiveness of the Victorian feminine ideal, she scandalously erupts into the novel her chaotic and assertive disorder. She fails in the most treasured of feminine occupations—that of mothering—and refuses to recognize the boundaries of her separate sphere, advising her husband on the rights, or rather wrongs, of investment. She suffers, like Freud's hysterical patients, mainly from reminiscences, and her speech, with its extraordinary free associations and surreal creativity, disrupts the plots, plans, the order and reason of her interlocutors. Constantly attempting consecutive narration, constantly failing, she has the talking but not the cure; 'mere memory becomes a kind of debauch'.[25] Like other Victorian hysterics, she is implicitly condemned for malingering, treachery, and immorality. What other than illicit sexual desires could cause her to be so interested in the exact shape of Frank Cheeryble's nose? Why else does she fail to recognize what exactly is being said to her with cucumbers and vegetable marrows? Why else does she persist in calling Madeline Magdalene?

Psychic conflict is often expressed in the book through somatic symptoms, most usually as emotional crisis accompanied by theatricality, what Freud was later to call paroxystic hysteria.[26] This is not just a female matter: Mrs Witittterly's soul, her husband tells us, 'swells, expands, dilates—the blood flows, the pulse quickens, the excitement increases—Whew!' (267–8) and having rubbed himself up to such a pitch of excitement at the thought of his wife's sensibility, Mr Wititterly blows his nose. Indeed, there is a small epidemic of nose-rubbing in the book. John Browdie, at Nicholas's suggestion that he might become a godfather following the Browdies' marriage,

chuckled, roared, half-suffocated himself by laughing large pieces of beef into his windpipe, roared again, persisted in eating at the same

---

[24] Sigmund Freud and Josef Breuer, *The Pelican Freud Library Volume 3: Studies On Hysteria* (Harmondsworth: Penguin, 1974), 216.

[25] Chesterton, *Charles Dickens*, 115. Freud's main papers on hysteria are collected in Freud and Breuer, *Studies On Hysteria*, and Sigmund Freud, *The Pelican Freud Library Volume 8: Case Histories I* (Harmondsworth: Penguin, 1977). See also Charles Bernheimer and Claire Kahane (eds), *In Dora's Case: Freud–Hysteria–Feminism* (Columbia: Columbia University Press, 1985).

[26] 'Emotional crises accompanied by theatricality': J. Laplanche and J. B. Pontalis, *The Language of Psychoanalysis* (London: Karnac, 1973), 194.

time, got red in the face and black in the forehead, coughed, cried, got
better, went off again laughing inwardly, got worse, choked, had his
back thumped, stamped about, frightened his wife and at last
recovered in a state of the last exhaustion and with the water still
streaming from his eyes, but still faintly ejaculating "A godfeyther,
Tilly, a godfeyther." (543)

The Gentleman in Small Clothes, the most clearly lunatic character in the book and Mrs Nickleby's inamorato, reprises so
many of its themes, as the fragments of imperial and commercial dignity meet the tetchy irritabilities of bourgeois life: 'Or is
it . . . in consequence of the statue at Charing Cross having been
lately seen on the Stock Exchange at midnight, walking arm-in-
arm with the Pump from Aldgate, in a riding habit?' (534). The
narrator of the Dotheboys scene himself is on the edge of hysterical laughter at the 'grotesque features' of the extreme suffering he describes, which are 'irresistibly ridiculous, but for the
foul appearance of dirt, disorder and disease' (88–9).

Like Mrs Gamp, Mrs Nickleby links, carnival-like, birth and
death. Peter Stallybrass and Allon White have shown the profound links between bourgeois hysteria and the carnivalesque:
'Carnival debris spills out of the mouths of those terrified
Viennese women in Freud's *Studies in Hysteria* . . . The broken
fragments of carnival . . . glide through the discourse of the
hysteric.'[27] The book, like so much of Dickens's fiction, has
many fragments of carnival embedded within it, and not simply
within the scenes of public festivity, like the scene at the racecourse at Hampton. Noggs has 'two goggle eyes and a rubicund
nose' (13); the policemen at the Crumpet scene resemble 'that
ingenious actor Mr Punch' (13); even Golden Square where
Ralph lives is a 'region of song and smoke' (7). The final over-
throwing of Dotheboys is in many ways a full-scale carnival
inversion, complete with eating of 'low' matter, reversal of hierarchy, and ritual violence, an unlicensed transgression from
which the institution will never recover. Mrs Nickleby too has
her carnival fragments, invoking that most grotesque and hybrid
of creatures the pig, whose 'open-mouthed squeal' is such an
important figure in the festive and sinister imaginary,[28] in the

[27] Stallybrass and White, *The Politics and Poetics of Transgression*, 171.
[28] Ibid., 47.

yet more hybrid and grotesque form of 'the pig-faced lady' (646). There are many such hybrid and grotesque creatures in the book, from Fanny Squeers's final insult to Matilda— ' "mermaid" ' (547)—to Mr Mantalini's endearments to his wife—' "pure and angelic rattlesnake" ' (428) and ' "demd savage lamb" ' (821). In a memory of a memory, about dismemberment, Mrs Nickleby sites the comic butchery of carnival between father and child:

"Roast pig! I hardly think we could ever have had one, now I come to remember, for your papa could never bear the sight of them in the shop and used to say that they always put him in mind of very little babies, only the pigs had much fairer complexions; and he had a horror of little babies too, for he couldn't very well afford any increase to his family, and had a natural dislike to the subject." (529)

Dismembering and remembering the distinction between animal and human, death and life, money and children, salvaging the torn shreds of carnival, making them once more the object of cathartic laughter.

III

It may appear that the ending of the novel, in which there is a strong movement to narrative closure in multiple marriages and Nicholas's purchase of his father's former home, weakens or undercuts the case I am making, the transitions and displacements of the book seeming to yield to a domesticity of repetition and return. Even those like Nicholas whose restless energy has impelled them forward through the book seem compelled to yield to a logic of stasis and return to origins. But repetition does not exist in any pure comic or psychic space in the novel: the Mantalinis, doubtless, would have been content to act out their repetitive drama of passion and rejection were it not for the unfortunate fact of their bankruptcy. And the return to or of a past state or time, or the meeting of an object or presence from it, as the book's many hauntings and returns show, is often a painful or impossible affair. The denouement of the book consists of a whole string of returning, embodied memories as the pathetic story of Smike's birth and fostering is laid bare; Snawley and Squeers return, as does Smike himself, to cause the suicide of Ralph, the exposure of Snawley, and the transportation of Squeers. The uncovering of the past and the attempt to restore a past familial order lead to the return of Madeline and Nicholas to his father's old house but also to Smike's impossible love for Kate and fatal illness.

Smike, both an orphan and a son, accompanies Nicholas almost throughout the novel, his double, counterpart, and cousin, his 'partner' and 'sharer' (762). The first time they speak alone together, Smike asks Nicholas if he remembers 'the boy who died here' (97) at Dotheboys. When Nicholas tells him that he was not there at the time, Smike recounts the anonymous child's death:

"When it was all silent he cried no more for friends he wished to come and sit with him, but began to see faces round his bed that came from home; he said they smiled, and talked to him; and he died at last lifting his face to kiss them . . . What faces will smile on me when I die! . . . Who will talk to me in those long nights! They cannot come from home; they would frighten me if they did, for I don't know what it is, and shouldn't know them." (97)

For Smike as for Mrs Nickleby the home and haunting are linked, but through absence and loss, not her plenitude of irrelevant recollection. This account of the death of the nameless dead boy at Dotheboys identifies the presence and creation of subjectivity with the possibility of being haunted by domestic presences. Smike feels that he himself cannot be haunted in this way, having no memory of family or home, indeed no memories (no hauntings) except of a certain empty room (where Ralph will hang himself) before the sloppy day he arrived at Dotheboys. Slightly later, when Nicholas has escaped from Dotheboys, he sees a kneeling figure before him, which he first feels is 'a creation of the visions that have scarcely left me' (159). It is Smike, who tells Nicholas 'you are my home' and offers to follow him 'to the churchyard grave' (159). When Nicholas wants to take him to meet Kate and his mother, Smike falters and draws back, telling him that he no longer yearns for any home on earth 'except one . . . the grave' (443). On each occasion, death, desire, and domesticity are inextricably bound together, synonyms almost.

Jacques Derrida in his discussion of the dialogue *Phaedrus* in *Dissemination* speaks of what he calls 'the logic of the Pharmakon' in Plato's text where the single Greek term signifies both

'poison' and 'cure'.[29] His whole discussion, concerned as it is
with ghosts and writing, inheritance and the relation of fathers
and sons, with orphans, teaching, and repetition, takes us very
close to this novel. 'Pharmakos' signifies both poison and cure;
'pharmakon' signifies the scapegoat, the degraded and useless
being, chosen, fed, and kept in the very heart of the home or polis
before being expelled, loaded with the sins and difficulties of the
community. There are several expulsions at the end of *Nicholas
Nickleby*—Squeers is deported to Australia, Ralph commits
suicide, Mantalini is found in the cellar doing the washing—but
it is Smike with whom the novel ends. In a way that is at first surprising, Smike fears as well as desires the entry he makes into
culture in the form of friendship with Nicholas, love of Kate,
and domestic bliss. Nicholas continually promises him a home
through the novel, but Smike believes that such a home can only
be death. Degraded but preserved, returned to the first Nicholas
Nickleby's house, he dies of that ambivalent disease consumption, but also of his impossible love for Kate. Almost from the
moment he leaves Dotheboys he seems to know that this is to be
his destiny, to carry out with his death the necessary loss, never
to know who his father is, to remain unhaunted by ancestral and
paternal presences, to remain without a home.

Ralph, we learn in the second chapter of the book, has a door-
knocker in the shape of an infant's fist, holding a skewer. Smike
is an infant, Ralph's child, who cannot knock and enter in the
novel, constantly remaining on the threshold between the brutality outside culture and domesticity and the dark hauntings
within, the child for whom death and the home are synonyms,
the ghost whom Ralph and Squeers have trained. The story of
Nicholas Nickleby is of course a comedy; unless one tells it from
the point of view of Smike, who is betrayed by his father, brutalized by Squeers and then finds the simultaneous possibility
and impossibility of desire, subjective identity, and a home in
one fell haunting. The final scene of the book is of Nicholas's
and Madeline's children placing flowers on their cousin's grave.
An act of expiation but also expulsion; patriarch and scapegoat,
Nicholas and Smike, poison and cure, cousins.

---

[29] Jacques Derrida, *Dissemination* (London: Athlone, 1981), 61–171.

CHAPTER FIVE

Nell's Crypt: *The Old Curiosity Shop* and *Master Humphrey's Clock*

I

THERE ARE MANY echoes of *Nicholas Nickleby* in the *Old Curiosity Shop*. Both begin with the impoverishment of their admirable but vulnerable central character (through Nicholas's father's bankruptcy and death and Nell's grandfather's gambling) which precipitates the hero out of the family home and into a series of loosely related encounters and adventures. Nicholas and Nell both have a foolish relative (Mrs Nickleby, Nell's grandfather), visit a country school, and meet sympathetically drawn travelling showmen who help them. Both have hostile relatives (Ralph Nickleby, Fred Trent) whose jealousy is expressed through disputes over money; both face greater danger from other, wild and monstrous villains (Squeers, Quilp); the central villain in both cases (Ralph, Quilp) is a rentier and money-lender. The contrasts, however, between the two novels are as great, for where Nicholas overcomes overwhelming odds to recover from his father's bankruptcy and his uncle's foulness to restore and re-inaugurate the lost family home and hearth, Nell fails to find anything but poverty, misery, and death. Nicholas comes out of the clear, controlled light of his novel's beginning; Nell haltingly frees herself from 'the deep, dark, silent closet' of *Master Humphrey's Clock*.[1] *Nicholas Nickleby* is a jubilant, triumphant book for the most part, the manic overcoming of disaster through resolution and good cheer; Nell's story is its melancholic supplement, leading to the tomb.

[1] Pilgrim, II, 4.

It is perhaps for this reason that, of the extraordinary group of novels of the 1830s and 1840s which give the lives and consciousness of children an unprecedented centrality—*Oliver Twist, Jane Eyre, Wuthering Heights, Dombey and Son, David Copperfield*[2]—it is *The Old Curiosity Shop* that the majority of critics and readers today are most uneasy with. Few of us are curious about the Curiosity Shop or care (which is another word for curiosity) about or for Little Nell.[3] It is, almost universally, thought to be a text of notorious sentimentality, morbid and uncontrolled, embarrassing and absurd by turns. Oscar Wilde said it would take a heart of stone to read the death of Little Nell without laughing and even those, like Chesterton, prepared to forgive Nell's death, cannot forgive the life that precedes it.[4] In many studies of Dickens, Nell is an early candidate for the critical chop, sacrificed on an early page to demonstrate the seriousness of the criticism that will follow. For F. R. Leavis, for example, 'to suggest taking Little Nell seriously would be absurd: there's nothing there. She doesn't derive from any perception of the real; she's a contrived unreality, the function of which is to facilitate in the reader a gross and virtuous self-indulgence.'[5]

Leavis's remark is a revealing one, not least because so much of what it says is true. Nell does not exist. She is a contrived unreality. But then so too are all fictional characters. There is nothing there with Nell, but then there never is, in reading

---

[2] The classic account of Romantic ideas of the child in English Literature is Peter Coveney, *The Image of Childhood* (Harmondsworth: Penguin, 1967).

[3] Curiosity, like care, is derived from the Latin, 'cura', meaning care. The term often appears in the novel, as when the landlady tells Nell after her collapse, 'Curiosity is the curse of our sex, and that's the fact' or when Nell is thought to be 'an important item of the curiosities' of Mrs Jarley (Charles Dickens, *The Old Curiosity Shop*, ed. Elizabeth M. Brennan (Oxford: World's Classics, 1998), 347, 214. All references will be to this edition and placed in the text.) Almost Nell's first action in the novel is to steal 'a curious look' at Master Humphrey (5). Immediately after the passage on allegory in chapter 1, Humphrey describes 'a curious speculation' which imagines Nell 'holding her solitary way among a crowd of wild, grotesque companions' (20). The whole novel is here prefigured as 'a curious speculation' by Humphrey.

[4] Violet Wyndham, *The Sphinx and her Circle: A Biographical Sketch of Ada Leverson, 1862–1933* (London: André Deutsch, 1963), 119. G. K. Chesterton, *Chesterton on Dickens* (London: Everyman, 1992), 54.

[5] F. R. Leavis and Q. D. Leavis, *Dickens the Novelist* (Harmondsworth: Penguin, 1972), 298.

fiction. And Dickens, I think, is a good deal more aware of the complexities of this truth than the majority of his critics. In this chapter, I want to explore the life and death of Nell in *The Old Curiosity Shop*; a figure and a text which on the one hand is unreal, where there is nothing there, and which may even lead to gross self-indulgence;[6] and which on the other hand is one of the more radical and sustained encounters with the otherness of the child, a text which refuses to take for granted the concepts, forms of narration, and notions of psychological development commonly associated with the depiction of childhood. Against childhood conceived of as symbolic of interiority and growth, we need to conceive of an aesthetic adequate to this text: what I shall call an allegorical aesthetic or an aesthetic of mortality.

Carolyn Steedman in her book *Strange Dislocations* has delineated the figure of the child in eighteenth- and nineteenth-century scientific, historical, and literary narratives that informs so much writing of the period: the child as representing or figuring interiority, growth, historicity, and development. Her major example of this is the figure of Mignon in Goethe's *Wilhelm Meister* and its many adaptations and resurfacings in nineteenth-century culture—Mignon the sexually androgynous, inarticulate, beautiful-and-yet-deformed child, richly and complexly symbolic.[7] The parallels between Mignon and Nell are clear, and were noticed early on in *The Old Curiosity Shop*'s history, so that John Forster in his biography of Dickens felt obliged to point out that Dickens had not actually read Goethe's book.[8] Dickens may well, though, have read one of the Scott novels influenced by it or seen one of the many stage adaptations in the 1820s or 1830s.[9] Like Mignon, Nell had very wide currency in the nineteenth century both in the novel itself and

[6] Karl Miller picks up Leavis's hint in his *Doubles* (Oxford: Oxford University Press, 1985), where he argues, apropos of Nell's death, that 'Sentimentality is to grief what masturbation is to a loving sexuality' (189). Quilp engages in a good deal of hand-rubbing in the presence of Nell (30), and Dick Swiveller, mourning the loss of Sophy Wackles, lies in bed and plays a solo on his flute (435). On this topic and the difficulty of maintaining Miller's distinction, see Jacques Derrida, *Of Grammatology* (Baltimore: Johns Hopkins University Press, 1976), 154–7.

[7] Carolyn Steedman, *Strange Dislocations: Childhood and the Idea of Human Interiority 1780–1930* (London: Virago, 1995).

[8] John Forster, *The Life of Charles Dickens*, ed A. J. Hoppé (London: Dent, 1966), II, 440.

[9] Steedman, *Strange Dislocations*, 29–31, 145–8.

in adaptations for children, popular illustrations, and many stage versions.[10] Nell is slightly older than Mignon, but she (like Mignon) is enigmatically encountered by a stranger, surrounded by mystery, and accompanied by an elderly relative who neglects and endangers her. Like Mignon she is drawn to popular performance, to Codlin and Short's Punch and Judy show and Mrs Jarley's waxworks. Like Mignon, Nell is a figure who seems predestined to die.

Nell, then, at first seems another version, variation, or continuation of the Mignon story, another episode in the growing interiorization of the Romantic Child. Yet it is striking how much she resists as well as enacts the forces that run through and comprise Mignon. There are some small differences: Nell is feminine where Mignon is androgynous; she is articulate where Mignon is not. But there are also larger differences that go to the heart of the way that the romantic and modern periods conceive the child, which involve the text's relationship to fictional form and to what Dickens calls the 'allegory' (20) of Nell, on the one hand, and, on the other, to conceptions of time and temporal change in the novel's near-obsessive concern with mortality: the mortality of Nell, but also of many other material objects and living things, and indeed of forms of writing and inscription. Nell, unlike Mignon, is not a figure of history, or of symbol, or the body; she has little to do with development, interiority, time, or change. On the contrary, insofar as language can create stasis, Nell is a static figure, who does not change, who is neither interior nor exterior, nor alive nor dead, who is both spirit and matter, and who is not really there at all, who exists, as Dickens says, 'in a kind of allegory' (20). A very different child, in short.

At the end of the first chapter of the novel, Nell is left alone by Master Humphrey, the reader, and her grandfather in her bedroom. It is a room in the Curiosity Shop and remarkably like a crypt, with 'suits of mail standing like ghosts in armour' (11). Master Humphrey then pictures to himself:

the child in her bed: alone, unwatched, uncared for, (save by angels,) yet sleeping peacefully ... I am not sure I should have been so

---

[10] See Paul Schlicke and Priscilla Schlicke, *The Old Curiosity Shop: An Annotated Bibliography* (New York: Garland, 1988), for a comprehensive listing.

thoroughly possessed by this one subject, but for the heaps of fantastic things I had seen huddled together in the curiosity-dealer's warehouse . . . I had her image, without any effort of imagination, surrounded and beset by everything that was foreign to its nature, and farthest removed from the sympathies of her sex and age . . . she seemed to exist in a kind of allegory. (19–20)

Here Nell the child in her bed exists alone, unwatched, uncared for except in Humphrey's imagination and ours. But the most striking phrase is the final one: 'she seemed to exist in a kind of allegory'. As the novel develops, this allegory of the child 'surrounded and beset' by everything foreign to its nature is confirmed. Nell's speech, her thoughts, even her dreams as the novel progresses (or fails to) are utterly conventional and uninflected. Her story moves on only to stand still, to re-encounter the same thing over and over and over again: mortality, death, the death of children in particular, and graveyards, as she moves through what Steven Marcus calls the 'vast necropolis' of England.[11] In chapter 15 she encounters an old man whose son had died; in chapter 16 she finds Codlin and Short in a graveyard; in chapter 17 she meets an old woman whose husband died in his youth; in chapter 25 the old schoolmaster whose favourite pupil dies. Mrs Jarley's waxworks is a kind of mobile cemetery of the illustrious dead, and when Nell finally escapes Birmingham and the Black Country, the village she goes to is full of tombs, crypts, and gravestones, and she herself will die there.

'Allegory' is a rare term in Dickens's fiction, and almost always used satirically. But it is also true that Dickens's work is full of certain kinds of figure and trope—and they are often among his most powerful and characteristic ones—that are explicitly allegorical or else come close to allegory, such as the figure of Shares in *Little Dorrit*, or the depiction of the railway as 'Death' in Dombey's consciousness in *Dombey and Son*. This is most clear in Dickens's best-known and most explicitly allegorical work, *A Christmas Carol*, where Want and Ignorance— two more allegorical children—appear from under the cloak of Christmas Present. The term 'allegory' does not appear in the first serial publication of *The Old Curiosity Shop* but is added

[11] Steven Marcus, *Dickens: From Pickwick to Dombey* (London: Chatto and Windus, 1965), 145.

by Dickens for its first volume appearance and is a response to or incorporation of Thomas Hood's remarks in his review of early sections of the novel, which describe the first picture of Nell as 'like an allegory of the peace and innocence of child-hood in the midst of violence, superstition and all the hateful or hurtful passions of the world'.[12] There are other allegorical figures in the novel. Several important characters—the Grand-father, the schoolmaster, the young scholar, the bachelor, the Marchioness—have no proper name. Sampson and Sally Brass, when they are released from prison, are 'the embodied spirits of Disease, and Vice and Famine' (548). The appearance of Punch on the gravestone (129) is like a figure from an emblem book, as is Nell gazing into the crypt (415). This allegory is carried in scenes and metaphors of writing and education: Nell's grand-father 'read the book of her heart from the first page presented to him, little dreaming of the story that lay hidden in its other leaves' (76). Kit is given a 'writing lesson' (33) by Nell, and the young scholar who dies is epitomized in the displayed tokens of his writing hand (189). The anonymous working man whom Nell encounters in her nightmare journey through the Midlands sees in the forge which he tends a 'book' that 'has its pictures' (335), and there are explicit parallels made between Nell's journey, *The Pilgrim's Progress*, and biblical typology.

The preface to *Oliver Twist* described Oliver as 'the principle of Good surviving through every adverse circumstance'.[13] Like Nell's, Oliver's presence is extremely close to allegory. Like Nell he exists not as allegory but 'in a kind of allegory', something

---

[12] Thomas Hood, review of *Master Humphrey's Clock*, *Athenaeum* (7 November 1840), 884–9, reprinted in Michael Hollington (ed.), *Charles Dickens: Critical Assessments* (Sussex: Helm Information, 1995), I, 284. Gabriel Pearson, 'The Old Curiosity Shop', in John Gross and Gabriel Pearson (eds), *Dickens and the Twentieth Century* (London: Routledge and Kegan Paul, 1962), 81, writes of 'the frantic forcing into maxim and emblem' in the novel, but there is often a strong resistance among critics to admit to allegory either in Dickens's writing or their own criticism. Characteristic, if unusually frank in its self-contradiction, is Gissing's simultaneous assertion and denial of allegorical intent in his own reading of the novel: 'Heaven forbid that I should attribute to Dickens a deliberate allegory; but, having in mind those helpless children who were then being tortured in England's mines and factories, I like to see in Nell a type of their sufferings; she, the victim of avarice . . . ever pursued by heartless self-interest, and finding her one safe refuge in the grave': *Charles Dickens: A Critical Study* (London: Gresham, 1902), 211.

[13] Charles Dickens, *Oliver Twist*, ed. Kathleen Tillotson (Oxford: World's Classics, 1982), xxv.

akin to allegory, a simile of an allegory, but not exactly one. That phrase—a kind of allegory—leads one to ask what kind of reading practice Dickens is expecting his readers to have of this text, and this child. And to ask what kind of allegory the text creates, what reading of the other, what other reading, what other child?[14] Is it simply a text that insistently, morbidly, obsessively, compulsively seeks to remind us of mortality, to take us to the edge of graves to tell us that all living things, even children, are marked with the stamp of death? Is it merely a banal pedagogy of mortality? Or is there something else at stake? What is the allegory of this allegory? What is the allegory of this child?

II

The case for a sexual or Freudian reading of this text (in which, as Peter Ackroyd writes, 'sexuality is everywhere present and nowhere stated'[15]) is quite strong. Nell is clearly an object of sexual interest to Quilp (who bounces on her bed) and also to Dick Swiveller who abandons Sophy Wackles in the hope of gaining her. But it is Nell's grandfather who is of most interest. He has been surprisingly little discussed in accounts

[14] On allegory generally, see Angus Fletcher, *Allegory: The Theory of a Symbolic Mode* (Ithaca: Cornell University Press, 1964), Paul de Man, *Allegories of Reading: Figural Language in Rousseau, Nietzsche, Rilke and Proust* (New Haven: Yale University Press, 1979). See also Walter Benjamin, *The Origin of German Tragic Drama* (London: Verso, 1977), 159–235; 166:

'Everything about history that, from the very beginning, has been untimely, sorrowful, unsuccessful, is expressed in a face—or rather in a death's head. And although such a thing lacks all "symbolic" freedom of expression, all classical proportion, all humanity—nevertheless, this is the form in which man's subjection to nature is most obvious and it significantly gives rise not only to the enigmatic question of the nature of human existence as such, but also of the biographical historicity of the individual. This is the heart of the allegorical way of seeing, of the baroque, secular explanation of history as the Passion of the world; its importance lies solely in the stations of its decline. The greater the significance, the greater the subjection to death . . . if nature has always been subject to death, it has always been allegorical.'

[15] Peter Ackroyd, *Dickens* (London: Sinclair-Stevenson, 1990), 333. A characteristic example is Mrs Jarley's account of the waxworks, which include 'Jasper Packlemerton of atrocious memory, who courted and married fourteen wives, and destroyed them all, by tickling the soles of their feet when they were sleeping in the consciousness of innocence and virtue . . . his fingers are curled as if in the act of tickling' (218).

of the novel, although the entire plot is motivated by his actions. The novel is often presented as if the central relationship and major sexual threat to Nell is from Quilp, but her life and death are in fact structured around her grandfather. In part, this lack of interest by critics may be because the relationship between the two is so mysterious to both the narrator and the reader. Her grandfather seems to over- and to undervalue Nell. He places her in great physical and moral danger—wandering the streets of London at midnight lost and alone as the novel opens, later at the racecourse, travelling with Codlin and Short, at the waxworks, and then on the barge journey and the walk to Tong. Yet at the same time as there is this apparent neglect he also overvalues her—his whole life as a gambler is a quest to gain the riches so that she will be 'rich one of these days, and a fine lady' (13), a figure in an allegory of Wealth. She is the sole point and purpose of his existence, as he so often reminds us and her—'"whoever loved a child," [he asks,] "as I love Nell?"' (12).

The grandfather's gambling is obsessive, neurotic, and stimulating, but also causes him to break into Nell's room one night to steal money, in a scene that is akin in the child's consciousness to an illicit sexual threat, with his wandering hands and 'breath so near her pillow' (233). The grandfather is one of Dickens's many debtors, and debt, Freud argues in his essay on Dostoevsky, can be read as a material manifestation of psychological guilt at a repressed or unacknowledged sexual desire.[16] It would not be hard to see his gambling as an expression of his desire for Nell, able to give him exclusive possession of her— they must flee together when she becomes an object of sexual interest to Dick Swiveller and Quilp—and as both the material form of guilty desire and the imaginary reparation for that desire. The grandfather punishes himself for the desire he can never acknowledge, while at the same time unconsciously permitting Nell to be placed in the danger of precisely the action

[16] Sigmund Freud, 'Dostoevsky and Parricide', in *The Pelican Freud Library Volume 14: Art and Literature* (Harmondsworth: Penguin, 1985), 456. John Forrester, 'Transference and the Stenographer: on Dostoevsky's *The Gambler*', in *The Seductions of Psychoanalysis* (Cambridge: Cambridge University Press, 1990), 260–86.

he himself most wants to carry out. The consequences of his behaviour are of course fatal for her.

But the threat to Nell seems a good deal less localized than this, and to embrace an entire social or metaphysical order. From the moment that Master Humphrey describes his walks through London at the beginning of the novel, it seems as if there is no place here for life or the life of a child. 'Think of a sick man', he writes on the first page, 'listening to the footsteps . . . think of the hum and noise being always present to his senses . . . as if he were condemned to lie, dead but conscious, in a noisy churchyard, and had no hope of rest for centuries to come' (8). It was perhaps this quality that drew Walter Benjamin and Theodor Adorno to Nell's story. For Adorno the importance of *The Old Curiosity Shop* was that it appeared to contain a very different Dickens and a very different nineteenth-century novel from the one he thought he knew.[17] Dickens, it is often assumed, creates a world in which poverty, despair, and death are the products of a bourgeois and commodified world, and to which only the traces of warmth and kindness in individual human relations can reconcile one. This novel, for Adorno, is much more akin to those baroque tragedies which Benjamin discusses in *The Origin of German Tragic Drama*, in which the individual—Nell in this case—is the bearer of a dark and obscure fate in a dead and commodified world. The romantic symbol, argued Benjamin, tends to obscure the disruptive effect of time on any effort to unify an ephemeral object with an eternal idea. Allegory, by contrast, he argues, allows nature to be seen not as 'idealised and transfigured' but as in a 'petrified, primordial landscape'.[18] Nell tries to flee and break out from the allegorical settings she encounters but cannot: everywhere she faces death.[19] Her final swoon occurs after her encounter with the starving unemployed poor of the Black Country. Nell knocks at a hovel door:

[17] T. W. Adorno, 'On Dickens' *The Old Curiosity Shop*: A Lecture', in *Notes to Literature* (Columbia: Columbia University Press, 1992), II, 170–7. See also Michael Hollington, 'Adorno, Benjamin and *The Old Curiosity Shop*', *Dickens Quarterly*, VI (September 1989), 87–95.

[18] Benjamin, *Origin of German Tragic Drama*, 166.

[19] Adorno, *Notes to Literature*, II, 175–6.

"What would you have here?" said a gaunt man, opening it.

"Charity. A morsel of bread."

"Do you see that?" returned the man hoarsely, pointing to a kind of bundle on the ground. "That's a dead child. I and five hundred other men were thrown out of work, three months ago. That is my third dead child, and last. Do you think *I* have charity to bestow, or a morsel of bread to spare?" (341)

Nell's relation, writes Adorno, to things is pre-bourgeois and she thus becomes an inevitable victim, unable to grasp that things are to be manipulated as dead commodities in this world: 'Because she is not able to take hold of the object-world of the bourgeois sphere, the object world seizes hold of her and she is sacrificed.'[20] The allegory of a child, in short, in a commodified world.

There is a good deal to be said in favour of Adorno's account. Humphrey, like one of Benjamin's flâneurs, links the archaic and the modern in his nocturnal city strolling.[21] In Nell's meeting with the rioting workers, the novel contains the most radical engagement in Dickens's early fiction with the social cost of Victorian capitalism. The commodity and the role of the commodity-form have a good deal of importance to the novel; it is, after all, as the title tells us, a story about a shop. The plot's action is motivated a good deal by matters of debt and credit and Nell dies at least in part because she is poor and because Quilp, an entrepreneurial rentier who has 'a share in the ventures of divers mates of East Indiamen' (34), has repossessed her home. The novel, like *Nickleby*, is full of the pressures of economic life and the many possibilities of lending, investing, borrowing, gambling, sponging, and stealing for profit. Mrs Jarley is a self-advertiser in the Squeers and Crummles class, but the economic dynamism of this novel (unlike that of *Nickleby*) is almost always frozen and arrested by death, and commodification is constantly associated with mortality. The shop of the title is more like a repository or a tomb than a place of sale, and Nell, immediately before learning of her grandfather's ruin,

---

[20] Ibid., 177.

[21] Walter Benjamin, *Charles Baudelaire: A Lyric Poet in the Era of High Capitalism* (London: Verso, 1976), 69–70. See also Ned Lukacher, 'Dialectical Images: Benjamin/Dickens/Freud', in *Primal Scenes* (Ithaca: Cornell University Press, 1986), 275–336.

looks out of the shop window to see 'a man passing with a coffin on his back' (74).[22]

There are also limitations to Adorno's reading. There is nothing in it, for example, of the comic and redemptive forces in the book, particularly those embodied in Dick Swiveller, that great human jukebox, and the Marchioness, the other child of the story, who together complexly refigure and retrope so much of the pathos of Nell. The novel's sense of a world open to transformative and creative change, its affirmative delight in linguistic and metaphysical play, is markedly different from the profoundly negative critique of modernity in Adorno. More importantly though, we should ask how far Nell's fate is a consequence of the commodity-form in the world. Does the critique of the commodity—Adorno's allegory of this allegory—provide an adequate reading of this text? Are the many death's-heads of the book merely displaced figurations of a final, economic cause never explicitly articulated?

A fuller account of the book would be more centrally concerned with the question of mourning. Some of the most interesting developments in this field have followed on from the work of Nicolas Abraham and Maria Torok, and their distinction between *incorporation* and *introjection*.[23] When introjection (as in the classic Freudian account[24]) fails in the work of mourning, Abraham argues, the psyche *incorporates* the lost object in what he terms a 'crypt', an inaccessible psychic space distinct from the unconscious, which is also cryptic in the other sense, as secret.[25] This leads to what Derrida has called in

[22] Nell also dies because she is a commodity and part of a commodity, created by Dickens to sustain himself, his family and house with five servants, and to support his father who (like Nell's grandfather) gets himself and his family into deeper debt and danger. This is the point of Ruskin's remark that Nell was 'killed for the market, as a butcher kills a lamb': *Works*, ed. E. T. Cook and Alexander Wedderburn (London: George Allen, 1903), xxxiv, 275n, cited in Philip Collins (ed.), *Dickens: The Critical Heritage* (London: Routledge and Kegan Paul, 1971), 100.

[23] Nicolas Abraham and Maria Torok, *The Wolf Man's Magic Word: A Cryptonomy* (Minneapolis: University of Minnesota Press, 1986). Nicolas Abraham, 'A Note on the Phantom: A Complement to Freud's Metapsychology', *Critical Inquiry*, 13 (Winter 1987), 287–92. Esther Rashkin, 'Tools for a New Psychoanalytic Criticism: The Work of Abraham and Torok', *Diacritics* (Winter 1988), 31–52.

[24] Sigmund Freud, 'Mourning and Melancholia', in *The Pelican Freud Library Volume 11: On Metapsychology* (Harmondsworth: Penguin, 1984), 245–68.

[25] Nicolas Abraham and Maria Torok, 'The Topography of Reality: Sketching a Metapsychology of Secrets', *Oxford Literary Review* (1991), 65.

various places 'semi-mourning', a mourning that can never be finished or complete, which becomes the type and figure of all mourning:

Mourning is an interiorisation of the dead other, but it is also the contrary. Hence the impossibility of completing one's mourning and even the will not to mourn are also forms of fidelity. If to mourn and not to mourn are two forms of fidelity and two forms of infidelity, the only thing remaining—and this is where I speak of semi-mourning—is an experience between the two. I cannot complete my mourning for everything I lose, because I want to keep it, and at the same time, what I do best is to mourn, is to lose it, because by mourning, I keep it inside me. And it is this terrible logic of mourning that I talk about all the time, that I am concerned with all the time . . . this terrible fatality of mourning; semi-mourning or double mourning.[26]

This state—of the simultaneous necessity and impossibility of mourning—is one that *The Old Curiosity Shop* constantly attempts to arouse in its readers.

The Old Curiosity Shop is one of the most complexly framed or supplemented of Dickens's novels, transformed (like Grimaldi the clown converted by Mrs Jarley into Lindley Murray the grammarian) from a miscellany—*Master Humphrey's Clock*— into a novel. It is tempting simply to ignore what is usually called, awkwardly enough, 'the *Clock* material', but knowing how much Dickens's imagination loved prosthetic things that belong and do not belong to the bodies to which they are attached, it is worth looking again at this strange supplement, this prosthesis of the novel, Little Nell's wooden leg.[27] And what we find in *Master Humphrey's Clock*, as in the novel it precedes and gives birth to, is an emphatic and obsessive mourning and

---

[26] Jacques Derrida, 'Dialanguages', in *Points . . . Interviews, 1974–1994* (Stanford: Stanford University Press, 1995), 152. See also Jacques Derrida, *Memoires: For Paul de Man* (New York: Columbia University Press, 1989), especially 28–36; 'Fors', *The Georgia Review*, 31 (1977), 64–116; *The Post Card from Socrates to Freud and Beyond* (Chicago: University of Chicago Press, 1987), 335 and Geoffrey Bennington and Jacques Derrida, *Jacques Derrida* (Chicago: University of Chicago Press, 1993), 146–8.

[27] Charles Dickens, *Master Humphrey's Clock and Other Stories*, ed. Peter Mudford (London: Everyman, 1997). All references will be to this edition and placed in the text. On the prosthetic in Dickens, see John Carey, *The Violent Effigy* (London: Faber and Faber, 1973), 80–104. On the prosthetic, see Allon White, 'Prosthetic Gods in Atrocious Places: Gilles Deleuze/Francis Bacon', in *Carnival, Hysteria, and Writing* (Oxford: Oxford University Press, 1993), 160–77.

semi-mourning. Humphrey himself is in a kind of mourning, although it is not clear at first for what. So too is his friend, the deaf gentleman, who like Humphrey is both mourning and failing to mourn (which are not different) a secret death which he does not acknowledge until it is too late. More than that, their own human status is not certain. Like a ghost, Humphrey exists in a world that treads the boundaries of life and death: 'I haunt the house where I was born . . . I prowl around my buried treasure (though not of gold or silver) and mourn my loss . . . I revisit the ashes of extinguished fires and take my silent stand at old bedsides' (*MHC* 58). Memory is a kind of haunting by 'long-buried thoughts [which] . . . steal from their graves' (*MHC* 58). Humphrey's friend Jack Bamber looks 'like some strange spirit, whose delight is to haunt old buildings' (*MHC* 113) and their companion Jack Redburn has withdrawn totally from the world and wears only a 'spectral-looking dressing gown' (*MHC* 60). They are a collection of semi-ghostly semi-mourners whom Humphrey describes as 'alchemists who would extract the essence of perpetual youth from dust and ashes', to whom 'Spirits of past times, creatures of imagination, and people of today are alike the objects of our seeking, and . . . we can ensure their coming at our command' (*MHC* 34). Narration is here conjuration, and one in which the boundaries between haunting and being haunted, and between the creatures of imagination and the people of today are by no means stable or secure ones.

The stories of *Master Humphrey's Clock* are, not surprisingly, usually about death and mourning, about buried corpses and the returning dead. Indeed, Dickens's original intent was to bring some of the best-known characters from his earlier works back into posthumous life.[28] Because of the magazine's lack of success, it is only Pickwick and Sam Weller who actually made it to the strange supplementary half- or afterlife of the *Clock*, but Dickens's idea was to create a magazine that would have to let nothing go, a place (like Heaven) where all the good dead will be found again, alive and transformed. The 'Gothic' stories told by the various narrators are mainly about death and the tendency of things from the past to return in the present. The

---

[28] Forster, *The Life of Charles Dickens*, 112.

second story shows this in stark form. Told by a murderer from the condemned cell ('my grave is digging' (*MHC* 67), he writes) who has out of envy drowned his nephew and buried the body in his garden, the story records how the corpse is discovered and grislily dug up by two bloodhounds. It is a tale full of ghosts. The dead child's mother 'haunted . . . like the memory of a dark dream' (*MHC* 67–8); the child itself as it drowns has '[h]is mother's ghost . . . looking from his eyes' (*MHC* 69); above all, the narrator is haunted by himself, obsessively returning to look at the site of the grave, and finally eating and drinking upon it, thus revealing its whereabouts to the dogs.

These concerns are continued into *The Old Curiosity Shop* itself, in which, in its astonishing first chapter, Humphrey introduces us to a sick man in St Martin's Court who hears the many noises in the city 'as if he were . . . dead but conscious' (8), like the narrator of Tennyson's *Maud* and many characters in the tales of Edgar Allan Poe, who reviewed this story in 1841.[29] And then, in his tour of the city, we meet the crowds on the bridges who dream of 'sleeping in the sun upon a hot tarpaulin, in a dull, slow, sluggish barge' and of death by drowning 'of all means of suicide the easiest and best' (8). London itself and life within it is like a crypt of the quasi-dead. If London is a tomb or crypt, its inhabitants already dead or quasi-dead, like Humphrey and his friends, then so too, and more intensely, is Nell's home. Nell's grandfather, Humphrey tells us, 'might have groped among old churches, and tombs and deserted houses and gathered all the spoils with is own hands' (11), a grave-robber in short, who makes the Curiosity Shop a tomb, albeit one as yet without a corpse, or with a secret corpse, like a crypt. And this semi-mourning of the first chapter of the story and its framing material is echoed (the ghosts of ghosts) in later scenes in the book: the streets when Nell and her grandfather flee are 'like bodies without souls' (120). When they arrive in the city that is probably Birmingham it seems 'as if they had lived a thousand years before, and were raised from the dead and placed there by a miracle' (329). There are many more examples, which figure not death, not life, but something more and

---

[29] Edgar Allan Poe, 'The Old Curiosity Shop', *Graham's Magazine*, XIX (February 1842), 124–9, reprinted in Hollington (ed.), *Charles Dickens: Critical Assessments*, I, 292–7.

less than both, which the reader and the narrator simultaneously summon up or conjure and mourn.

Narration, then, in both *Master Humphrey's Clock* and *The Old Curiosity Shop* is a form of conjuration on the one hand and semi-mourning on the other. The whole novel is one of commerce with the dead, a nightwalking story, full of ghosts. But this is not simply a matter of the characters, but also of the narrator, and the text itself. For *Master Humphrey's Clock* is also both dead and alive, a text that came alive, only to be killed off and abandoned by Dickens, but which still exists. It is, as Dickens says in his preface to *The Old Curiosity Shop*, 'one of the lost books of the earth' (5), but also to be found edited by Peter Mudford and published by Everyman, alive and dead. Humphrey too is alive and dead, both the narrator of the story and not the narrator, both a character within it and not a character at all, a narrator who relinquishes his hold on the story and who is then briefly and implausibly resurrected too late to save Nell; and who has a curious half-life that no one believes in as the grandfather's brother, which is then excised in later editions.[30]

Dickens's preface carries out for his own book precisely that same structure of semi-mourning that is so compulsively enacted elsewhere in the text. Like all Dickens's prefaces, it is a remarkable document, but I shall simply point to two ghosts in it. The first is that of Thomas Hood, who had first seen (even before the author himself) the story as an 'allegory' in which 'gentleness, purity and truth' are 'dormant but never dead'[31] (another figuring of semi-mourning, life-death), and whom Dickens later saw 'going slowly down into the grave' (6), and whom he thus binds in the preface to Little Nell, who also goes down slowly into the grave. The second, more daring ghost is found in the citation of a literary text, indeed the greatest text in our culture about mourning and the impossibility of mourning— Shakespeare's *Hamlet*. The ghost and the citation come from the

---

[30] The Penguin edition of the novel, edited by Malcolm Andrews (Harmondsworth: Penguin, 1972), 679–80, conveniently reprints the passage in *Master Humphrey's Clock* in which Humphrey admits to being the single gentleman. See Rosemary Mundhenk, 'Creative Ambivalence in Dickens's *Master Humphrey's Clock*', SEL: *Studies in English Literature 1500–1900*, 32 (1992), 645–62.

[31] Hood, in Hollington (ed.), *Charles Dickens: Critical Assessments*, I, 284.

moment that Hamlet meets his own father on the battlements of Elsinore—dead and yet strangely alive—a figure whom he alone must mourn but can never successfully mourn. In the preface to *Master Humphrey's Clock* Dickens, mourning his own failure to make his periodical live, describes himself as 'like one whose vision is disordered [who] . . . may be conjuring up bright figures where there is nothing but empty space' (*MHC* 25). Like Hamlet, like Humphrey, like the reader, like all narrators and readers of fiction and non-fiction alike, like ghosts and those who see ghosts, Dickens desires and fears the capacity to conjure up bright figures where there is nothing but empty space. For what is novel-reading and novel-writing but conjuring up where there is nothing but empty space?

This then is a text about presence and absence, about encountering a ghost, and knowing the right place to encounter a ghost—like Hamlet 'on a more removed ground'[32]—and then to continue these acts of mourning which can never be complete. Dickens brings Nell to life, he kills Nell, he brings her back to life in the spirit (which is what she always was anyway), and he mourns and fails to mourn for her. As too does the reader, who brings Nell to life in reading, kills her in reading, brings her back to life in spirit in reading, and mourns and fails to mourn her. As too does Humphrey, who himself cannot mourn, or be mourned, and yet must do so. The preface to the novel is a kind of mourning for a lost book, 'more precious [like a lost child] than any that can be read for love or money', a mourning for something that is and is not dead, which Dickens must let go and cannot let go, which will live for ever because it is by Dickens and contains two of his immortal characters (Mr Pickwick and Sam Weller, brought back to life), and which is thoroughly dead because it is writing after all which is always dead and because nobody much liked the idea of a miscellany, and yet it is alive because it gave birth to the immortal Nell and yet it is dead because Nell and *The Old Curiosity Shop* are detached from it. So it dies in childbirth, as it were, but then

---

[32] Shakespeare, *Hamlet*, Act 1, Scene 4, cited by Dickens in the preface to the 1848 Cheap Edition of *The Old Curiosity Shop* (6). *Hamlet* is cited parodically at Quilp's wake (Quilp is of course still alive at this point) by Sampson Brass, who asks 'When shall we look upon his like again?' (370). Immediately before Quilp's re-appearance, he is likened by Brass to 'the Ghost of Hamlet's father' (371).

the child it gave birth to (Nell) is dead and is going to die as you read the book, and so Dickens is letting the *Clock* go and at the same time and in the same gesture refusing to mourn and not letting it go, helping it on to a ghostly half-life. As we are too.

These paradoxes of mourning and failing to mourn in the novel are encapsulated in that notorious scene which we all think we know, the death of Little Nell, which, strikingly, does not happen in the novel. Little Nell does not die in the story, for she is already dead when Kit and the others arrive at her funeral home. The scene that is so well known in parody and half-memory—the hushed mourners, the final words, the departing breath and soul—one of the most famous and notorious scenes in literature, does not occur in the novel. Dickens, who throughout the text has figured Nell as both alive and dead, continues to do so at her end. It is not that Nell does not die, or that Nell is not dead, but that there is no 'death of Little Nell'. The last time we see her alive is at the end of chapter 55 when she is shown the crypt. When, sixteen chapters later, Kit Nubbles finds her, she is already dead and has been so for two days. He is thus cheated both of her life and death, as is the reader too, a semi- or double dispossession. At the beginning of the next chapter, there are four brief retrospective paragraphs which begin 'She had been dead two days' and continue 'she died soon after daybreak' (539). She was clinging to her grandfather when she died so that the onlookers 'did not know that she was dead' as she 'faded like the light upon a summer's evening' (539–40). There is a subtle play of tenses in this section, which Dickens uses not to increase narrative suspense, but to make the moment of revelation to the reader and the moment of passage for Nell uncertain and constitutively retroactive. We learn not that Nell is dead, but that she has died. Her death is not docile to time. It is an effect akin to Freud's *Nachträglichkeit*, retrospective action or retrospective causality.[33] Mourning does not follow death here, but anticipates it; we have the consequence before the cause, and a deep troubling of the distinction between the two. We are asked to mourn here, but also to mourn mourning. It may be this defiance of some important metaphysical distinctions—the differences between

---

[33] J. Laplanche and J. B. Pontalis, *The Language of Psychoanalysis* (London: Karnac, 1988), 111–14.

life and death, and cause and effect, and the importance of clear temporal sequence—rather than any horror at Nell's fate or the narrator's little touches of sentiment, that has so offended readers and caused this great novel of allegory and mourning to be so often traduced.

The *Clock* and the *Shop*, then, are books of mourning or semi-mourning, in which 'the living maintain the dead, play dead, busy themselves with the dead, let themselves be entertained and occupied and *played* or *tricked* [*jouer*] by the dead, speak *them* and *to them*, bear their name and hold forth in their language'.[34] A work of semi-mourning which I allegorize first (following Freud) as the consequence of illicit desire, second (following Benjamin and Adorno) as the consequence of the commodification of the world, and in a third circle of mourning for the text allegorize it (with Derrida) as the consequence of language and narrative themselves, that 'monumentality which we . . . see linked to death'.[35]

What, though, of the obsessive and ostentatious religiosity that seems to modern readers so to disfigure the text? What of passages such as this at Nell's death?

When Death strikes down the innocent and young, for every fragile form from which he lets the panting spirit free, a hundred virtues rise, in shapes of mercy, charity and love, to walk the world, and bless it. Of every tear that sorrowing mortals shed on such green graves, some good is born, some gentler nature comes. In the Destroyer's steps there spring up bright creations that defy his power, and his dark path becomes a way of light to Heaven. (543)

---

[34] Jacques Derrida, *Specters of Marx: The State of the Debt, the Work of Mourning and the New Internationl* (London: Routledge, 1994), 113.

[35] Bennington and Derrida, *Jacques Derrida*, 45. Writing, for Derrida, entails a necessary relationship to death:

'Writing communicates my thoughts to far distances, during my absence, even after my death. At the moment of reading my letter, the addressee knows that I might have died during the time, however minimal it might be, between the moment at which the letter was finished and the moment of its reception . . . it is not necessary for me to be dead for you to read me, but it is necessary for you to be able to read me even if I am dead . . . my mortality (my finitude) is thus inscribed in everything I write' (50–1).

Reading and interpretation thus become forms of mourning: 'every determinate addressee, and thus every act of reading is affected by the same "death" . . . a text never comes to rest finally or in a unity or meaning finally revealed or discovered. This work must also be a work of mourning . . . in truth, only this situation allows a text to have a "life" or as we shall say later an "afterlife"' (56).

Is not the radical form and social critique of the novel dissipated by such verbose religiosity?[36] It is not, it should be pointed out, a particularly Christian passage. There is a good deal of citation in the novel of scripture—Matthew, Isaiah, the Psalms, Romans, John—and of *The Pilgrim's Progress*. But as several Christian commentators pointed out on its publication, there is very little directly Christian ideology or consolation in the book. *The Christian Remembrancer*, for example, called it 'a tissue of fantastic sentiment', and Harriet Beecher Stowe was heard to observe that Dickens did not seem to have heard of 'such a person as Jesus Christ'.[37]

For Dickens, it is a question of spirit—and Nell's spirit—rather than that of faith or doctrine that is at the centre of the book. In the preface to *Master Humphrey's Clock*, in which Dickens engages in this scene of mourning for Nell and his own text, he speaks of the 'gentle spirits' (*MHC* 25) of the abandoned journal. It is a curious passage at the beginning of a curious book about a curious child—'curious' meaning 'strange, singular, queer', all terms with good reason near the centre of contemporary critical debate. It is also one of many passages in the novel in which the term 'spirit' occurs: Quilp is 'an evil spirit' (178) and Mrs Quilp 'hasn't the spirit to give him a word back' (38); Nell is 'spiritual' (19) to the narrator and appears to her grandfather 'as if she were a spirit' (322); Dick Swiveller is 'a choice spirit' (178) when he is not 'out of spirits' (322). High and low, comic and pathetic, the novel is a world of spirits, there, vividly present, and not there at all, both alive and dead, like Nell and *Master Humphrey's Clock*. So we need to see Nell's spirit in the context of a much wider discourse of spirit in the book, which is as much about the peculiarities of what is called human life and fictional life as about faith or truth. In Jacques Derrida's recent work that wish, which this text attempts to

---

[36] 'The retreat to Nature in Dickens is for the most part a negative gesture, associated with death and regression to childhood, social disengagement rather than social paradigm': Terry Eagleton, *Criticism and Ideology* (London: Verso, 1976), 127.

[37] 'Modern Novels', *The Christian Remembrancer*, 14 (December 1842), 581–96. Harriet Beecher Stowe, in Edward Wagenknecht, *Harriet Beecher Stowe: The Known and the Unknown* (New York: Oxford University Press, 1965), 150. See Schlicke and Schlicke, *The Old Curiosity Shop: An Annotated Bibliography*, entries 90 and 205.

incite in us, to be able and willing to walk and talk with spirits, with all things such as Little Nell and Master Humphrey, Charles Dickens and you and me, dear reader, who tread and undo in language and signification the boundaries of life and death, the human and the inhuman, that wish is identified with the very possibility of justice.[38] As it is in this novel, with the summoning of the hope of a justice that cannot be reduced to that 'wholesale and retail shop of criminal law' (445) behind whose counter Sampson Brass and his monstrous sister stand.

III

The Old Curiosity Shop is a deeply repetitive novel. So many of the characters feel compelled to repeat themselves in words or action. The grandfather's gambling, Quilp's violence, Dick Swiveller's verbal mannerisms, and Sally Brass's persecution of her illegitimate daughter—all repeat and repeat. But whereas the early novels such as *Pickwick* and *Nickleby* were committed to the repetitions of the pleasure principle, here the novel seems to hand itself over to the entropic compulsions of its Beyond.[39] As Steven Marcus has written, 'The strongest impulse within the novel is for inertia',[40] a spectre of a world like the one that Nell finds in the Black Country 'presenting that endless repetition of the same dull, ugly, form, which is the horror of oppressive dreams' (338). This nightmare vision is strongest in Nell's consciousness, which is compelled, at moments of trauma, eternally to repeat in imagination what she most fears, a pitiless compulsion without mastery or relief. Sleeping among the waxworks, she 'tortured herself—she could not help it—with imagining a resemblance, in some one or other of their death-like faces, to the dwarf' (222). The gambling of her grandfather

---

[38] 'A deconstructive thinking, the one that matters to me here, has always pointed out the irreducibility of affirmation and therefore of the promise, as well as the undeconstructibility of a certain idea of justice (dissociated here from law)': Derrida, *Specters of Marx*, 90.

[39] Freud, 'Beyond the Pleasure Principle', in *The Pelican Freud Library Volume 11: On Metapsychology*, 269–338. For a discussion of this text, see Richard Boothby, *Death and Desire: Psychoanalytic Theory in Lacan's Return to Freud* (London: Routledge, 1991), and Derrida, *The Post Card*, 259–409.

[40] Marcus, *Dickens: From Pickwick to Dombey*, 142.

is similarly a repetitive 'torture' of which she is 'the innocent cause' (229). Whatever she tries to escape—Quilp, her grand-father's gambling—returns. The novel is about flight, but it is flight that always finds again what it has fled. And this psychic compulsion is, as Dickens writes, worse precisely because it is psychic. Lying in bed, fearing the return of her grandfather, she imagines his return: 'It was but imagination, yet imagination had all the terrors of reality; nay, it was worse, for the reality would have come and gone, and there an end, but in imagina-tion it was always coming, and never went away' (234).

But pure or perfect repetition is never possible. The same thing may recur, but perforce in a different time and/or place, and so it is not the same, but subject, in Derrida's terms, to 'dif-férance'.[41] This is not, though, a necessarily consoling thought, for when we are in the presence of something that is both the same and not the same, familiar and not familiar (as when Nell feels the 'dim uncertain horror' (234) at finding her grandfather in her room at night 'so like and yet so unlike him' (235)), we are in the presence of the uncanny.[42] There are many uncanny moments and creatures in the novel. Sampson and Sally Brass are an 'exact . . . likeness' (250) of each other, although one is male, the other female. Sally herself is 'a strange monster' (256) and a 'curious animal' (255–6). The waxworks, 'so like living creatures' (222), are uncanny for Nell, who gazes at them in 'a kind of terror of them for their own sakes' (222), as if they too could suffer and feel. Waxworks are a notorious sign of uncan-niness, disturbing things which trouble the boundaries between the living and dead and the animate and inanimate. Quilp is a similarly disturbing, 'fantastic and monkey-like' figure, 'like an evil spirit', appearing to Nell as if he had 'risen from the earth' (211) and disappearing as quickly, a drinker of boiling fluids, able to reappear at his own wake, 'a dismounted nightmare' (372) to his wife.

---

[41] The best discussion of this term is in Bennington and Derrida, *Jacques Derrida*, 70–84. On repetition, see J. Hillis Miller, *Fiction and Repetition: Seven English Novels* (Cambridge: Harvard University Press, 1982).

[42] Freud, *The Pelican Freud Library Volume 14: Art and Literature*, 335–76. There is a handy checklist of uncanny qualities in Andrew Bennett and Nicholas Royle, *An Introduction to Literature, Criticism and Theory: Key Critical Concepts* (Oxford: Blackwell, 1995), 34–7. See also Nicholas Royle, *Telepathy and Litera-ture* (Oxford: Blackwell, 1991).

There is, however, another form of repetition in the book, which is neither the repetition of the uncanny nor the death-wish. So much of the comedy and indeed power of the novel stems from its willingness to repeat in parodic form the material we are asked to take seriously in Nell's story. Indeed, this process begins as early as *Master Humphrey's Clock*, as Mr Weller's Watch counters and parodies Humphrey's gloomy and sentimental tales. Both Tony and Sam Weller tell stories about wills, one about a will written inside a chest, the other, more surreally, about a barber kept alive only by his own love of hair-cutting, who eventually shaves the head of the lawyer drawing up his will. Tony also tells a story about a woman who is 'the wery picter' (*MHC* 124) of a wax dummy. A young hairdresser falls in love with her, exclaiming in a parody of the sentimentalism we will later be encouraged to feel about Nell, ' "here's a community o' feelin', here's a flow o' soul!" ' (124). The romance is not successful, whereupon the barber breaks the dummy's nose and then melts it down, and the young lady reads 'a deal o' poetry and pined away', although Tony tells us that ' "she an't dead yet" ' (124). So much of the material we are asked to take seriously in the *Old Curiosity Shop*—a beautiful young woman like a waxwork, people poised between life and death, sentimentality, what and how we inherit from the dead—is already at play with the Wellers.

There are many examples of the novel's ability to conduct complex transpositions and retropings between the main Nell plot and the many sub-plots (or counter-plots) of Quilp, the Brasses, and Dick Swiveller. Swiveller often invokes something akin to the idealism that surrounds the depiction of Nell, kindling 'the fire of soul . . . at the taper of conwiviality' and invoking a world of 'choice spirits' from which Quilp is for ever excluded (178). There is, for example, a remarkable transition from chapter 55 to 56. Nell has just been shown the crypt and tomb which so neatly epitomize her allegory and plight, whereupon the next chapter Swiveller goes to Sampson Brass's 'with his hat very much over one eye, to increase the mournfulness of the effect' (417) and tells them, pastiching Thomas Moore, ' " 'Twas ever thus—from childhood's hour I've seen my fondest hopes decay, I never loved a tree or flower but 'twas the first to fade away. I never nursed a dear Gazelle, to glad me with its soft black eye, but when it came to know me well and love me, it was sure to marry a market-gardener"' (417). This is very funny in itself, and a very rapid and daring transition, which takes all the serious sentiment of the preceding chapter and makes it comic and absurd. Then Dick's friend Chuckster comes in and they quote from the witches in *Macbeth* about the graves giving up their dead, at which the narrator comments, 'such morsels of enthusiasm were common among the Glorious Apollos, and were indeed the links that bound them together, and raised them above the dull cold earth' (419), the dull cold earth we have just seen Nell heading towards, and above which we will later be asked to believe that she will be raised, having, like Swiveller's trees and flowers, decayed and faded away.

There is a good deal that draws attention to the processes of writing and signification in both *Master Humphrey's Clock* and the *Shop* itself. Humphrey's best friend, the deaf gentleman, requires everything to be written for him and Mr Pickwick communicates with him by means of 'the finger alphabet' (*MHC* 112). Almost the first time we see Nell is when she is giving Kit Nubbles a writing lesson, a scene that is echoed at the very end when Dick Swiveller sends the Marchioness to school. So much of the pathos of Harry, the young scholar who dies, is carried by his beautiful writing, which invokes his pathetic presence by its ability to live on and beyond him. Mrs Jarley cannot read, but employs Slum the poet to re-create popular ditties such as 'Over the Water to Jarley' as advertisements for her waxworks (206), or adapt a dialogue between the Emperor of China and an oyster or the Archbishop of Canterbury and a Dissenter on the subject of Church rates for similar purposes. Miss Monflathers too claims the authority of literary quotation when she calls Nell 'wicked' and idle (239), by quoting Isaac Watts at length. Swiveller, though, is a greater literary figure than either of these two, able to fall asleep and still write 'divers strange words in an unknown character with his eyes shut' (264–5), embodying so much of the 'figurative and poetical character' (59) of the novel, full of figures, tropes, metaphors, puns, impersonation, song, verse, pantomime, and dumb-show, recognizing no distinctions between song and speech or authentic utterance and plagiarism, but composing and recomposing his self and world out of quotations, parodies, and allusions. Like one of Harold Bloom's strong poets, he defines himself through his creative mis-citation, richly and complexly retroping his father-poets—Burns, Byron, Thomas Moore, and many others—in tessera, clinamen, askesis, and swivel,[43] a man of so many quotations that when he takes the Marchioness to school he is taken to be 'a literary gentleman of eccentric habits' (550).[44]

Swiveller is also one of the best examples of the rich metaphysical significance that Dickens's work so often finds in popular life. John Carey has shown how often and how much leading figures of modern literature have despised the world of suburban clerks.[45] How strong is the contrast with this novel, in which a lawyer's clerk married to an illegitimate scullery maid become its most strongly affirmative presence—'those two sane, strong, living and loveable human beings', in Chesterton's words—and the hinge that swivels the book from despair to secular redemption. The parallels between Nell's story and Swiveller's romance with the Marchioness are many: both Nell and the Marchioness are thirteen years old, both are orphans (or thought to be in the Marchioness's case), and both suffer a good deal of physical pain. But whereas Nell is gradually drawn down into her crypt, the Marchioness is liberated from her chthonic existence beneath the Brass's house. Swiveller too is an orphan and, like Nell, he gets very ill, but, like the Marchioness, he survives and escapes.[46]

The Marchioness nicknames Swiveller 'Liverer', just as he renames her 'Sophronia Sphynx'. They are richly allegorical names, bestowed by two poor people on each other, as Swiveller, who for so long has had to play by himself, at last finds someone to play with. A liverer is someone who lives, and more than lives, who lives on in his name and beyond his name, as well as swivelling on and living on and living through

---

[43] Harold Bloom, *Kabbalah and Criticism* (New York: Seabury, 1975), 28.

[44] Walter Benjamin wished to produce an entire book composed of quotations: *Illuminations* (London: Jonathan Cape, 1973), 47. Where Nell's grandfather collects curious objects in his shop, Swiveller collects quotations.

[45] John Carey, *The Intellectuals and the Masses: Pride and Prejudice among the Literary Intelligentsia* (London: Faber, 1992).

[46] 'The real hero and heroine of *The Old Curiosity Shop* are, of course, Dick Swiveller and the Marchioness': Chesterton, *Chesterton on Dickens*, 56.

swivelling.[47] The new name of the Marchioness is even better. Half of her new name is 'Sphynx', that inscrutable figure, half-woman, half-lion, found in the sands of Egypt and in the Oedipus story, and half is 'Sophronia', the Greek virtue of moderation and self-restraint, and so her name contains both the necessary price and virtue of civilized life and whatever in human culture precedes and questions it, all in a nickname for 'a small slipshod girl in a dirty coarse apron and bib' (260). So many things meet, fold together, and unfold in this couple, 'the one true romance in the whole of Dickens',[48] a 'comic Oedipus'[49] and his wife, in whom Nell's spiritual heaven is answered and outplayed by the Swiveller-Sphynxs' material and romantic heaven of having enough to eat and drink, and some fun.

The Old Curiosity Shop is a curious book, at first appearing to be Dickens's most remorselessly transcendent and idealizing text, a novel trembling on the brink of allegory, a story about to become a picture. Nell walks in the cemetery among 'the houses of the dead' (133) and this book too seems a house of the living dead, Dickens's house that he is required to build, in response to public demand, around the absent body and ever-present little name of Nell, a book which is also a clock that both measures and arrests time in narrative, which is also a shop that sells everything and nothing, which is also a tomb and a waxworks exhibition of a 'waxworks child' (239) and a crypt and a funeral procession. The book is also an hilariously and triumphantly self-defeating story, and when Nell's tale is retold in the final paragraphs of the novel by Kit and Barbara to their still-living children, who thus become the final mourners in Nell's long cortège, the children first cry but then laugh and are 'again quite merry' (554).

---

[47] On living on, see Jacques Derrida, 'Living On: Border Lines', in Harold Bloom, Paul de Man, J. Hillis Miller, and Jacques Derrida, *Deconstruction and Criticism* (New York: Seabury, 1979), 135–6.

[48] Chesterton, *Chesterton on Dickens*, 56.

[49] Marcus, *Dickens: From Pickwick to Dombey*, 168.

CHAPTER SIX

History's Grip: *Barnaby Rudge*

I

IN MARCH 1841, Dickens was having some problems. He had recently become a father for the fourth time, and was also deeply troubled by his own father, who was once more borrowing money on his name. He did however find time from some of the difficulties he was having with his current novel, which was not going well, to read an unpublished manuscript, lent to him by his friend, Basil Hall. It was by the late Lady De Lancey, and described the tragic death of her husband, following his horrific wounding at the Battle of Waterloo, an heroic story of military bravery and feminine devotion set against the background of an epic historical event of a generation before. Dickens was profoundly moved by the description of De Lancey's mortal wounds, which detached several ribs from his spine and drove one into his lung, and deeply affected by the care given to him by his wife of a mere six weeks:

To say that the reading that most astonishing and tremendous account has constituted an epoch in my life—that I shall never forget the lightest word of it—that I cannot throw the impression aside and never saw anything so real, so touching, and so actually present before my eyes, is nothing . . . What I have always looked upon as masterpieces of powerful and affecting description, seem as nothing in my eyes. If I live for fifty years, I shall dream of it every now and then from this hour to the day of my death.[1]

This passage from Dickens's letter of thanks to Hall is testament to the remarkable things history and historical narrative can do to one. Dickens praises the vividness and truthfulness of the description, but this leads him to a vocabulary—astonishing, tremendous, frightful, powerful, affecting—close to that of

[1] Pilgrim, II, 235.

the literary sublime, to what defies, exceeds, and defeats expression in language.[2] Lady De Lancey's writing is so real, so true, and so present that it becomes preternaturally so, more real than real, and even to say this is to say 'nothing'. So truthful is her writing that it transports the reader to a condition beyond the possibility of representation in language, to exhilarating, distressing, and contradictory idioms and states of mind, compared to which, other texts seem 'as nothing'. When reading the deathbed scenes, writes Dickens, 'I am husband and wife, dead man and living woman, Emma and General Dundas, doctor and bedstead, everything and everybody (but the Prussian Officer—damn him) all in one'.[3] The reader of successful historical narrative loses his or her identity and the very possibility of identity, transported into a state that recognizes no distinction between self and other, text and reader, life and death, male and female, or indeed doctors and bedsteads. It is only this that can drive the effects of the text in and through conscious experience into 'the most frightful reality' of unconscious recollection in dreams.[4]

At the end of *Barnaby Rudge*, the historical novel Dickens was struggling with at the time, the insane Lord George Gordon, leader of the anti-Catholic riots that bear his name and which are the notional subject of the book, is arrested for libel and imprisoned until he dies. During that time, writes Dickens, 'he applied himself to the study of history'.[5] It is a strange ending to Gordon's career and to the novel, this demented and incar-

---

[2] There is an extensive literature on the literary sublime. The standard account is Samuel H. Monk, *The Sublime: A Study of Critical Theories in XVIII-Century England* (Ann Arbor: University of Michigan Press, 1935). For more recent treatments, see, for example, Peter de Bolla, *The Discourse of the Sublime: Readings in History, Aesthetics and the Subject* (Oxford: Basil Blackwell, 1989). On the relation between revolutionary events and the discourse of the sublime, see Geoffrey Bennington, *Lyotard: Writing the Event* (Manchester: Manchester University Press, 1989), 164–6 and Terry Eagleton, *The Ideology of the Aesthetic* (Oxford: Basil Blackwell, 1990), 53–6. On Dickens and the sublime, see Jonathan Loesberg, 'Dickensian Deformed Children and the Hegelian Sublime', *Victorian Studies*, 40, 4 (Summer 1997), 625–54. There is no copy of Edmund Burke, *Philosophical Inquiry into the Origin of the Sublime and the Beautiful* (1757) in the 1844 inventory of Dickens's library reprinted in Pilgrim, IV, 711.

[3] Pilgrim, II, 235.

[4] Ibid.

[5] Charles Dickens, *Barnaby Rudge*, ed. Gordon Spence (Harmondsworth: Penguin, 1973), 733. All references will be to this edition and placed in the text.

cerated pursuit of historical knowledge, but it is of a piece with the affinity the novel makes between the experience of history and irrational, excessive, and deviant states of mind. Critics of Dickens have often seen *Barnaby Rudge* as a flawed work because, as John Forster influentially put it, of its lack of 'singleness of purpose, unity of idea, or harmony of treatment', and critics of the historical novel have often dismissed it in a few brief paragraphs, on the grounds that Dickens had no real knowledge of or interest in historical processes.[6] Although the riots were, as Linda Colley puts it, 'the largest, deadliest and most protracted . . . in British history' and the novel's subject-matter—the scapegoating and violent attack on Catholics—one central to the project of national self-formation in the eighteenth and early nineteenth centuries, *Barnaby Rudge* still seems to lack the qualities that would allow it a secure place in the pantheon of the historical novel.[7] Those who have admired the book have often worked hard to make it seem a coherent 'epical novel with a philosophy of history behind it',[8] but as the irony of Gordon's fate as an insane and imprisoned student of history may suggest, the novel may have a very different view of history and its relation to fiction from its contemporary and later readers, one that, like the reading of Emma De Lancey's manuscript, takes witnesses, participants, narrators, and readers of historical events to places and states of mind not assimilable to the orthodoxies of historical fiction and its criticism.[9]

---

[6] John Forster, *The Life of Charles Dickens*, ed. A. J. Hoppé (London: Dent, 1966), I, 144. George Lukács, *The Historical Novel* (Harmondsworth: Penguin, 1969), 290–2. For Chesterton, Dickens 'Undoubtedly . . . knew no history': *Chesterton on Dickens* (London: Dent, 1992), 70. For Steven Marcus, Dickens's knowledge of history was 'both grotesquely unformed and defective': *Dickens: From Pickwick to Dombey* (London: Chatto and Windus, 1965), 142. 'When he writes of . . . even . . . the late eighteenth century . . . he did so with an amused contempt', using the past as 'an additional field for his genius in describing the unpleasant': Humphry House, *The Dickens World* (Oxford: Oxford University Press, 1941), 34–5.

[7] Linda Colley, *Britons: Forging the Nation 1707–1837* (London: Vintage, 1996), 23–4. See also pp. 352–4.

[8] '[T]he hearty romance became an epical novel with a philosophy of history behind it': Jack Lindsay, 'Barnaby Rudge', in John Gross and Gabriel Pearson (eds), *Dickens and the Twentieth Century* (London: Routledge and Kegan Paul, 1962), 94.

[9] In sharp contrast to the popular acclaim that had greeted its precursors, it 'went almost entirely unnoticed' on its first appearance: Kathryn Chittick, *Dickens and the 1830s* (Cambridge: Cambridge University Press, 1990), ix.

Barnaby Rudge tells a story about an ambiguous set of events, an uprising that is both political and unpolitical, religious and secular, radical and reactionary, dangerous and absurd.[10] The Gordon Riots are at various points in the novel a popular movement, a religious pogrom, and an attempted *coup d'état*, and they are led by such uncertain and troubling figures as an aristocratic demagogue, a rioting hangman, and a poetic idiot.[11] The riots occur for a number of deeply contingent reasons, but the novel wishes them also to represent an important historical development or contrast, in uncertain analogy with both Chartism and the French Revolution.[12] This political complexity is made more complex by the family dynamics of the story, in particular the desperate conflicts of fathers and sons which are such a pronounced feature of the book, and the unclear relationship of them to the larger historical picture. And the political and familial material is made yet more troublesome by the narration of the story, which frequently uses Gothic motifs to tell a tale full of haunting, trauma, and uncanny repetition, dramatized

[10] On the history of the riots, see J. P. De Castro, *The Gordon Riots* (Oxford: Oxford University Press, 1926); George Rudé, *The Crowd in History: A Study of Popular Disturbances in France and England 1730–1848* (2nd edition, London: Lawrence and Wishart, 1981), 57–9; John Stevenson, *Popular Disturbances in England, 1700–1832* (2nd edition, London: Longmans, 1992), 94–113; and Nicholas Rogers, 'Crowds and Power in the Gordon Riots', in Eckhart Hellmuth (ed.), *The Transformation of Political Culture: England and Germany in the late Eighteenth Century* (Oxford: Oxford University Press, 1990), 39–55.

[11] For the description of the riots as a 'pogrom', see Avrom Fleishman, *The English Historical Novel: Walter Scott to Virginia Woolf* (Baltimore: Johns Hopkins University Press, 1971), 105.

[12] Marcus, *Dickens: From Pickwick to Dombey*, 172, discusses 'the analogy ... with Chartism' following earlier discussions by Edmund Wilson, Edgar Johnson, Humphry House, T. A. Jackson, and Kathleen Tillotson. See also Paul Stigant and Peter Widdowson, 'Barnaby Rudge—A Historical Novel?', *Literature and History*, 2 (October 1975), 2–44. Patrick Brantlinger, *The Fiction of Reform: British Literature and Politics, 1832–1867* (Cambridge: Harvard University Press, 1977), 85, sees the novel as 'an analysis of Chartism', although John Lucas (*The Melancholy Man: A Study of Dickens's Novels* (London: Methuen, 1970), 103) is 'not at all convinced that the threads of Chartism and Unionism were uppermost in his mind'. The most comprehensive treatment of the novel as 'a fully articulated political allegory' of the potential alliance in the early 1840s of radical and reactionary political forces is Thomas J. Rice, 'The Politics of *Barnaby Rudge*', in Robert Giddings (ed.), *The Changing World of Charles Dickens* (London: Vision, 1986), 51–74. On the relationship between the Gordon Riots and the French Revolution, see Chesterton, *Chesterton on Dickens*, 71–3.

through a heavily melodramatic excess. This allegedly historical novel has at its absent centre an idiot and a raven, surrounded by ghosts, shadows, and monsters, who question and
trouble some deep assumptions about the nature of historical
events and their representation in fiction—their uniqueness,
causal sequence, and the possibility of a truthful description—
that are common both to the nineteenth century and our own.
Is Dickens's first historical novel simply hasty and confused, or
does it contain the possibility of a more radical, disturbing, or
originary understanding of historical narrative, one that is also
uncanny, self-effacing, abyssal?

Ideas of history and historical fiction were changing at a rapid
rate in the decades of Dickens's youth and early manhood, as
a newly professionalizing historicism sought to loosen itself
from the taint of the amateur and literary.[13] Stephen Bann in
The Clothing of Clio describes the 'exemplary'[14] creation by du
Sommerard of the Cluny Museum in Paris in the 1830s, at
precisely the time of the writing of *Barnaby Rudge*, and its
change from a collection of 'part-objects . . . disjoined from each
other and from any transcendent value' to its re-creation in a
more modern form as a collection of 'part-objects . . . linked
sympathetically both to an architectural whole and to the
mythic system of "History" '.[15] The once-random collection of
antiques is arranged by du Sommerard thematically into such
groupings as the 'Chambre de Francois Ier', to create not just a
better-ordered museum but a qualitatively 'new experience'[16] of
historical understanding. Bann sees this as representative of a
wider transformation in the period, which makes historical
objects into specimens not relics, related not haphazardly but
assimilated into a rational economy of knowledge.[17] Bann's
contrast is a useful one with which to begin to analyse

---

[13] Phillipa Levine, *The Amateur and the Professional: Victorian Historians and
the English Past* (Cambridge: Cambridge University Press, 1982).

[14] Stephen Bann, *The Clothing of Clio: A Study of the Representation of History
in Nineteenth-Century Britain and France* (Cambridge: Cambridge University Press,
1984), 78. See also A. Dwight Culler, *The Victorian Mirror of History* (New Haven:
Yale University Press, 1985), and Hayden White, *Metahistory: the Historical Imagination in Nineteenth-Century Europe* (Baltimore: Johns Hopkins University Press,
1973).

[15] Bann, *The Clothing of Clio*, 108.   [16] Ibid., 82.   [17] Ibid., 87.

Dickens's work as an historical novelist in *Barnaby Rudge*, for heuristic purposes at least. Before the creation of his museum (in an illustration reproduced by Bann) du Sommerard is painted as an antiquary surrounded by the lumber of his collection of medieval antiquities, 'a chaotic assemblage crammed into a small space, with armour and fire arms invading the carpet' which represents for Bann the old *epistēmē*. Dickens's previous novel, *The Old Curiosity Shop*, had created a remarkably similar space for Little Nell and her antiquarian grandfather—the Curiosity Shop itself—and Dickens's description of it is complete with armour, fire-arms and a chaotic sprawl like that which surrounds du Sommerard. That novel had itself emerged from an equally chaotic lumber room, *Master Humphrey's Clock*, the periodical in which both *The Old Curiosity Shop* and *Barnaby Rudge* first appear, and both the *Clock* and the stories that precede the two novels are much like the narrative equivalent of the old Cluny museum, a group of little stories, set in a variety of past times, told by various odd narrators, with no regulating idea or central point of view, seized fragments, narrative part-objects, junk. They are set for the most part in the past, but not one that could be called historical in any modern sense. Instead they belong to a world of temporal allegory, for *Master Humphrey's Clock*'s founding idea is of an old clock-case in which the stories which comprise the journal are discovered, an explicit allegory of Time and Narration. How far does *Barnaby Rudge* belong to this world of temporal allegory, the world of Nell and Humphrey? Or is it more like a novel by Scott or a text by Carlyle, wanting to tell a coherent story in a systematic way, to bring fragments together into an architectural whole, related to a wider conceptual understanding of 'History'?

Walter Scott, in almost all accounts of the historical novel, is its great founding father. Dickens clearly thinks a good deal about Scott, and *Barnaby Rudge* has often been taken as his attempt to imitate him. As Chesterton puts it: *Barnaby Rudge* 'is a very fine, romantic historical novel: Scott would have been proud of it'.[18] This is a commonplace of many critics of Dickens who, looking for a predecessor of similar literary and popular

---

[18] Chesterton, *Chesterton on Dickens*, 66.

European success, find Scott.[19] There is, however, an important contrast between the two men and the two bodies of work, which is brought out well in a review by Scott of the fiction of Ernst Theodor Hoffmann, an article deeply hostile to 'the FANTASTIC mode of writing—in which the most wild and unbounded licence is given to an irregular fancy, and all species of combination, however ludicrous or however shocking, are attempted and executed without scruple'.[20] Scott, although willing to countenance some use of Gothic effects in fiction, wished to subordinate the use of supernatural effects and devices to a predominantly historical narrative method.[21] Although 'Gothic modes of history . . . survive in the Waverley Novels', Dickens uses them in a more integrated and disturbing

[19] Barnaby Rudge the character seems to owe a good deal, in physical appearance at least, to Madge Wildfire in Scott's *The Heart of Midlothian*, and critics have seen other parallels between Scott's oeuvre and Dickens's novel. See John Butt and Kathleen Tillotson, *Dickens at Work* (London: Methuen, 1957), 78. Angus Wilson argues that 'in the final version there is only a skeleton of Scott's world surviving': *The World of Charles Dickens* (London: The Book Society, 1970), 147. See also Gordon Spence's introduction to the 1973 Penguin edition of the novel, 18–19. Chittick argues that Dickens wished to make his novel 'resemble those of both Sir Walter Scott and *Master Humphrey's Clock*': *Dickens and the 1830s*, 167. Robert L. Caserio argues that *Barnaby Rudge*'s plot is 'dominated by a jealous hostility to Scott' and comprises an 'attempt to fight off the influence of Scott's storytelling practice', in his 'Plot and the Point of Reversal', in Harold Bloom (ed.), *Modern Critical Views: Charles Dickens* (New York: Chelsea House, 1987), 163–4, first published in Robert L. Caserio, *Plot, Story and the Novel* (Princeton: Princeton University Press, 1979). See also S. J. Newman, '*Barnaby Rudge*: Dickens and Scott', in R. T. Davies and B. G. Beatty (eds), *Literature of the Romantic Period 1750–1850* (Liverpool: Liverpool University Press, 1976), 171–88. Dickens himself went some way with the Scott identification, for it is clear that he was pleased (in his early years at least) that his father-in-law, George Hogarth, had been an intimate friend of the elder novelist. He enjoyed the adulation of Edinburgh in 1841 and spent a whole day at Abbotsford, Scott's home, and there are a good many complimentary references to Scott in Dickens's letters. See Pilgrim, I, 576, 'A Legend of Montrose, and Kenilworth which I have just been reading with greater delight than ever' (letter of 21 August 1839). Scott wrote in his Journal of March 1829, 'I meditate doing something on the popish and protestant affray': *The Journal of Sir Walter Scott*, ed. W. E. K. Anderson (Oxford: Clarendon 1972), 533, quoted in Fiona Robertson, *Legitimate Histories; Scott, Gothic, and the Authorities of Fiction* (Oxford: Clarendon, 1994), 9.

[20] Walter Scott, 'Novels of Ernest Theodore Hoffmann', in *The Prose Works of Sir Walter Scott* (Edinburgh: A. and C. Black, 1881), 18, 270–332, first published in *The Foreign and Quarterly Review* (July–November 1827), 60–98. Scott spends a large part of the essay summarizing and then condemning the story 'The Sandman', which then becomes the centrepiece of Freud's essay on 'The Uncanny', in Sigmund Freud, *The Pelican Freud Library Volume 14: Art and Literature* (Harmondsworth: Penguin, 1985), 339–76.

[21] On Scott's relation to Gothic, see Robertson, *Legitimate Histories*, 21.

way.[22] It seems likely that he knew the work of Hoffmann and related German romantic fantasy-writers and both *Barnaby Rudge* and its precursors contain a widespread use of Gothic and 'fantastic' narrative elements.[23] Barnaby for example has 'phantom-haunted dreams' (107), and in the accompanying illustration he is surrounded by demonic and grotesque figures—heads without bodies, a creature with a flute for a nose, and numerous pairs of eyes, massively out of proportion to or wholly detached from the faces and bodies to which they belong, like something out of a painting by Hieronymus Bosch. We are also asked to believe in prophetic dreams, coincidence of dates, the importance of ghosts and spectres, and a number of other characteristically Gothic or fantastic motifs.[24]

The necessary contrast can be made through the very different prefaces of Dickens and Scott. The paratextual apparatus of historical fiction—its prefaces, notes, and framing devices—are widely recognized to be of considerable importance in the interpretation of the texts they surround.[25] Dickens's 1849 preface to *Barnaby Rudge* does not claim to have discovered a black letter manuscript or to be in the hand of an interesting fictional persona like Scott's Dryasdust. It seems by comparison a rather slight thing, telling two stories, the first about two ravens, the second about Mary Jones, who was hung in 1770 for theft. The ravens, writes Dickens, are the 'two great originals' of the raven in the novel we are about to read and Mary Jones 'no effort of invention'. Their lives all end in sudden death; the first raven, like its author and Ann Page, a character in *The Merry Wives of Windsor*, 'of good gifts . . . improved by study and attention',

---

[22] Robertson, *Legitimate Histories*, 7–8.

[23] Dennis Walder, Introduction to *Sketches by Boz* (Harmondsworth: Penguin, 1995), xxv.

[24] See Michael Hollington, *Dickens and the Grotesque* (London: Croom Helm, 1984), 96–122, and Juliet McMaster, ' "Better to be silly": From Vision to Reality in *Barnaby Rudge*', in Michael Hollington (ed.), *Charles Dickens: Critical Assessments* (London: Helm Information, 1995), II, 444–58, first published in *Dickens Studies Annual*, XIII (1984), 1–17. On fairy-tale motifs, see Harry Stone, *The Invisible World: Fairy-tales, Fantasy, and Novel-Making* (Bloomington: Indiana University Press, 1979).

[25] There is a large literature on this topic. See Edward Said, *Beginnings: Intention and Method* (New York: Basic Books 1975); A. D. Nuttall, *Openings* (Oxford: Clarendon, 1992); Jacques Derrida, *Dissemination* (London: Athlone, 1981), 1–59. On Scott, see Robertson, *Legitimate Histories*, 118–19.

commits 'a youthful indiscretion'—eating a pound or two of white lead—which 'terminated in death' (39). His successor, 'an older and more gifted raven' but 'too bright a genius to live long', also dies, without known cause (39–40). And then, across a caesura in the preface, we move from the story of birds who can speak what we like to think of as human language and to whom, jokingly it seems, the author ascribes human intentions and qualities rather like his own, to the story of a woman who speaks only to say that she does not understand what she did, and who is treated, like so many of her class and sex, worse than an animal or bird. The first raven buries 'cheese and halfpence in the garden' and the second digs them up again (39). Dickens digs up the story of Mary Jones from its resting place in parliamentary history, a story about small quantities of food and money, and tells us the story of someone whose husband is press-ganged, whose children have nothing to eat, and who steals some cloth to make a few shillings to feed them. She is not yet nineteen when she is hanged, and we could call her deed, like the raven's, 'a youthful indiscretion' for which she (like him) dies. But it is only the ravens, those richly realized comic individuals, who can be described in such a sportive and light-hearted way, for in sober historical truth, we are told, Mary Jones died under the Shoplifting Act, like many others, 'for the comfort and satisfaction of shopkeepers in Ludgate Street' (42).

The preface tells a story, or pair of stories, about youth and death, food and money, language and burial, tales about the limits or ends of the human in talking animals and judicial execution. But they also begin an historical novel, one which settles accounts with, moves beyond or, alternatively, lamely imitates the historical fiction of Walter Scott. The second raven of the preface, who succeeds the first, is 'more gifted' than his predecessor, but spends most of his short brilliant life undoing all the first bird's work, disinterring 'all the cheese and halfpence' the other raven had buried (39). To do this he has to carry out, like the good historical novelist, 'a work of immense labour and research', but only as a preface to his 'acquisition of stable language' (39), which he then uses (in one of Dickens's best puns) in the stable to drive 'imaginary horses with great skill, all day' (39). Dickens has done his research for the book, and one can list his reading and references;[26] the first chapter will have a horse driven through it, in stable, unstable language. Nothing seems to follow or succeed in the preface. A third raven is introduced in the 1858 revision, but the bird is clearly a disappointment to Dickens, who tells us frankly that 'it is not a genius' (745), its only accomplishment an ability to bark like a dog. We are not told what happened to Mary Jones's child, who, as we learn in the final words of the preface, 'was sucking at the breast when she set out for Tyburn' (42). The only thing that does follow is the novel itself, which culminates in the judicial execution of a bastard child, Hugh the Maypole, whose mother too was 'hung up . . . at Tyburn for a couple of thousand men to stare at' (241). They all die young and gifted: the first raven 'in the bloom of his youth' (39), the second not long after, and Mary Jones 'was very young (under nineteen), and most remarkably handsome' (41) when she died, the first of many young people in the book—Barnaby, Hugh, Joe Willet— who die or nearly die, or lose their legs like Sim Tappertit. And Dickens too is young and handsome when he writes this novel, twenty-four years old or so at most at its inception.

The first paragraph of the novel proper also acts as a kind of preface, one that is all about history and the truth of history, as witnessed and read in its archives and monuments. The Maypole which it describes is an inn, but also the sign of an inn, one of many (such as 'The Dragon' in *Martin Chuzzlewit*) where Dickens seems as interested in the sign as its referent. The chapter is full of the forces that traverse and constitute the book: reading and writing (the Maypole has a sign for the many travellers who could then do neither); legend, tradition and fairytale, and their relation to fact; democracy and belief; truth and violence. We begin, like the good historian, with what seem to be sure dates and clear facts: it is 1775, and the inn is exactly twelve miles from London. But the inn, unlike its unequivocal and iconic sign, an upright and erect symbol of fertility whose meaning is clear to all who can or cannot read or do or do not

---

[26] They are conveniently listed in the 1973 Penguin edition of the novel, 741–3. Ackroyd, *Dickens* (London: Sinclair Stevenson, 1990), 343, notes that 'his copy of Waterton's *Essays on Natural History* has pencil marks beside the chapter on ravens'. There are a number of letters about Dickens's pet ravens. See Pilgrim, II, 230–7 and 266–7.

know stable language, is a troublesome and capricious referent, composed of 'fantastic shapes' (43). The narrator, once he starts to narrate, can give us only gossip and legend: there is 'said to have been' and 'there was a legend' which is also 'apocryphal . . . tradition' (43). When he does move to an undisputed fact— 'the Maypole was really an old house'—it is immediately recaptured by 'fairy-tale' and 'fancy' in narration (44). We instantly encounter conflicts of interpretation, about history and the history of the inn, between 'the large majority' of traditionalists who believe in its legends and 'matter-of-fact' people who do not and are invariably defeated, whereupon we are told, at the beginning of a novel whose central action is about the claims of true belief in conflict, the 'believers exulted as in a victory' (43).

We are about to be told a tale which divides or is broken in the middle, which has an apparently 'private' first part, full of Gothic and uncanny events and characters (shortly we will meet the first of many ghosts), which then passes over five years in silence before being swept up in a 'public' historical event which exists in a troubled and occluded relationship to what precedes or prefaces it. Just as the preface is broken in the middle, as we pass from the private world of Dickens's pet ravens to the grossly public death of Mary Jones, so the novel is divided in the middle by a deep caesura, both in time—it occurs five years later—and in subject-matter, for there is nothing of Gordon or the riots in the preceding three hundred or so pages before, 'as suddenly as he appears in these pages after a blank of five long years, did he and his proceedings begin to force themselves . . . upon the notice of thousands of people' (348).[27] This is a remarkable entry into the novel which, far from attempting to link the private history that we have so far encountered with the public events which follow, flagrantly refuses to do so. Nor can the two parts of the book be assimilated to a pattern of

---

[27] Edgar Allan Poe wrote when the book first appeared that the riots were 'altogether an afterthought' with 'no necessary connections with the story': in Philip Collins (ed.), *Dickens: The Critical Heritage* (London: Routledge and Kegan Paul, 1971), 109, from a review in *Graham's Magazine* (February 1842), xix, 124–9. There have been a number of attempts to establish the thematic coherence of the text, of which the most important are Harold F. Folland, 'The Doer and the Deed: Theme and Pattern in *Barnaby Rudge*', *PMLA*, 74 (1959), 406–17 and James K. Gottshall, 'Devils Abroad: The Unity and Significance of *Barnaby Rudge*', *Nineteenth Century Fiction*, 16 (1961), 133–46.

stable irony or dialectical progression. On the contrary: the novel carefully builds up causal connections and links in time, while dissolving and violating those connections at crucial points. Gordon appears in history without cause, precedent, or reason, as arbitrarily as he appears in a story that so far has seemed to have had no possible link to him. *Barnaby Rudge* is thus very different from the sort of historical novel that wishes simply to bind intimately together private and public life, to establish causal chains and sequences in order to understand their relation. Dickens, by contrast, stresses the contingency of the links between public and private life, historical action and individual fate, a contingency explicitly linked to the making and reading of fictions: 'Just as he has come upon the reader, he had come . . . upon the public' (348).

II

If the novel resists developing causal relations between historical actions and individual fates, it does establish relations of analogy between private and public events. As Steven Marcus has convincingly argued, it is a novel concerned 'with authority in political and social terms, as well as in personal and private ones'.[28] Such a reading can be reinforced by the thematic and figurative continuity across the two halves of the novel. There is, for example, a remarkable play of eyes, faces, and visibility throughout the book: in the first chapter Solomon Daisy 'seemed all eyes from head to foot' (48) and Joe Willet gazes earnestly at Rudge; later, Varden will do the same (63), insisting on seeing the murderer's face, which looks like death's. Many disguised, distorted, failed, and blind gazes fill the book: both Rudge's and Edward Chester's faces are covered at their first appearance, and Rudge's is again when he encounters Chester and Varden on the road; when Varden tells Emma

---

[28] Marcus, *Dickens: From Pickwick to Dombey*, 172. James Kincaid argues that there is an essentially rhetorical or ironic relationship between the two parts: 'It is a novel based on reversal; the second half reverses the tendencies of the first half and negates its assurances': *Dickens and the Rhetoric of Laughter* (Oxford: Clarendon, 1971), 107. Wilson, *The World of Charles Dickens*, 147, argues that Dickens, 'having established authority in Part One, . . . destroys it in Part Two'.

Haredale of Edward Chester's fate, she is at a masked ball, and Varden 'slips him on a mask' (83) to tell her the news. Haredale distrusts Chester's 'masked faces' (144) and Chester's face is so like a mask that he might have sat 'for an equestrian portrait' (126); Hugh is accused of having 'an evil eye' (329) and Barnaby is brought before Sir John Fielding, blind magistrate and brother of a seeing novelist. This is both a public and private matter, as the important speech of the blind Stagg on the many kinds of blindness—'connubial blindness . . . wilful and self-bandaging blindness . . . the blindness of party, ma'am, and public men . . . the blind confidence of youth . . . physical blindness . . . blindness of the intellect' (422)—makes explicit. It at first appears as if this concern with sight and blindness forms a straightforward pattern of norm and deviancy. Gabriel Varden, who has the most moral authority in the book, sees clearly, and his power is related to this. Deviancy and disorder are expressed through misapplied or perverse gazes—as when Miggs spies on Tappertit or when Tappertit, proud of the 'power of his eye' (79), attempts to inflame the passion of Dolly Varden with his 'big looks' (85). In this, the novel seems to repeat a familiar set of oppositions: phallic, paternal power symbolized in Varden's clear and lucid gaze, surrounded by various deviant, distorted, and perverse gazes and blindnesses, both literal and metaphoric, such as Sim's narcissistic overvaluation of his own sight, and John Willet's blindness to everything except the boiler to which his gaze obsessively returns.

There is also an inordinately large number of keys and locks in the book. Varden himself is a locksmith and the original title of the book was to have been *Gabriel Varden: The Locksmith of London.*[29] Tappertit has a large key (108) and he smites his trouser pocket to check that it is safe from danger. The whole scene in which Tappertit escapes to the Apprentice Knights and is spied on and then locked out by Miggs is a matter of eyes and keys, the signs and stakes of the conflict of desire and power (124). The relationship to keys in the book is similar to the relationship to sight: Varden is the Master Locksmith and others, such as Miggs and Tappertit, overvalue or misuse them. Sim wants

---

[29] Butt and Tillotson, *Dickens at Work*, 63. On locks, see John Carey, *The Violent Effigy* (London: Faber, 1971), 120.

to be 'the master spirit at the head of' the Apprentice Knights (80), and his power over them comes from his ability to manufacture keys. There are countless scenes of the locking and unlocking of both private and public buildings, from Mrs Rudge's house to the House of Commons, a motif which runs through the book until Miggs ends her days as a female turnkey, poking keys into her charges' backs (734–5). This too is both a public and private matter, for narrators also break locks: chroniclers, we are told, 'are privileged to enter where they list, to come and go through keyholes' (119); these scenes climax at the gates of Newgate when Varden refuses to open the lock he has made (101).

This thematic cluster—sight, blindness, keys, and locks—has led some readers of the novel, naturally enough, to think of the Oedipus complex, and this seems convincing when we note the importance the novel gives to the relationships of fathers and sons.[30] In contrast to the earlier novels, which have few significant father–son relationships (except Ralph Nickleby and Smike, who never meet, and the Wellers' mutual benign neglect), Rudge, Chester, and Willet are tyrannical fathers who attempt to oppress and diminish their sons.[31] This is often figured in terms of castration: John Willet, 'having snipped off a flemish ell' (292) of his son's liberty, continues 'trimming off' and 'shearing away' (292) at him; his clique of friends accuse Joe of 'Wringing the very nose off his own father's face' (51); when Willet advertises for Joe, he cuts off 'from eighteen inches to a couple of feet' off his height (317). Simon Tappertit is cut off too: his name is cut short to 'Sim' by almost everyone and even his little bow is 'cut short off at the neck' on his first appearance in the book.[32] This chopping-off is explicitly linked to

---

[30] Marcus asserts that the novel 'contemplates only one kind of personal relationship—that of father and son': *Dickens: From Pickwick to Dombey*, 184. Jeremy Tambling argues that 'The gallows is the national phallus' in his *Dickens, Violence and the Modern State* (London: Macmillan, 1995), 134. On the Oedipus Complex, see Sigmund Freud, *The Interpretation of Dreams* (Harmondsworth: Penguin, 1976), 362–6 and 471. On blindness and castration, see Freud, 'The Uncanny', 349–52.

[31] As Marcus points out, Barnaby and his father even meet, like Laius and Oedipus, in a struggle at a crossroads at the beginning of the story: *Dickens: From Pickwick to Dombey*, 192.

[32] 'To decapitate = castrate': Sigmund Freud, 'Medusa's Head', in *The Standard Edition of the Complete Psychological Works of Sigmund Freud*, trans. James Strachey (London: Hogarth, 1955), XVIII, 273.

sexual desire. When Joe is riding with Dolly, he would have touched her hand even if 'there had been an executioner behind with an uplifted axe ready to chop off his head if he touched that hand' (226); when he returns from war, he tells Dolly that he 'would rather have lost my head—than to have found you dead' (652). Tappertit, as punishment for his illicit sexual desires, loses his legs, although he has earlier had the small compensating pleasure of 'rubbing up his hair till it stood stiff and straight on end all over his head' (231).

There are many Gothic and fantastic motifs and events within *Barnaby Rudge*, in particular that of haunting.[33] Rudge, for example, is told in the first chapter that Geoffrey Haredale, the brother of the murdered man, 'is not alive, and he is not dead . . . Not dead in a common sort of way' (53). In meeting on the road with Varden, Rudge himself is a 'bloodless ghost' on whose skin hang 'heavy drops like dews of agony and death', like Death on a pale horse. When Edward Chester appears to be near death, the narrator remarks, comparing Chester and Barnaby, 'the absence of soul is far more terrible in a living man than in a dead one'. Hugh is 'a animal' according to old Willet (140), who cannot read or write, and Haredale is a 'human badger' to Chester (148). Rudge is repeatedly a ghost in the book, 'a ghost upon the earth' (185), 'the apparition of a dream' (183), pursued by 'those curst beings of another world, who will not leave me' (185), and an 'ill-looking figure who might have fallen from a gibbet' (101), the father as ghost. The released prisoners from Newgate in the climax to the riots seem 'as if they had risen in their shrouds' (594), and the dead men killed

[33] Eve Kosofsky Sedgwick, *The Coherence of Gothic Conventions* (New York: Methuen, 1986), 24, defines the 'radical Gothic' as a form in which 'violence pertains to an approach—from within or without—to the interfacing surface'. There is a great number of such surfaces violently approached in the book. After their abduction, for example, there is a repeated concern with the possible violation of the bodies of Dolly Varden and Emma Haredale and a corresponding representation of their 'delicate bodice . . . streaming hair' and 'neglected dress' (541). There are many images of things about to burst forth and break through their containing surfaces: Tappertit threatens to 'burst out one of these days' (116); Hugh, as Willet puts it, has 'got all his faculties . . . bottled up and corked down' (140); Joe threatens to break out: 'I shall be driven to break bounds' (68). The narrator at one point speaks of men who, 'self possessed before, have given a sudden loose to passions they could no longer control' (62). Grip's favourite song is 'Polly put the kettle on', and his favourite party trick the pulling out of imaginary corks.

in the riots are given weapons 'to make them look as if alive'
(599). Dennis, about to be executed, thinks of himself as 'a
being in the likeness of a man' (688).

At such moments, the novel seems close to those texts and
events analysed by Freud in his essay on the uncanny, 'that class
of the frightening which leads back to what is known of old and
long familiar', which contains 'doubts whether an apparently
animate being is really alive' and is characteristically marked by
'the fear of going blind' as 'a substitute for the dread of being
castrated'.[34] The uncanny is marked by a compulsion to repeat,
as in Rudge's compulsion to return to the scene of his crime,
and the Newgate criminals' return to the prison from which they
have recently been released. Sim Tappertit, in more comic form,
believes in his ability to use the power of thought to control
rabid dogs and seduce women, a parody of a characteristically
uncanny belief. The Warren itself is 'the very ghost of a house,
haunting the old spot in its outward form' (154). There is a frequent uncertainty in the book about the distinctions between
the living and the dead, and the human and the inhuman, in the
many depictions of the phantoms and shadows that surround
human life. When Barnaby is born he receives an uncanny
stigma, a strange mark like 'a smear of blood but half washed
out' (87), from his mother's sight of her bloodstained husband,
fresh from the murder. The father's engendering crime marks
and wounds the son, a form of transgenerational haunting
written on the body.[35]

More importantly, *Barnaby Rudge* also depicts public historical events as a further manifestation of uncanny hauntings.
When Gordon appears for the first time, the narrator remarks
that 'bygone bugbears which had lain quietly in their graves for
centuries were raised again to haunt the ignorant and credulous'
(348). For Gashford, the threat of Catholic emancipation means
that 'Queen Elizabeth . . . weeps within her tomb and Bloody
Mary, with a brow of gloom and shadow, stalks triumphant'
(33). The dead live, as repetition is layered upon repetition, each
event both invoking and running over multiple and competing
frames of temporal reference. The events leading up to the riots

[34] Freud, 'The Uncanny', 340, 347.
[35] See Esther Rashkin, 'Tools for a New Psychoanalytic Criticism: The Work of
Abraham and Torok', *Diacritics* (Winter 1988), 31–52.

simultaneously echo those of the English Reformation, the Glorious Revolution, and of the first part of the book. Martha Rudge warns Barnaby that 'there are ghosts and dreams abroad' (431) and the riots—'a dream of demon heads and savage eyes ... phantoms not to be forgotten all through life' (465)—are a fulfilment of Barnaby's earlier dream. The gibbet on which Barnaby is to be hung haunts its street 'like a spectre' (689), its construction 'ghostly unsubstantial work' (688). There are also prophetic dreams: Gordon has an accurate prophetic dream about becoming a 'bearded Jew' (349), and Haredale's dream of finding Barnaby once more is also the fulfilment of 'a dream or vision' (399).[36] At the end of the novel, Haredale, haunted by Chester, is drawn inexplicably to the Warren, where he meets in the flesh 'the phantom of last night' (737). At such points, the novel seems unwilling to accept the distinctions, which may be essential to historical understanding, between what happens first and what happens later, and between what is alive and what is dead, distinctions that it troubles and disturbs, seeking out marginal and problematic events—like the death of Rudge, which happens twice—and figures who both are and are not alive or human.

At one point in the book, Gabriel Varden, entangled in the mystery of Rudge's ghostly reappearance, asks himself: '"What dark history is this!"' (98). The question occurs when Edward Chester, assaulted the previous night by Rudge, is recovering in Martha Rudge's house, twenty-two years to the day after the murder took place. So it is, in classically uncanny fashion, a doubled and redoubled doubling of that night—in location, in personnel and in a second assault, twenty-two years on. It is also a moment of anagnorisis or revelation when Varden realizes that Edward's assailant is the same man he himself had collided with earlier and whom he had just seen downstairs. Varden asks the question of himself, but he is answered by 'a hoarse voice' which replies '"Halloa! ... Halloa, halloa, halloa! Bow wow wow. What's the matter here! Hal-loa!"' (98). The speaker of this enigmatic reply to Varden's questioning of 'dark history', which makes him 'start as if he had been some supernatural agent', is Barnaby's pet raven Grip, who 'listened with a polite attention

---

[36] McMaster, '"Better to be silly"', 447–52.

and a most extraordinary appearance of comprehending every word' (99). This disturbing creature, 'one hundred and twenty' years old at this point, according to Varden, speaks like a human being but does so as if his voice 'seemed to come through his thick feathers rather than out of his mouth' (99), in an idiom which parodies, subverts, and deletes the voices of the haunted, self-deluded actors and narrators of the history and fiction that surround him: ' "I'm a devil, I'm a polly. I'm a kettle. I'm a protestant . . . We'll all have tea. I'm a protestant kettle. No popery!" ' (519). It is only the raven, history's Grip, it seems, who can answer Varden's question about this 'dark history'.[37]

III

Barnaby Rudge has been compared to tragedy, but it is much more akin to melodrama.[38] It is often thought to be an unsatisfactory novel for this reason, insistently drawn to the static and picturesque, to heightened polar emotions and implausible coincidence. It is more clichéd in expression than other Dickens novels—time runs like a mighty river (684), people have the vigour of lions (593), are felled like oxen (644), curse the hour they were born (661), and howl like wolves (576). Lips are sealed (255), heaven is invoked as a witness (255), and 'pretty fools' are told to 'Hush' (660). This is not only a matter of local expression, but of the whole ethos and construction of the book. The narrator remarks at one point on the 'appetite for the marvellous and the terrible' in humanity (492), and often seeks to gratify it with exorbitant and melodramatic effects. 'Hyperbolic figures, lurid and grandiose events, masked relationships and disguised identities, abductions, slow-acting poisons, secret societies, mysterious parentage'[39] are characteristic marks of melodrama, and *Barnaby Rudge* has them all, except slow poisoning. Melodrama notoriously works in and through starkly polarized contending forces and throughout the book Dickens uses

---

[37] The letter which tells of Dickens's reading of De Lancey's manuscript also notifies Hall of the death of Dickens's pet raven Grip.

[38] Marcus, *Dickens: From Pickwick to Dombey*, 191, 195.

[39] Peter Brooks, *The Melodramatic Imagination: Balzac, James, Melodrama, and the Mode of Excess* (New Haven: Yale University Press, 1976), 3.

implausible coincidence to engineer scenes of stark manichaean contrast and conflict: Barnaby shares a cell with his own lost father, Dennis with Hugh whom he has betrayed; Gashford, captured by Joe Willet, 'is like sin subdued' (646); Martha Rudge must suffer in silence and virtue. The language of the book moves to absolute expression, to a perfect externalization of primordial, excessive, and hyperbolic emotion. Rudge is not merely mysterious and secretive. He is 'a spectre at . . . licentious feasts; a something in the midst of their revelry and riot that chilled and haunted them', a ghost who, it is thought, 'has sold himself to the devil' (180–1). When Rudge meets his wife in the scenes of starkest moral dichotomy in the book, the novel becomes a drama on a metaphysical stage:

"I that in the form of a man live the life of a hunted beast; that in the body am a spirit, a ghost upon the earth, a thing from which all creatures shrink, save those curst beings of another world, who will not leave me" . . .

"Remove this man from me, good Heaven!" cried the widow. "In thy grace and mercy, give him one minute's penitence, and strike him dead!"

"It has no such purpose," he said, confronting her. "It is deaf." (185)

Martha Rudge even fears that the walls of her house will start to drip blood at the mention of her name (255).

Melodrama in *Barnaby Rudge* depicts events, situations, and forces not usually or easily encompassed within orthodox historical narratives, in particular the force of historical *trauma*. The whole novel is built around traumatic events: Solomon Daisy finds the sight of Rudge inconceivably horrific; John Willet must watch the complete destruction of his whole world when the Maypole is sacked; Haredale returns to find the Warren in ruins; Joe Willet goes to war and is wounded; Dolly Varden and Emma Haredale are abducted and fear rape; Varden is carried off to the gates of Newgate; Rudge himself is traumatized by hearing the bell again at the Warren; a single glimpse of the condemned men escaping from Newgate is 'an image of force enough to dim the whole concourse; to find itself an all-absorbing place, and to hold it ever after' (594). There is a good deal of paradox and oxymoron in the book—Dolly Varden is 'made up of . . . many contradictions' (306); Mrs Varden is at 'a higher pitch of genius than Macbeth, in respect of her ability to be wise, amazed, temperate and furious, loyal and neutral in an instant' (102)—but in trauma and intense suffering this attains peculiarly heightened states: Martha Rudge is 'guilty, and yet innocent; wrong, yet right' (256);[40] Rudge in prison is 'fearful alike, of those within the prison and of those without; of noise and silence; light and darkness; of being released and being left there to die' (586); almost the final word of the narrator on the riots is to say that many of the anti-Catholic rioters 'owned themselves to be Catholics' (698).

At such points, the novel repeatedly emphasizes the difficulty or impossibility of relying upon the evidence of one's senses, in particular the authority of visual knowledge (498). Many things occur in the riots 'like nothing we know of, even in our dreams' (587). It is John Willet, the most stupid character in the book, who insists on the importance of reason and 'the evidence of my senses' (493). The sacking of the Maypole is the ruin of them both. There is a frequent recoil from language to dumb show, in particular the gazing on silent things that are horrific or mysterious.[41] The most important of these is the face of Mrs Rudge which has 'some extraordinary capacity for expressing terror . . . the faintest and palest shadow of some look, to which an instant of intense and most unutterable horror only could have given birth' (87). Barnaby has the same look as his mother; the 'same stamp . . . seen in a picture', writes Dickens, 'would have haunted those who looked upon the canvas' (87). These looks, like Barnaby's mark, date from the terrible secret of the murder of Haredale and the simultaneous birth of Barnaby, an abyss of knowledge and understanding which Varden for all his phallic and paternal visual power cannot fathom.

Barnaby Rudge thus attempts to depict the experience of history as constitutively sublime, and to demonstrate its consequent resistance to historical narration and to assimilation to any law or causal explanation. The most significant events in the book, both private and public, are not temporal ones: for John Willet, once the Maypole is sacked, 'as far as he was concerned, old Time lay snoring, and the world stood still'; Haredale in the twenty-eight years following his brother's murder 'has never changed . . . never grown older, nor altered

---

[40] Brooks argues that paradox is a characteristic device of melodrama: *The Melodramatic Imagination*, 31.
[41] On dumbness, see ibid., 60–1.

in the least degree' (560). Spatial ordering too is contradictory: in Varden's house, for example, 'no one window seemed to have the slightest reference to anything beside itself' (76). The windows are a language or code without reference, as too is the shop: 'The shop . . . was, with reference to the first floor, where shops usually are; and there all resemblance between it and any other shops stopped short and ceased' (76). It belongs and does not belong to the category of shops, just as the windows are windows and are not.[42] It is as inconceivable as the 'monstrous and absurd' events of the riots, which, comments the narrator, 'but that we know them to be history', would be received as 'wholly fabulous and absurd' (492). There is no law to which they can be assimilated, but nevertheless they can only be spoken of by means of such a law. In a characteristic passage, Dickens tells us of Rudge, the dead man come alive, living on in prison, with 'an uneasy sense of guilt' which 'pursues him through his dreams . . . and yet is no bodily sense, but a phantom without shape, or form, or visible presence, pervading everything, but having no existence, recognisable everywhere, but nowhere seen, or touched, or met with face to face' (557–8). A presence that is not a presence, a form without form, a thing with no existence, neither an embodied sense nor a thought in the mind of a man who is continually described as if he were dead: this is so often the aporetic attempt to think or to live the historical event in the novel.

IV

This concern with the exorbitant, transgressive, and sublime is also a political matter.[43] The principal characters of the book— Gordon, Barnaby, Hugh, and Tappertit—represent not

[42] On the depiction of space in the book, see Steven Connor, 'Space, Place and the Body of Riot in *Barnaby Rudge*', in Steven Connor (ed.), *Charles Dickens: A Longman Critical Reader* (London: Longman, 1996), 211–29.

[43] This is emphasized in the vocabulary of political theory—of rights, the laws of 'nature and Providence' (45), of 'treason' (50) and 'what is godly and righteous' (512), of 'rule and rebellion' (69), of 'liberty, will and the right to speak' (68)—that permeates the private life of the novel. This is most clear in the early Maypole scenes, but also in Chester's interest in 'management' and 'diplomacy' (214) and Sim Tappertit's concern with 'the constitution' (115), 'the church, the State and everything established' (115), 'oppression', 'restoration' (115), and 'rights, privileges and immunities' (112).

archetypal psychic forces,[44] but, through their adolescence, illegitimacy, illiteracy, and idiocy, what exceeds or goes beyond the laws and conventions of political community in the novel. Barnaby both belongs and does not belong to the category, law, or the genre of the human and the responsible in the book. He is brought before the law and to the point of execution for his actions in the riots, but then is released, to become 'a ghost among the living' (711). This often leads the book to effects that at first seem sharply at odds with Dickens's apparent political affiliations. It shows, for example, that much of the existing authority in eighteenth-century England—John Willet, the country magistrate, Sir John Chester MP—is neglectful or abusive. But the motivation for revolt, even under such provocation, is consistently described as meaningless or futile, as Dickens's initial plan for the rioters to be led by three escaped Bedlamites makes clear.[45]

Thus, Dickens's most explicitly political novel of his early period also appears to be his most reactionary one. This stems mainly from the problem of reconciling his use of popular melodramatic form with a historical narrative. It is not accidental that Dickens's two most flagrantly melodramatic works are both historical novels, for it is difficult in historical fiction to create the perlocutionary dimension that is such a strong feature of his fictional radicalism. The novels wish to move and incite their readers to act, by persuading them of an abuse or outrage that must be remedied, but this is particularly difficult to achieve with an historical narrative. The country magistrate is one of the most obnoxious representations of social and political authority in Dickens's work, but he is not presented as a living abuse to the novel's readers, and the rhetoric of the book does

[44] 'Dennis the hangman is a kind of super-ego . . . Hugh . . . is the id . . . Barnaby is a paradigm of the defective ego': Marcus, *Dickens: From Pickwick to Dombey*, 211.

[45] Forster, *Life of Dickens*, I, 142. If not mad, then theatrical. There is frequent recourse to theatrical metaphors for understanding history in the book. Dennis thinks of the gibbet as a kind of stage: 'I've heard a eloquence on them boards' (591); Chester is an 'actor' (680); Barnaby is 'an actor in a show' (682); Willet watches the destruction of the Maypole 'as if it were some play or entertainment' (497); Sir John is 'like . . . a weary actor' (680); the Warren seems the 'predestined theatre' (154) for the murder. Tappertit, above all, lives his life as a collection of theatrical and literary conventions: ' "Lead on," said Mr Tappertit, with a gloomy majesty' (109).

not try to persuade us to do anything about him. The rhetoric of rage and change, which is so powerfully at work against the abuses of Squeers at Dotheboys and Scrooge at the counting-house, is not used in this novel, but is substituted by the rhetoric of prophecy. *A Tale of Two Cities* ends with Carton's prophecy of a better world; here there are only the less climactic and less plausible prophetic curses of Hugh on the society that has created him: ' "Upon these human shambles, I, who never raised this hand in prayer till now, call down the wrath of God! On that black tree, of which I am the ripened fruit, I do invoke the curse of all its victims past, and present, and to come" ' (695). The endings to Dickens's novels characteristically depict a form of restoration and restitution, but few are as full as this story's last view of the Varden household, a scene in which 'nothing was forgotten and everything by some means or other brought back to a conclusion' (716). Barnaby, after an offstage peripety, is restored to his mother, Miggs is ritually expelled, and Varden at this point becomes little short of the embodied Logos itself, 'the rosiest, cosiest, merriest, heartiest, best-contented old Buck in England . . . the sun that shone upon them all: the centre of the system: the source of light, heat, life and frank enjoyment in the bright household world' (714). At such moments, the novel seems at its most conservative, ending the book with a deeply deterministic conclusion which starkly poses law against madness, chaos against order, and sees no middle way between them. *Barnaby Rudge*, as melodrama does, seems at such points to 'sacralise Law itself' in 'a perfect justice of reward and punishment'.[46]

But there are also forces working sharply against this logic, transcoding the serious material of the book into other, more absurd forms. One of the funniest occurs when Tappertit escapes Varden's house to go to a meeting of the Apprentice Knights. Pocketing his large key, he enters a 'blind court' (108) and is met at the door by Stagg (who appears later as the persecutor of Barnaby and his mother, and the sinister agent of the elder Rudge), who is blind. When Tappertit 'eyes him over', the

---

[46] 'Melodrama must at last sacralise Law itself, a perfect justice of punishment and reward, expulsion and recognition': Brooks, *The Melodramatic Imagination*, 204. Dickens will later radically transform melodrama into a future-oriented form in *A Christmas Carol*.

blind man exclaims '"He's got his eyes on me . . . I feel em though I can't see em"', whereupon Tappertit agrees to remove his 'ocular screw' from Stagg, who then falls to his knees and, in a passage which in any anthology of the comedy of legs and wooden legs would be rivalled only by Silas Wegg's wooden erection in *Our Mutual Friend* and Pecksniff's alcoholic effusion in *Martin Chuzzlewit*, gently smooths the calves of Tappertit, exclaiming: '"That I had but eyes . . . That I had but eyes, to look upon these twin invaders of domestic peace!"' (111). Tappertit affects to be embarrassed at this effusion, at which Stagg continues: '"When I touch my own afterwards . . . I hate 'em. Comparatively speaking, they've no more shape than wooden legs, besides these models of my noble captain's"' (111). He later protests with tears in his eyes, on hearing Tappertit dance, that 'he had never truly felt his blindness until that moment' (118). Here Dickens puts into play the Oedipal material that the novel elsewhere takes so seriously; tragedy returns as farce.

More disturbing is the novel's wish to establish relations between the violence of popular insurrection on the one hand and paternal violence against children on the other, and its presentation of the continuing force of the ghosts of those violences in the present. This frequently leads to a deeply paradoxical depiction of the law in the book, the epitome of which is the appearance of Dennis the hangman, that 'representative man' (453) and 'functionary of the law' (568) at Newgate, into which he breaks, not in order to free the condemned prisoners but to gloat over their fate. Revolt is not outside the law here, but enacted through its central representative, just as Chester as an MP foments the violence in a paradoxical legality of violence.

These two evasions or transcodings of the paternal law come together in a key scene of the most destructive and violent relationship of a father and son in the book, that of Joe and John Willet. Before Joe rebels, his father has restricted his activity by placing him, as he puts it, 'upon his patrole . . . not to leave the premises' (284). 'Patrole' is a strange word, one like Derrida's 'différance', which only matters when it is written down.[47]

---

[47] Jacques Derrida, *Margins of Philosophy* (Brighton: Harvester Wheatsheaf, 1982), 3–27.

Dickens dwells on this strange coinage, mispronunciation, or invention by the elder Willet, a linguistic deviancy or wandering designed to prevent wandering and deviancy, a speech act that both works—Joe stays at home—and, as J. L. Austin might have put it, 'misfires', for it causes Joe's wandering and wounding.[48] Of course, what Willet wants to say is that his son is on parole, on his word, a word that is also a deed, like naming a ship or saying 'I will' in the marriage ceremony. Yet the word never arrives safe and sound, but goes off on a sort of parabola or tangent, set off by itself, as if it were on patrol indeed, and comes back the same but different, like a man (like Joe Willet) who has lost an arm. Patrole, parole, as J. Hillis Miller has shown, is another form of parabola, or parable.[49] Dickens's parable of history, which includes Joe's parabola and his father's, is also a speech act with a good deal of deviancy and wandering, both in and from this story of a father and son and all stories of fathers and sons.[50] Dickens here is out on patrole, on and off his word and his honour, way ahead of us, never coming back, quite out of patrole.

A good deal goes back to fathers at the end of this story: Gabriel Varden returns as 'the centre of the system' of his household; Barnaby, if only briefly, meets his father; Joe Willet returns to create a second Maypole Inn like his father's. There is a restoration of property, possession, and inheritance, and a return to the brutal enforcement of the law in the executions of Hugh and Dennis,[51] but it is by no means a full restoration: John Willet ends up speechless;[52] there is no revelation of Hugh's paternity and no real reconciliation between the Willets and Chesters, father and son; Barnaby and his father fail to meet in meeting and do not share a common death. Each historical and

---

[48] J. L. Austin, *Philosophical Papers* (Oxford: Clarendon, 1979), 238.

[49] J. Hillis Miller, *Tropes, Parables, Performatives* (Brighton: Harvester Wheatsheaf, 1990), ix, 147–8.

[50] In the middle of writing *Barnaby Rudge* Dickens had attempted to put his own father 'on patrole', on his word and honour, not to stay at home, but to keep away from it. See Pilgrim, II, 225.

[51] '[T]he classical historical novel . . . realised the *general laws of large epic* in a model form': Lukács, *The Historical Novel*, 422. 'The truth that speaks (to) itself within the logocentric circle is the discourse of *what goes back to the father*': Derrida, *Dissemination*, 48–9.

[52] See Natalie McKnight, *Idiots, Madmen and Other Prisoners in Dickens* (New York: St Martin's, 1993), 90.

quasi-Oedipal relation is interrupted, turned aside, diverted—
by blind men, hanging, wounding, death, and patroles. And this
is true also of the novel itself. A good deal goes back in *Barnaby
Rudge* to the genre of the historical novel and its father, Scott,
but much more escapes and evades that filiation. *Barnaby
Rudge*, like the shop in Varden's house and its windows, is both
an historical novel and not, and resemblance between it and
other historical novels, to that genre, at a certain point stops
short and ceases. This does not of course stop it from being an
historical novel.[53] Like Dennis the hangman in Newgate, it is
both of and outside the law, belonging to it and breaking it in
the same ambiguous gestures. G. K. Chesterton, seeking not
quite to dismiss the book, gets it, as he does so often, right: 'It
is no more a historical novel than Sim's secret league was a political movement.'[54] No more, and no less. And what remains at
the very end of the novel is nothing but a parasitic beast, a
raven, history's Grip, who imitates or doubles human speech in
empty, sinister words without human intent, which repeat and
re-repeat themselves, in and out of this and other contexts,
saying ' "I'm a devil, I'm a devil, *I'm* a devil" ' (738). It is something quite meaningless but also thoroughly evil, both the end
to a great historical novel and an absurd little bit of mimicry.
What the Dickens—what the devil—is going on here?

---

[53] On genre, see Jacques Derrida, 'The Law of Genre', in Derek Attridge (ed.),
Acts of Literature (London: Routledge, 1992), 223–52. On Dickens and genre, see
J. Hillis Miller, 'The Genres of *A Christmas Carol*', *The Dickensian*, 431: 89, 3,
(Winter 1993), 193–206.

[54] G. K. Chesterton, *Charles Dickens* (London: Methuen, 1906), 125: 'but they
are both beautiful creations'.

CHAPTER SEVEN

The Genealogy of Monsters:
Martin Chuzzlewit

Martin Chuzzlewit is the strangest, most demanding, and funniest of Dickens's earlier fictions, and one of the most important of all nineteenth-century novels. The title-page emphatically tells us that the book is going to be about families and inheritance: 'The Life and Adventures of Martin Chuzzlewit, his relatives, friends and enemies . . . showing, moreover, who inherited the family plate, who came in for the silver spoons, and who for the wooden ladles. The whole forming a complete key to the House of Chuzzlewit.'[1] The first chapter seems to fulfil this promise with its lengthy genealogy of the Chuzzlewit family since the time of the Creation. Yet, in fact, the nature of inheritance and family obligation are often of only marginal concern to the book that follows, and several members of the Chuzzlewit family appear only once, then to disappear for good. This contradiction between the framing material of the title-page and first chapter on the one hand and the rest of the novel on the other, the simultaneous assertion and denial that *Martin Chuzzlewit* is about families and inheritance, is a form of paradox or oxymoron. There is a good number of such paradoxical or oxymoronic assertions in the novel, not least when it comes to matters of personal identity: we are asked to believe, for example, that apparently quite different characters—Tigg Montague and Montague Tigg, Bailey Junior and Young Bailey—share the same identity, and that two quite different people—the Martins Chuzzlewit—can share the same name. Aside from the profoundly innocent and deluded Tom Pinch, to be a person in this novel is to be a persona and to possess a character is to wear a mask. In old

[1] Charles Dickens, *Martin Chuzzlewit*, ed. Margaret Cardwell (Oxford: World's Classics, 1982), ii. All references will be to this edition and placed in the text.

Martin's deception, Mark Tapley's virtue, Jonas Chuzzlewit's courtship, the Anglo-Bengalee Disinterested Loan and Life Insurance (or Assurance) Company, and above all in Seth Pecksniff and Sarah Gamp, character becomes a play of masks, social relationships a set of displaced identifications, and the world a vertiginous play of personification and apostrophe.

After the allegory of *The Old Curiosity Shop* and the uncanny history of *Barnaby Rudge*, *Martin Chuzzlewit* seems to represent Dickens's return to the depiction of contemporary society in the manner of *Oliver Twist* or *Nicholas Nickleby*, the novel it superficially most resembles. But the action in *Martin Chuzzlewit* is liberated much more fully than that of any of its predecessors from the constraints of the past, and its characters in consequence seem to inhabit a world existing within a continuous and hyperbolic present tense.[2] There is no movement backwards in the narration, for example, to reveal deep causes of plot or hidden springs of motivation, as when we learned that Monks was brother to Oliver Twist or that Smike was Ralph Nickleby's son; the action in *Martin Chuzzlewit* is forward-moving nearly all the time. Even the main mystery of the plot—Jonas's seeming murder of his father—occurs within the time of the narration. This is only one of several ways in which *Martin Chuzzlewit* shows its affinity with later novels, in particular those central to literary modernism. The questions that lie at the heart of the book—the nature of a commodified and self-commodifying culture and the role of finance capital within it; the possibilities of secrecy, surveillance, and detection within modern urban space; the radical autonomy of the self and its capacity for re-invention within such a world; the genealogy of ethical behaviour in such conditions—become the themes and topics of a vast later literature. In the shape of those two representative figures, Gamp and Pecksniff, working-class woman and bourgeois man, in the representative institution of the Anglo-Bengalee and in the representative nation of the modern world, the United States, Dickens gives us one of the first and most prescient of modern novels, and a key harbinger of

---

[2] 'The arena of *Martin Chuzzlewit* is the present, a present which is irrevocably cut off from the past': J. Hillis Miller, *Charles Dickens: The World of his Novels* (Cambridge: Harvard University Press, 1959), 103.

modernism. No doubt this is why it is so disturbing, and has so often been disliked.[3]

I

The first chapter of Martin Chuzzlewit (which purports to be a genealogy of the Chuzzlewit family, going back to Adam and Eve) is one of the most remarkable of any novel. As puzzling as its unsettling, almost nihilistic, energy is the contempt with which it has been treated by most critics of the book.[4] It is a strange hors d'oeuvre or preface to a novel, subverting as it does patriarchal filiation, class identity, reference in language, historical understanding, and the distinction between the human and the animal. It seems to propose that history is either a matter of bad puns and misread evidence, or of oral tradition, rewritten by the ignorance, folly, or will-to-power of the present, and which exists only to tell stories of 'violence and vagabondism' (1), suffering and starvation, through bizarre catachreses and demented paronomasia. The chapter is concerned with the interpretation of documents and how, with 'the exercise of a little ingenious labour on the part of a commentator' (3), anything can be made to mean anything else. It claims to have a great belief in 'just interpretation . . . authority of all the

---

[3] 'Never again would he compose in so slapdash a way, be so prodigal with his material, or allow himself to waste his genius instead of taxing and extending it': John Lucas, The Melancholy Man (London: Methuen, 1970), 113. See also, for the earlier critical reception, George H. Ford, Dickens and his Readers (New York: Norton, 1965), 44; Philip Collins (ed.), Dickens: The Critical Heritage (London: Routledge and Kegan Paul, 1971), 186–97.

[4] George Gissing, Charles Dickens: A Critical Study (London: Gresham, 1902), 55, calls it 'a very dull, long-drawn piece of ridicule'; and Barbara Hardy a 'tiresome exercise in sarcasm': 'Martin Chuzzlewit', in John Gross and Gabriel Pearson (eds), Dickens and the Twentieth Century (London: Routledge and Kegan Paul, 1962), 107–20. Sylvère Mood, who assembles a large number of disparaging remarks in his Martin Chuzzlewit (London: George Allen and Unwin, 1985), 18–19, calls it 'ponderous facetiousness . . . mediocre stuff'. More sympathetic accounts are by Alexander Welsh, From Copyright to Copperfield (Cambridge: Harvard University Press, 1987), Myron Magnet, Dickens and the Social Order (Philadelphia: University of Pennsylvania Press, 1985), 204–13, and V. S. Pritchett, 'The Comic World of Charles Dickens', in George H. Ford and Lauriat Lane Jr (eds), The Dickens Critics (Ithaca: Cornell University Press, 1961), 323. See also Kathleen Wales, 'The Claims of Kinship: The Opening Chapter of Martin Chuzzlewit', The Dickensian, 83 (1987), 169–79.

books . . . proof . . . documentary evidence . . . testimony' (3–5), but it does so simply to show how absurd such interpretation, authority, evidence, and testimony is. It is, in short, a deconstruction, or Dickenstruction, of some central beliefs and assumptions not just of Victorian culture and our own, but of Western metaphysics more generally. Causes do not produce effects here, for example, but effects causes. The Chuzzlewits create their 'aristocratic' ancestors through misunderstanding and falsification, as we are told in the spirit more of a comic Nietzsche than a Fielding.[5] History is a matter of absurd interpretation and bad puns stretched over a meaningless catalogue of accidents, vice, poverty, and violence. Interpretation is here, as Nietzsche put it, a matter of '[f]orcing, adjusting, abbreviating, omitting, padding, inventing, falsifying, and whatever else is of the *essence* of interpreting'.[6] Dianne Sadoff has argued that Dickens 'associated writing with figurative fatherhood', but here writing is a force not of fatherhood and lawful patriarchal succession, but of wild dissemination both of family ties and of meaning and significance in language and history.[7]

The title-page of the book (which promises 'a complete key to the House of Chuzzlewit') is as deceptive as its first chapter. It promises a story about inheritance, that complex knot where law, property, families, and psychic needs meet and quarrel, but the novel gives us almost nothing of this sort: the Chuzzlewit name is squandered and spread abroad on minor and trivial characters, such as George Chuzzlewit, whom the author intro-

---

[5] On parallels with Fielding, see Monod, *Martin Chuzzlewit*, 19. For Nietzsche, compare Friedrich Nietzsche, *On The Genealogy of Morals*, trans. Walter Kaufmann and R. J. Hollingdale, in *On the Genealogy of Morals and Ecce Homo*, ed. Walter Kaufmann (New York: Random House, 1969), 77:

'the cause of the origin of a thing and its eventual utility . . . lie worlds apart; whatever exists, having somehow come into being, is again and again reinterpreted to new ends, taken over, transformed, and redirected by some power superior to it; all events in the organic world are a subduing, a *becoming master*, and all subduing and becoming master involves a fresh interpretation, an adaptation through which any previous "meaning" and "purpose" are necessarily obscured or even obliterated . . . the entire history of a "thing", an organ, a custom can in this way be a continuous sign-chain of ever new interpretations and adaptations.'

[6] Nietzsche, *On The Genealogy of Morals*, 151.
[7] Dianne F. Sadoff, *Monsters of Affection: Dickens, Eliot and Brontë on Fatherhood* (Baltimore: Johns Hopkins University Press, 1982), 38. On dissemination and the father, see Jacques Derrida, 'Dissemination', in *Dissemination* (London: Athlone, 1981), 287–359.

duces and then promptly forgets; the plot wanders off in pseudo-intrigues and a pseudo-murder; the name of the central character does not even know to whom it belongs, certain only that it does not belong to the father, but to the father's father or his grandson, that strangely doubled paternal relation, marked by a doubled name. John Lucas criticizes Dickens for allowing his characters to 'take over' the novel and 'upset' and 'destroy' it, like insurrectionists in the streets or lunatics taking over the asylum.[8] Celebrating the 'ungovernable sense of life' in Dickens's novels, Chesterton sees Dickens's characters as 'spoilt children' who 'shake the house like heavy and shouting school-boys'. The rebellious, insurgent characters of *Martin Chuzzle-wit*, knowing no law but language, disseminate and scatter the novel's plot and major themes, as they 'smash the story to pieces like so much furniture'.[9]

The task of interpretation, like that of family history, is to control issue, whether textual or bodily, but the issue of the preface, and the issues of the text, are not easily ordered or restrained. There are attempts to control both children and inter-pretation in the novel, but as the relationship of Martin Chuzzlewit and Martin Chuzzlewit asks, how does one control, not issue, but the issue of issue, the child who is known as a grand-child? As young Martin says of his quarrel with old Martin, 'words engendered words' (85), just as children engender chil-dren and interpretation interpretations. The first chapter shows the Chuzzlewits seeking to control inheritance, on the one hand, by making their ancestors what they want them to be (creating, retrospectively, the causes of the effects that they are now) and, on the other, by controlling their children by passing on their false and misleading stories. It is thus strikingly different from the melodramatic or mythical social world that we are often told Dickens creates, a world that 'consolidates the middle class, its identity and values'.[10] This chapter, by contrast, tells, and fails to tell, a different kind of story, and permits and imposes in the process very different pleasures and responsibilities on its inter-preting readers. The original epigraph to the book was to have been 'Your homes the scene, yourselves the actors, here!' until it

[8] Lucas, *The Melancholy Man*, 118.
[9] G. K. Chesterton, *Charles Dickens* (London: Methuen, 1906), 14–15.
[10] Christina Crosby, *The Ends of History: The Victorians and 'The Woman Question'* (London: Routledge, 1991), 96.

was censored by Dickens's friend John Forster.[11] It is as disturbing a swipe as Eliot's borrowing from Baudelaire in *The Waste Land*: ' "You! hypocrite lecteur!—mon semblable,—mon frère!" '[12] Chapter 1 subverts many of the forms of historical and patriarchal obligation and indebtedness that were so important to *Barnaby Rudge*. There are no all-powerful fathers here, or oppressed and rebellious sons. There are, it is true, the relation of Jonas and Anthony Chuzzlewit and old Martin's conflict with his grandson, but the novel recognizes how fictitious familial relations are, how much they rest on narrative, linguistic, and figurative operations. The preface to the novel does see the 'sordid coarseness and brutality' of Jonas Chuzzlewit as 'the legitimate issue of the father upon whom those vices are seen to recoil' (719), and Dickens even uses a phrase to describe the power of inheritance and upbringing—'As we sow, we reap'— that echoes a favourite phrase of his own improvident father.[13] But the novel has a much richer and more contradictory sense of both financial and familial inheritance: this is most clear in the plot's central thread—the bizarre conceived-but-not-committed murder of Anthony by Jonas, a sort of murder 'under erasure', an Oedipal murder sure enough, but one that is simultaneously enacted and disavowed by the novel, just as the first chapter simultaneously asserts that the idea that we inherit things from our family history is absurd, and that it is true.[14]

The novel begins as bourgeois satire, guying aristocratic affectation:

It is remarkable that as there was, in the oldest family of which we have any record, a murderer and a vagabond, so we never fail to meet,

---

[11] John Forster, *The Life of Charles Dickens*, ed. A. J. Hoppé (London: Dent, 1966), I, 296.

[12] T. S. Eliot, 'The Waste Land', in *The Complete Poems and Plays of T. S. Eliot* (London: Faber and Faber, 1969), 63.

[13] Peter Ackroyd, *Dickens* (London: Sinclair-Stevenson, 1990), 13; 'If *Martin Chuzzlewit* is indeed a novel about selfishness . . . then surely one can interpret it in the light of a remark he made a little later to the effect that "the greater part of my observation of parents and children has shewn selfishness in the first, almost invariably" ' (419).

[14] Disavowal is Freud's term for the simultaneous recognition and denial of some (usually traumatic) event or thing. Psychologically it is a matter of 'holding two incompatible positions at the same time': J. Laplanche and J. B Pontalis, *The Language of Psychoanalysis* (London: Karnac, 1988), 119, and is akin to the rhetorical figures of paradox and oxymoron.

in the records of all old families, with innumerable repetitions of the same phase of character. Indeed it may be laid down as a general principle, that the more extended the ancestry, the greater the amount of violence and vagabondism. (1)

English aristocrats, like the Chuzzlewits, are the 'unconscious inheritors' (52) of a tradition of conceit, violence, hypocrisy, and theft. But the satire reaches well beyond its immediate target of aristocratic pretension ('the immense superiority of the house to the rest of mankind' (1)) to a much wider subversion of the norms of social being and historical understanding. Michel Foucault has written of a 'parodic' use of history by Nietzsche that 'opposes the theme of history as reminiscence or recognition', and Dickens too gives us parodic history which misreads and misrecognizes itself and the past.[15] Families exist through their ability to repeat themselves in succeeding generations in different form, and to recognize themselves in that repetition. This is largely accomplished through acts of speech, writing, and interpretation. In the preface, this is seen as an absurd and fatal affair, the erection of a 'goodly tumulus . . . above the Family grave' (5). Within the Chuzzlewit tumulus, we find a bleakly funny account of human culture in which history is merely a displaced, absurd set of repetitions of the will-to-power, in which they (and, by implication, we) all behave (as Dickens suggests through his invocation of J. F. Blumenbach and Lord Monboddo) like pigs and monkeys. The Chuzzlewits are poor, pretentious, and grasping; there is no possibility of their ever knowing or saying anything true about themselves. The chapter releases a set of disturbing questions and suggestions that run through the rest of the novel in the many 'counterparts and prototypes' (5) of the Chuzzlewits: the concern with mythical and misleading origins will be later seen in Pecksniff's self-presentation as Adam (331) and in the 'grim domains' (325) of Eden; strange and misinterpreted fragments of letters and documents surface throughout the book. Together they build a novel which comes to centre on two deaths, a murder and a suicide. Here at the threshold of the story is placed not the human or the living, nor true meaning and interpretation, but

---

[15] Michel Foucault, 'Nietzsche, Genealogy, History', in Paul Rabinow (ed.), *The Foucault Reader* (Harmondsworth: Penguin, 1984), 93.

a sort of tumulus or sepulchre of falsification and death in the shape of documents ravaged by moths, 'the general registers of the insect world'. It is not a reassuring opening, nor is this a consoling fiction, which may be one reason why so many people defend themselves so strongly against it, but it is a fitting start to such a wild, free, and funny modern novel. Steven Marcus has written of the force of language in Dickens and its kinship to the Logos, the divine and creating word; but this chapter and novel give us a fallen, un-creating, disseminating word, a text full of deceit, death, hilarity, absence, and aporia.[16]

II

Martin Chuzzlewit was written in 1843–4, not long before Charles Baudelaire's clarion call of modern art in his essays on the Paris salons of 1845 and 1846. There are striking parallels between the two works, which lie in their shared sense of a break in tradition, 'of the discontinuity of times and . . . a feeling . . . of vertigo in the face of the passing moment' and of the important place of the city in these changes.[17] Baudelaire's Paris is a very different city from Dickens's London but, like Baudelaire, *Martin Chuzzlewit* finds 'the life of our city . . . rich in poetic and marvellous subjects':[18]

As there are a vast number of people in the huge metropolis of England who rise up every morning, not knowing where their heads will rest at night, so there are a multitude who shooting arrows over houses as

[16] Steven Marcus, 'Language into Structure: Pickwick Revisited', in Harold Bloom (ed.), *Twentieth Century Views: Charles Dickens* (New York: Chelsea House, 1982), 132.

[17] Michel Foucault, 'What is Enlightenment?', in *The Foucault Reader*, 39. Charles Baudelaire, 'The Salon of 1845' and 'The Salon of 1846', in *Art in Paris*, trans. and ed. Jonathan Mayne (London: Phaidon, 1965). See also Walter Benjamin, *Charles Baudelaire: A Lyric Poet in the Era of High Capitalism* (London: Verso, 1983); Marshall Berman, *All that is Solid Melts into Air: The Experience of Modernity* (London: Verso, 1982); T. J. Clark, *The Absolute Bourgeois: Artists and Politics in France 1848–1851* (London: Thames and Hudson, 1982).

[18] Baudelaire 'The Salon of 1846', in *Art in Paris*, 119. There is an extensive literature on Dickens's representation of the city. See in particular Miller, *Charles Dickens: The World of his Novels*, xv–xvi; Raymond Williams, *The Country and the City* (London: Paladin, 1975), 189–201; Alexander Welsh, *The City of Dickens* (Oxford: Clarendon, 1971), and Michael Hollington (ed.), *Charles Dickens: Critical Assessments*, IV (Sussex: Helm Information, 1995), 277–337.

their daily business, never know on whom they fall. Mr Nadgett might have passed Tom Pinch ten thousand times; might even have been quite familiar with his face, his name, pursuits and character; yet never once had dreamed that Tom had any interest in any act or mystery of his. Tom might have done the like by him, of course. But the same private man out of all the men alive, was in the mind of each at the same moment; was prominently connected, though in a different manner, with the day's adventures of both; and formed, when they passed each other in the street, the one absorbing topic of conversation. (505)

This is a remarkably early, new understanding of the city and urban space. It is not simply that the city is random and massive, full of anonymous faces and bodies, but that it is also an essentially uncanny place. The city is uncanny because it troubles and disturbs so many of the distinctions and definitions by which we understand ourselves and the world. Nadgett might be familiar to Tom, who may have seen him a thousand times, but he is also radically unfamiliar. City life undoes the distinctions between the known and the unknown, just as it undoes those between private and public, chance and destiny, mystery and act. Although there is an attempt to control and understand the city's strangeness through Nadgett's ability to follow and understand Jonas's murderous plotting, this simply displaces and intensifies the uncanniness, both because Nadgett's ability to track down Jonas is itself uncannily successful, and because the murder and its pursuit lead Jonas to a state of mind in which he becomes his own self-divided and uncanny double: 'his own ghost and phantom . . . at once the haunting spirit and the haunted man' (619).

This passage also shows the novel's prescience in understanding how important surveillance is within modernity.[19] Nadgett, the first detective in an English novel, working for Tigg, financier and master of fictive capital, has near-supernatural powers of observation: every button on Nadgett's coat 'might have been an eye: he saw so much' (505). Such surveillance, the ability to penetrate the mystery of the city, comes at the price of the even deeper mystery of Nadgett's own profoundly secret self and need to 'preserve his own mystery' (505). 'Nothing' has an interest to Nadgett 'that's not a secret' (509).

[19] For Michel Foucault's account of surveillance as a defining feature of modern society, see his *Discipline and Punish* (Harmondsworth: Penguin, 1979).

He both belongs to the community of the novel, indeed plays a crucial role within it, and yet does not belong to it at all. The company that employs him, the Anglo-Bengalee, has no reserves whatsoever; it exists simply as expenditure, display, and performance. Nadgett by contrast is all reserve, circulating nothing, spending nothing, saying nothing, locking away whatever (if anything) he might be in his own vault. The city and Nadgett's surveillance are not reducible to a matter of social discipline, for they embody a much more radical change in the nature of subjective experience, aesthetic practice, and ethical life. Surveillance here both reinforces and creates the uncanniness of the city and of modern life. It may produce some transparency—we do after all learn that it is Jonas who has committed the murder—but such social clarity and light on crime is shadowed by effects that do not recognize the distinction between light and dark, observation and being observed, or self and other.

Nowhere is this more clear than on the roof of Todgers's, at the heart of the urban labyrinth (which is not a heart at all, merely the place where the Pecksniffs end up) where the transformations that the city wreaks on subjective experience become dizzying:

Whoever climbed to this observatory, was stunned at first from having knocked his head against the little door in coming out . . . The man who was mending a pen at an upper window over the way, became of paramount importance in the scene, and made a blank in it, ridiculously disproportionate in its extent, when he retired. The gambols of a piece of cloth upon the dyer's pole had far more interest for the moment than all the changing motions of the crowd. Yet even while the looker-on felt angry with himself for this, and wondered how it was, the tumult swelled into a roar; the host of objects seemed to thicken and expand a hundredfold; and after gazing round him, quite scared, he turned into Todgers's again, much more rapidly than he came out; and ten to one he told M. Todgers afterwards that if he hadn't done so, he would certainly have come into the street by the shortest cut: that is to say, head-foremost. (115)

The man mending a pen is of 'paramount importance' to the scene, and like the phallus in Jacques Lacan's influential account of Freud, makes a ridiculously disproportionate blank when it stages its disappearance.[20] But this (absent, departed) centre of

---

[20] Jacques Lacan, 'The Signification of the Phallus', in *Ecrits* (London: Tavistock, 1977), 281–91.

signification is only a part of the jaunty, ghostly phallicism of the whole passage—in the man, the pen, the dyer's pole, and the swelling tumult. And when it stages the simultaneous pro-liferation of urban objects and the disappearance of the 'para-mount' object in it, the effect is vertiginous, like a painting without perspective or stable point of view.[21] Why should this man and his pen be of such importance? In one way, it is simply a quotidian detail, but it draws attention to the fact that this description of the city exists as writing, and only as writing. The man mending a pen is preparing to write, engaged not in writing but the material preparation for the act of inscription. Through this figure and its absence, which is also the figure of writing's simultaneous absence and presence, its materiality and non-materiality, the perception of the urban scene becomes a vertigo of displacements, a dream or haunting.

In the most important passage of 'The Salon of 1845', Baude-laire speaks of 'the heroism of *modern life*' and invokes 'the true painter . . . who can snatch its epic quality from life today, and can make us see and understand . . . how great and poetic we are in our cravats and patent-leather boots'.[22] Dickens too is concerned with the potentially heroic in modern life, and like Baudelaire wishes to link it to the fact of the modern city. For Baudelaire, the task of the modern artist was to make moder-nity heroic: 'to extract from fashion whatever element it may contain of poetry within history . . . to distil the eternal from the transitory . . . by modernity I mean the ephemeral, the fugitive, the contingent; the half of art whose other half is the eternal and the immutable'.[23] Dickens too attempts to unite the eternal

---

[21] Compare Baudelaire in 'The Painter of Modern Life', in Charles Baudelaire, *The Painter of Modern Life and Other Essays* (London: Phaidon, 1964), 16:

'An artist with a perfect sense of form but one accustomed to relying above all on his memory and his imagination will find himself at the mercy of a riot of details all clamouring for justice with the fury of a mob in love with equality. All justice is trampled under foot; all harmony sacrificed and destroyed; many a trifle assumes vast proportions; many a triviality usurps the attention. The more our artist turns an impartial eye on detail, the greater is the state of anarchy. Whether he be long-sighted or short-sighted, all hierarchy and all subordination vanishes.'

On the much-discussed Dickens passage, see Dorothy van Ghent, 'Dickens: the View from Todgers', in Ford and Lane (eds), *The Dickens Critics*, 213–32 and Miller, *Charles Dickens: The World of his Novels*, 112–13.

[22] Baudelaire, 'The Salon of 1845', 32.

[23] Baudelaire, 'The Painter of Modern Life', 12.

and the temporal, but in more mobile and ironic form. It is the preposterous Tigg, for example, who tells us that 'the peculiarity of my friend Slyme is that he is always waiting round the corner. He is perpetually round the corner' (43). At such moments, *Martin Chuzzlewit*'s characters are determined to live for ever, not to accept the petty restrictions of a fallen world, but to attain a life transcendent and ideal. Chesterton half-captures this quality when he sees Dickens as 'a mythologist rather than a novelist . . . [who] did not always manage to make characters men, but . . . always managed, at the least, to make them gods'.[24] This desire to be a modern heroic character is ironized by the novel, laid bare, like a Brechtian device, by the comic characters—Gamp, Slyme, Tigg—who both movingly articulate it and make it absurd.

When Mark Tapley and young Martin return from America, they appear magically transformed:

When they had feasted, as two grateful-tempered giants might have done . . . [e]ven the street was made a fairy street, by being half-hidden in an atmosphere of steak, and strong, stout, stand-up English beer. For on the window-glass hung such a mist, that Mr Tapley was obliged to rise and wipe it with his handkerchief, before the passengers appeared like common mortals. (472)

We have good reason to think of Mark and Martin as genuinely heroic at this point—they have, after all, survived the hell-hole of Eden. More usually, the book shows heroism to be more bathetic than sublime. Heroism easily fails in this novel, relying as it does on luck, chance, and others' willingness to comply with it. One of the most absurd, but also dementedly heroic, characters of the book is Augustus Moddle, Charity Pecksniff's fiancé, the epitome of the failed modern hero, who aggrandizes his emotions by screwing them up to an operatic pitch: rejected by Mercy, he informs Mrs Todgers 'that the sun had set upon him; that the billows had rolled over him; that the car of Juggernaut had crushed him; and also that the deadly Upas tree of Java had blighted him. His name was Moddle' (439). More

[24] At times Chesterton completely endorses the metaphysical or spiritual interpretation of Dickens's characters, as when he tells us that 'Mr Pickwick was a fairy', but at others is closer to Baudelaire's sense of modern character: Pickwick is 'human enough to wander, human enough to wonder, but still sustained . . . by that hint of divinity': Chesterton, *Charles Dickens*, 91.

uneasily poised between heroism and absurdity is Mrs Todgers herself:

Commercial gentlemen and gravy had tried Mrs Todgers's temper; the main chance . . . had taken a firm hold on Mrs Todgers's attention. But . . . [w]hen boarding house accounts are balanced with all other ledgers, and the books of the Recording Angel are made up for ever, perhaps there may be seen an entry to thy credit, lean Mrs Todgers, which shall make thee beautiful! (502)

The climax of this ironic heroism is the spectacle of young Bailey transformed into Mr Bailey Junior, who:

eclipsed both time and space, cheated beholders of their senses, and worked on their belief in defiance of all natural laws. He walked along the tangible and real stones of Holborn Hill; and yet he winked the winks, and thought the thoughts, and did the deeds, and said the sayings, of an ancient man, he became an inexplicable creature: a breeched and booted Sphinx. (363)

An ironic Sphinx and a real small modern hero who, by demanding an unnecessary shave, eclipses time and space, ends sense-certainty, and hilariously defies and confounds natural law and explanation.

The depiction of modernity is not simply a matter of ironic heroism and a particular kind of city life, for the novel is also very interested in finance and credit, in particular the relationship between social and economic life. Nadgett, for example, 'belonged to a class; a race peculiar to the city; who are secrets as profound to one another, as they are to the rest of mankind' (386). Nadgett is part of the city, but also part of the City, the mercantile and financial centre of the country and Empire. He carries 'contradictory cards' defining his identity, but all of them—'coal merchant . . . wine merchant . . . commission-agent . . . collector . . . accountant' (386)—are forms of financial and trading activity. Nadgett's multiple identities demonstrate both how important economic transactions are to the novel, and how they are also profoundly fictional in form. Nadgett's identity is not simply an assumed or disguised one, as Tigg's is; it is a complete absence of identity, an abyss of meaning without intent. Tigg, the great secondary reviser of himself, is all ornament, his place of business a temple of the fetishes of capital, his rhetorical and social gifts a matter of public display; Nadgett, by contrast, has no ornament and almost no spoken language, quietly going about his sinister business. This is not simply a personal thing, as the satire in these sections is dedicated to showing the fictional nature of all capitalistic enterprise. As in good business practice ever since, the Anglo-Bengalee's public façade tells us almost nothing of its real dirty work. The circulation of debt and credit is a matter of performance and fiction, in which Tigg 'the great capitalist' (374) is merely an actor and performer, who works in the company's 'inventive and poetical department' (372). We have already seen Dickens's interest in institutions in *Nicholas Nickleby*, but *Chuzzlewit* enacts a more profoundly radical understanding of the 'light-hearted little fiction' (374) that is entrepreneurial capitalism.

The novel plays and puns throughout on central terms of financial exchange, most noticeably in Mark Tapley's search for 'credit' throughout the book, a very different credit from the kind of 'credit' that the Anglo-Bengalee rests on. The word 'capital' is played with too:

"It was a capital thought, wasn't it?"

"What was a capital thought, David?" Mr Montague inquired.

"The Anglo-Bengalee," tittered the secretary.

"The Anglo-Bengalee Disinterested Loan and Life Insurance Company is rather a capital concern, I hope, David," said Montague.

"Capital indeed!" cried the secretary, with another laugh—"in one sense."

"In the only important sense," observed the chairman; "which is number one, David."

"What," asked the secretary, bursting into another laugh, "what will be the paid-up capital according to the next prospectus?"

"A figure of two, and as many oughts after it as the printer can get into the same line," replied his friend. "Ha, Ha!"

At this they both laughed. (370–1)

The power of 'capital' is linked to a comic hyperbole in the uncontainable laughter that keeps bursting out of the two men as they contemplate the vertiginous inflation of capital, credit, and print.

Nowhere are the essentially fictional and performative conventions upon which capitalist activity rests more clear than in Pecksniff, rentier, archetypal bourgeois, and simulacrum of virtue. Pecksniff's economic life has no other motive than the collection of premiums and rents, and even his relationship with his family becomes 'a mere money relation' in the book.[25] Like the families of *Nicholas Nickleby*—Squeerses, Crummleses, Mantalinis—the Pecksniffs are a family business, a corporation. Like Squeers, Pecksniff never loses a chance to advertise, even in the bosom of his family: ' "Oh Pa!" cried Mercy, holding up her finger archly. "See advertisement!" ' (13) after one effusion from her father. Drunk as a lord and attempting to seduce Mrs Todgers he asks for ' "A word in your ear. To Parents and Guardians . . . an eligible opportunity now offers, which unites the advantages of the best practical architectural education with the comforts of a home." ' (132). Pecksniff is, in the words of George Gissing, 'a tradesman, dealing in a species of exhortation which his hearers have agreed to call spiritual, and to rate at a certain value in coin of the realm'.[26] Whereas Marx believed that the bourgeoisie 'for exploitation, veiled by religious and political illusions . . . has substituted naked, shameless, direct, brutal, exploitation . . . stripped of its halo every occupation . . . torn away from the family its sentimental veil',[27] Dickens shows how the veils multiply, layer upon layer. As Marshal Berman says, 'old modes of honour and dignity do not die; instead they get incorporated into the market'; Pecksniff puts the sacred to work, takes the holy to market, sanctifies a desanctified world.[28]

III

The practices of language and writing are central to *Martin Chuzzlewit*. Like *Bleak House*, 'it is a document concerned with the interpretation of documents'.[29] Todgers, for example, can only be reached by 'clinging tenaciously to the postman' (113), as if the very existence, or at least the attaining, of place in the

---

[25] Karl Marx and Friedrich Engels, *The Communist Manifesto*, with an introduction by A. J. P. Taylor (Harmondsworth: Pelican, 1967), 82.
[26] George Gissing, *Charles Dickens: A Critical Study* (London: Gresham, 1902), 140.
[27] Marx and Engels, *The Communist Manifesto*, 82.
[28] Berman, *All That is Solid Melts into Air*, 111; see also p. 157.
[29] J. Hillis Miller, Introduction to Charles Dickens, *Bleak House* (Harmondsworth: Penguin, 1971), 11.

city depended on the post. At times, the many figures of writing in the book serve the interests of clarity and lucidity, as when Tom Pinch is described as smiling in a way that is 'as plainly a confession of his own imperfections . . . as if he had drawn one up in simple language and committed it to paper' (67), but the majority of them make it appear futile or self-destructive. An early scene shows old Martin writing out his will and then burning it to cinders, without a trace. Pecksniff is like 'a direction-post, which is always telling the way to a place, and never goes there' (11). Mark Tapley identifies himself with language itself: ' "A Werb is a word as signifies to be, to do, or to suffer . . . and if there's a Werb alive, I'm it. For I'm always a bein, sometimes a doin and always a sufferin"' (625). Nadgett's mystery (which is also the mystery of modernity, surveillance, and the city) is explicitly a matter of writing and erasure: Nadgett distrusts word of mouth and 'wrote letters to himself about him constantly; and when he found them in his pocket put them in the fire' (505). Tamaroo, Bailey's replacement at Todgers, 'was a perfect Tomb for messages and small parcels; and when despatched to the Post-Office with letters, had been frequently seen endeavouring to insinuate them into casual chinks in private doors, under the delusion that any door with a hole in it would answer the purpose' (438). Most surreal of all is Young Bailey's aggressively self-defeating greeting of the Pecksniffs: 'I thought you wos the Paper, and wondered why you didn't shove yourself through the grating as usual' (109).

Many of the characters try to resist the strange fates that writing leads to, and both narrator and characters seek to invest their utterances with a force that is not simply linguistic. At the end of the fourth chapter, a deaf cousin of the Chuzzlewit clan, in order to show her disgust with Mr Pecksniff and his dissembling, on leaving his house, scrapes her shoes upon the scraper and 'distributed impressions of them all over the top step, in token that she shook the dust from her feet before quitting that dissembling and perfidious mansion' (57). Her action, with which she leaves both the Pecksniff household and the novel, is a kind of moral pantomime, a making literal of a metaphor, a conscious symbolic acting out. This is something that many people in the book do, drawing on biblical and moral typology to heighten and emphasize their own social actions. Pecksniff himself is a master of it: he casts off Chevy Slyme 'as Saint George might have repudiated the Dragon' (42); his smile 'proclaimed the words "I am a messenger of peace!"' (49). At such moments, as in the emblem books which underwent a significant revival in the nineteenth century, language and visual appearance reinforce one another in a literal and figurative embodiment of a proverbial truth. Word, deed, and intention are embodied in a single archetypal display. Who could doubt at such a moment the cousin's feelings about Pecksniff, or the justice of her rejecting him? He is a type of hypocrisy and deceit; she an apostle, symbolically departing a place of blindness and sin. The secular and popular equivalent of such activity in the book is pantomime, an extra-linguistic resource of which young Bailey is a master, at one moment 'touching his nose with a corkscrew, as if to express the Bacchanalian character of the meeting' (128), at another 'counterfeiting in his own person the action of a high-trotting horse' (361), at another letting the world know how badly he has been tipped by giving 'several sharp slaps upon his pocket and other facetious pantomime' (163).

Proverbs are a key form of such reinforcement, invoking a common store of knowledge to make linguistic meaning appear more solid and certain, as when Jonas says: 'Here's the rule for bargains—"Do other men, for they would do you"' (158), or when Mould the undertaker reassures Mrs Gamp that '"Use is second nature"' (270).[30] So too is the characters' desire to see themselves as figures in an allegory, an impulse shared by the narrator. Pecksniff often presents his life in allegorical terms, telling Tom Pinch that, should he fall ill, he will 'convey him to the hospital in Hope, and sit beside his bed in Bounty!' (72). About to leave for Todgers's, he says to young Martin: ' "We shall go forth tonight by the heavy coach—like the dove of old,

---

[30] There are many more examples: 'At length it became high time to remember the first clause of that great discovery made by the ancient philosopher for securing health, riches and wisdom; the infallibility of which has been verified by the enormous fortunes, constantly amassed by chimney sweepers and other persons who get up early and go to bed betimes' (75); 'It is the duty of man to be just before he is generous' (192); 'reason in . . . roasting of eggs' (213); 'An ancient proverb tells us that we should not expect to find old heads on young shoulders' (153); 'Change begets change. Nothing propagates so fast' (255); 'Does anyone doubt the old saw, that the Devil (being a layman) quotes scripture for his own ends?' (151).

my dear Martin—and it will be a week before we deposit our olive branches in the passage. When I say olive branches," observed Mr Pecksniff, in explanation, "I mean our unpretending luggage"' (77). At least the luggage is unpretending here. There is something paradoxical about Pecksniff's allegorizing: on the one hand, he transforms all things and occasions to his advantage, but does so through turning them into the fixed object of a moral exemplum, homily, or parable, from the christening of his children Mercy and Charity onwards. '"What are we?" said Mr Pecksniff, "but coaches? Some of us are slow coaches . . . some of us are fast coaches. Our passions are the horses; and rampant animals too! . . . and Virtue is the drag. We start from The Mother's Arms, and we run to The Dust Shovel"' (103). Tigg, when he attempts to borrow money from young Martin and Tom Pinch, falls instantly into the habit: '"Upon my soul, I am grateful to my friend Pecksniff for helping me to the contemplation of such a delicious picture as you present. You remind me of Whittington, afterwards thrice Lord Mayor of London . . . You are a pair of Whittingtons, gents, without the cat"' (90). Mark Tapley allegorizes the American Eagle as 'like a Bat, for its short-sightedness; like a Bantam, for its bragging; like a Magpie, for its honesty; like a Peacock for its vanity; like a Ostrich for putting its head in the mud' (471).[31] On the one hand, allegory and proverbs promise an end to the displacements of signification and the creation of stable meaning and sure interpretation; on the other, by their arbitrariness, absurdity, and proliferation, they compound the problem they are intended to resolve.

This use of emblem, pantomime, proverbs, and allegory is part of the book's wish both to enact and resist the power of rhetoric. By some distance the most rhetorically sophisticated of Dickens's early novels, *Martin Chuzzlewit* both embodies powerful rhetoric in its own narration, and is concerned with the dangerous effects of rhetorical skill and power in the world. Dickens, like Shakespeare, grants much of his own rhetorical power to the characters he creates, and even the most poor in

---

[31] Not all the allegory is parodic: 'a dark and dreary night . . . Want, colder than Charity, shivering at the street corners' (211).

money are rich in the capacity to frame their desires in language.[32] Their characteristic tropes are revealing. Hyperbole is one of the most common, as it is in most Dickens novels: Pecksniff, the narrator assures us, is 'the best of architects and land surveyors' (57); Chevy Slyme, according to Tigg, is 'without an exception, the highest-minded, the most independent-spirited; most original, spiritual, classical, talented; the most thoroughly Shakspearian, if not Miltonic; and at the same time, the most disgustingly-unappreciated dog I know' (43); if his debts are not paid, 'a situation as tremendous, perhaps, as the social intercourse of the nineteenth century will readily admit of' (91) will arise; on the departure of the Pecksniffs, 'It would have been impossible to surpass the unutterable despair' (161) of the gentlemen of Todgers's.[33] This hyperbole is matched by an equal interest in the oxymoronic. We see this most clearly in and around Mark Tapley. In Eden he is 'wery bad myself, and jolly to the last' (446) and Martin's transformation there, and thus the anagnorisis and peripety on which the novel turns, is explicitly antithetical: 'So low had Eden brought him down. So high had Eden raised him up' (453). The characters are frequently driven to paradoxical and oxymoronic expressions: Pecksniff gives 'a motion of the head, which was something between an affirmative bow, and a negative shake' (164); Tapley smiles at Martin's selfishness 'with surprising ghastliness' (211), and Mrs Hominy's headdress makes her look like 'Mr Grimaldi . . . in the lappets of Mrs Siddons' (318), the clown costumed as tragedian. The landscape going towards Eden is 'half growing, half decaying' (323); Jonas meeting old Martin is a 'mixture of defiance and obsequiousness, of fear and hardihood, of dogged sullenness and an attempt at cringing and propitiation' (334); Miss Mould we glimpse 'sporting behind the scenes of death and burial' (346) and her father offers 'a queer attempt at

---

[32] 'I am unable to take Mr Pecksniff's hypocrisy seriously. He does not seem to me so much a hypocrite as a rhetorician': G. K. Chesterton, *Chesterton on Dickens* (London: J. M. Dent, 1992), 101.

[33] The 1867 preface both draws attention to and disavows the novel's characteristic hyperbole in its opening claim that 'What is exaggeration to one class of minds and perceptions, is plain truth to another' (719). See also Patrick J. McCarthy, 'The Language of *Martin Chuzzlewit*', *SEL: Studies in English Literature 1500–1900*, 20 (1980), 639–40.

melancholy . . . at odds with a smirk of satisfaction' (270); the week of Anthony's funeral is 'a round of dismal joviality and grim enjoyment' (275). Language and rhetoric at such moments are melancholy and deceiving things, constantly contradicting themselves.

Perhaps the most common trope in the book is irony, which is all-pervasive. We sometimes speak of 'corrosive irony', but there is nothing corrosive about the irony of this book, which does not rust or eat away at Mr Pecksniff or Montague Tigg but shines them up all the brighter. At times truth can only be spoken ironically, as when Westlock tries to tell Tom Pinch how much Pecksniff is exploiting him: ' "*He* never scraped and clawed into his pouch all your poor grandmother's hard savings . . . *he* never speculated and traded on her pride in you . . . Not he, Tom!" ' (21). Westlock and language are here at a point at which they can only say what they say by denying that they are saying it. A hostile early reviewer of the novel said 'the funny language is as flat as funny language about nothing is apt to be' and there is a constant danger that the book might be about nothing at all.[34] Hyperbole is pushed to such extremes that everything turns, like Pecksniff's morality, into nothing, simply the fragments and scraps of rhetoric. Against the hyperbole that surrounds him, Bailey's gift is litotes, or affirmation by negation. Driving Tigg's magnificent chariot, Bailey 'seemed to say, "A barrow, good people, a mere barrow; nothing to what we could do, if we chose!" ' (368). The narrator consciously reaches for an ironic aporia—the figure of impossibility of linguistic expression—to describe the Pecksniffs: 'What words can paint the Pecksniffs in that trying hour? Oh, none: for words have naughty company among them, and the Pecksniffs were all goodness' (50). Chuffey is so old and so infirm that he is 'looking at nothing, with eyes that saw nothing, and a face that meant nothing . . . an embodiment of nothing. Nothing else' (155). The rhetorical inflation of the book, like the financial inflation of the Anglo-Bengalee, often leads to a bankruptcy of sense and meaning. Plenitude leads to emptiness: in Nadgett's secrecy, Chuffey's silence, old Martin's silence, and Pecksniff's conscience, 'a perfectly

---

[34] From an unsigned article, *National Review*, XIII (July 1861), 134–50, in Collins, *Dickens: the Critical Heritage*, 193.

blank book ... in which entries were only made with a peculiar kind of invisible ink' (282). When Anthony Chuzzlewit dies, 'He seemed to utter words, but they were such as man had never heard. And this was the most fearful circumstance of all, to see him standing there, gabbling in an unearthly tongue' (264).

In the novel, the United States is at the heart of this, a great machine for the production of rhetoric, as powerful as it is ungrounded. All the characteristic figures and tropes of the book here find their most heightened form. It is a deeply hyperbolic country in which everyone is 'as remarkable a man as any in our country' (310) and 'every alligator basking in the slime is himself an Epic, self-contained' (314). It is full of paradox and oxymoron: Eden is an 'awful lovely place ... And frightful wholesome' (300), in which Scadder's face is like 'the compound figure of Death and the Lady at the top of the old ballad' (309); Americans frequently use emblems, as when Scadder offers his hands to Mark 'for examination in a figurative sense, as emblems of his moral character' (307); prosopopoeia and apostrophe are characteristic features of language there, especially in public address: ' "Bring forth that Lion!" said the young Columbian. "Alone, I dare him! I taunt that Lion. I tell that Lion, that Freedom's hand once twisted in his mane, he rolls a corse before me, and the Eagles of the Great Republic laugh 'Ha, Ha'!" ' (310). Colonel Diver lives his life as an allegory, in which his entire discourse and psychic life is a play of allegorical figures: ' "the Palladium of rational Liberty ... Human civilisation ... National Prosperity ... the Great Republic ... Young Desire ... the Hydra of Corruption ... the lance of Reason" ' (221–5).

The most interesting depiction of the hegemony of rhetoric in the book occurs in chapter 17, shortly after Mark Tapley and Martin have arrived in New York, after Mark has met a former slave now working in the city. When Martin returns from his journey, Mark, 'taking him aside and speaking confidentially' (242), tells him of the man's story—how 'he was shot in the leg; gashed in the arm; scored in his live limbs, like pork; beaten out of shape; had his neck galled with an iron collar, and wore iron rings upon his wrists and ankles', but then, under another master, was able to buy his freedom and how he is now saving to buy his daughter's.[35] Tapley, in order to tell Martin that the man has been a slave, does not go straight to the point: first he uses periphrasis—' "one of them as there's picters of in the shops, a man and a brother" '—giving at the same time a little pantomime of Wedgwood's famous icon of the anti-slavery movement, 'so often represented in tracts and cheap prints' (242). Mark is cautious about saying what Cicero is, insistent on non-linguistic signs—pictures, pantomime, Cicero's own body—to convey his meaning. By this stage in the book, he, like the novel's readers, have witnessed the various rhetorics of Pecksniff, the Chuzzlewits, Montague Tigg, and the editor of the *New York Rowdy*, and learned to distrust them, not least when they claim to be speaking in literal and straightforward ways.

What, though, of the man who is the subject of their discussion, which takes place within his presence but not, it seems, within his hearing? Martin does not address the former slave, but asks Mark about him. The black man, the silent topic of the discussion, is speechless throughout the scene, spoken of and for by Tapley.[36] There is only one, very brief, moment of interchange between him and the two Englishmen, where Mark addresses him by his name for the first and only time in the book—' "Now, Cicero." ' (243) Cicero does not reply, for Martin immediately interrupts, asking Mark ' "Is that his name?" ' ' "That's his name, sir," ' is the reply. And Cicero, 'grinning assent' (243), then carries out the luggage of the two men, to leave the novel for ever. The former slave, now servant of a

---

[35] Dickens, it is well known, was shocked and horrified by slavery in the southern states on his visit to the USA in 1842, and *American Notes*, his travel book based on his journeys, condemns slavery in stark terms. The later sections of the book contain a long transcription of advertisements for runaway slaves, the pathos of which contrasts sharply with Dickens's more usual exuberant rhetoric. In *Martin Chuzzlewit* the anger is equally clear, and is linked by Tapley to a central ideological term of both political liberalism and capitalism—'liberty': 'they're so fond of liberty in this part of the globe, that they buy her and sell her and carry her to market with 'em. They've such a passion for Liberty, that they can't help taking liberties with her' (243). It is a condemnation not simply of an abuse in the system, but one that questions one of the central ideological terms of the system itself, the alleged link between political and economic liberty.

[36] Suvendrini Perera, 'Wholesale, Retail and for Exportation: Empire and the Family Business in *Dombey and Son*', *Victorian Studies*, XXXIII (Summer 1990), 610, has argued that the depiction of Major Bagstock's servant 'The Native' in *Dombey and Son* 'enacts the certainties of imperial mastery' and demonstrates '[t]he utter negation of the colonial subject'.

servant, does not speak; but his name says a good deal. Cicero, after whom he is named, was the most famous of all Roman orators, a citizen of an earlier republic, and the author of, among many other books, five studies of rhetoric. This second Cicero is silent, his eloquence written not in language but with the marks and brands on his body, shown to Tapley when ' "he stripped off his coat, and took away my appetite" ' (242). It is of course ironical, to call a man who is silent after a prodigiously eloquent orator, but irony is the dominant trope of the whole passage; unless one calls it sarcasm, that word from Rabelais for speaking bitterly, gnashing the teeth, or tearing the flesh (as this Cicero's flesh was torn).

Why is Cicero silent? It may be that Dickens felt that he could not reproduce his speech effectively without patronizing him or making him sound comic, or believed that in a novel where language is so often deceptive, silence is more eloquent than words, and the scarred body more telling than any utterance. But Tapley's other activities while Martin has been away add another layer of meaning. For Mark has carved his name on the door of the *New York Rowdy* office, signing his initials and date, to create something like a picture painted by Tapley, an illustration and allegory of America and slavery. There is an illustration by Phiz of this scene of Tapley, Cicero, and the signed door, a picture of a picture, an allegory of an allegory, of a servant, a slave, writing and signature in an editorial office. It is a silent, speaking allegory in which Tapley is whistling a (silent) song, whose words we know from Dickens's text, but which we also know breaks off just before an unspeakable word—'slaves'. Tapley whistles 'Rule, Britannia!' and stops at the words 'never, never, never' leaving the reader to complete the quotation (which was never begun because he is, after all, only whistling) 'shall be slaves'. Tapley tells Mark that he wants to keep Cicero with him as an object of contemplation, a kind of *memento servire*, to keep himself 'jolly'. In the same scene he discusses with Martin a woman they met on the boat out, whom he jokingly calls 'the mad woman', and her husband who went out to America before her and is 'not altogether dead'. A slave, a servant, silence, a signature, an illustration, all in and through Dickens's language and rhetoric which seek to reach beyond language and rhetoric, and a mad woman with a husband who

exists in a space between the living and the dead; this is deep
irony, paradox, or oxymoron, that word from the Greek for
sharply or pointedly foolish.

IV

Martin Chuzzlewit is a novel deeply concerned with the nature
of moral behaviour in the world, and it presents modern ethical
life as deeply disturbed and disturbing. Questions of 'self' are
at the heart of this investigation, but it is not at all clear what
the novel understands the 'self' to be. 'Self' is a troubling and
difficult word in English, with at least two major senses. On the
one hand, 'self' refers to something that is peculiar to a particular individual or subject—my single solitary self. On the other
hand it can connote not uniqueness but sameness—it is the self-
same thing, as when a piece of a garment is made of the same
material as the main piece. It can also mean a person whom one
loves as oneself, or who is a counterpart of oneself. So 'self' can
refer on the one hand to uniqueness and peculiarity; on the
other, to sameness and identity; and then again to uncanny
figures who are both the same and different, self and other. In
Martin Chuzzlewit we find that not just the city but the self too
is profoundly uncanny. This is most clear in the motif of doubles
and others in the book: Mercy is referred to as 'the other one'
(107) by Jonas, her identity wholly defined as her sister's other;
Tigg has two identities, Montague Tigg and Tigg Montague;
Jonas himself becomes 'his own ghost and phantom' (619) after
he kills Tigg; Pecksniff is endlessly duplicitous; Mrs Gamp
wrapped in a great coat 'became two people' (355) and divides
herself into two in her imaginary dialogues with Mrs Harris.

This uncanniness in the novel is partly the result of the constant production of the self as a set of performances, that
'outward show of life' of which Baudelaire speaks.[37] The Pecksniff family compose little dramatic tableaux to greet their visitors, as does Tigg at the Anglo-Bengalee and, less convincingly,
Mrs Gamp for her clients. It is not that the novel forgets or fails

[37] Baudelaire, 'The Painter of Modern Life', 24. See also Erving Goffmann, *The
Presentation of Self in Everyday Life* (Harmondsworth: Pelican, 1971), and Alasdair MacIntyre, *After Virtue* (London: Duckworth, 2nd edition 1985), 115–17.

to sustain the theme of the self in the novel, but that the self is always dissolving into gesture and performance.[38] And performance and theatricality are not merely an affair of the morally unjust characters, like Tigg and Pecksniff, for as the novel develops, the virtuous—Tapley and old Martin—learn the importance of dissimulation and performance to further their moral ends. Theatrical performance does not simply require competent and plausible acting in order to succeed; it also requires an audience willing and able to sustain the illusion by ascribing human life and human intentions to the actors' words, deeds, and gestures. This is true of the theatre, but also true of performances outside theatres. Pecksniff is a consummate and brilliant improvising performer, but he would act in vain were Tom Pinch and others not willing to ascribe to him the life and intentions he feigns. The Anglo-Bengalee would be nothing without the willingness of its clients to ascribe virtue, solidity, and wealth to Bullamy's waistcoat.

The rhetorical name for this willingness or ability to ascribe human life to persons and things is prosopopoeia, one of the most important tropes in the book. Dickens in *Pictures from Italy* wrote that the visitors to the Colosseum in Rome could, if they wished, 'have the whole great pile before them, as it used to be, with thousands of eager faces staring down into the arena'.[39] This belief in the power of the human imagination is also testament to a faith in the power of prosopopoeia, that figure of speech 'which gives the ability to act and move to insensate things, as well as speech to absent or present persons or things, sometimes even to the dead'.[40] It is a key 'signature' of Dickens's work and is prominent from the very beginning of this narrative. Prosopopoeia is often disparaged, or praised

---

[38] Lucas, *The Melancholy Man*, 118. Foucault,'What is Enlightenment?', in *The Foucault Reader*, 41–2:

'Modernity for Baudelaire is not simply a form of relationship to the present; it is also a mode of relationship that has to be established with oneself . . . To be modern is not to accept oneself as one is in the flux of the passing moments; it is to take oneself as object of a complex and difficult elaboration . . . Modern man, for Baudelaire, is not the man who goes off to discover himself, his secrets and his hidden truth; he is the man who tries to invent himself.'

[39] Charles Dickens, *Pictures from Italy*, ed. Leonée Ormond in *American Notes and Pictures from Italy* (London: Everyman, 1997), 397.

[40] Alex Preminger and T. V. F. Brogan (eds), *The New Princeton Encyclopedia of Poetry and Poetics* (Princeton: Princeton University Press, 1993), 994.

simply as an ability to liven up a dull passage of writing, but in J. Hillis Miller's and Paul de Man's more ample sense it encompasses literature's central ability to ascribe 'a name, a face or a voice to the absent, the insensate, or the dead'.[41] In the opening chapter of the book, for example, almost everything is thought of as living in some quasi-human way and is frequently ascribed human intentions. This is of course in one way quite conventional, but Dickens uses the figure in more interesting ways: the village forge, for example, 'came out in all its bright importance. The lusty bellows roared "Ha! Ha!" to the clear fire, which roared in turn' (7–8). This creates a double prosopopoeia, in which the inanimate bellows summon up life in the equally inanimate fire. If inhuman things can be treated as human, as when the dogs in Salisbury 'were strongly interested in the state of the market and the bargains of their masters' (63) or when Tom Pinch handles volumes of Shakespeare 'with as much care as if they were living and highly cherished creatures' (88), they can be used in more disturbing ways to make the distinction between the human and non-human a less certain and sure one. When Jonas goes to commit the murder of Tigg, '[t]here was not a blade of growing grass or corn, but watched' (614); it is the necessary prelude to the complete breakdown of Jonas's subjectivity, and his own becoming thing-like: 'not only fearful *for* himself but *of* himself; for being, as it were, a part of the room: a something supposed to be there, yet missing from it: he invested himself with its mysterious terrors' (619). Jonas is both present and absent, both human and a thing, both subject, object, and what undoes the distinction between them. Such is the power of prosopopoeia.

Closely allied to prosopopoeia is the figure of apostrophe, which consists in addressing an absent or dead person, a thing, or an abstract idea as if it were alive and present before us. Apostrophe is an interesting and exceptional trope or figure. It is, as Jonathan Culler has argued, a figure of pathos, but also a metapoetic figure by which authors can address their own utterance.[42]

---

[41] J. Hillis Miller, *Versions of Pygmalion* (Cambridge: Harvard University Press, 1990), 47.

[42] Jonathan Culler, *The Pursuit of Signs* (London: Routledge and Kegan Paul, 1981), 146. Welsh, *From Copyright to Copperfield*, 26, notes the use of apostrophe in the novel but believes that Dickens reserves it only for Tom Pinch.

Apostrophe is used in many different ways in *Martin Chuzzle-wit*. The narrator, for example, uses it to address his own characters, most often Tom Pinch: 'blessings on thy simple heart, Tom Pinch, how proudly dost thou button up that scanty coat . . . as with thy cheerful voice, thou pleasantly adjurest Sam the hostler . . . Who could repress a smile—of love for thee, Tom Pinch . . . Who . . . would not cry "Heaven speed them"?' (58). The narrator can also use the trope ironically: 'O blessed star of Innocence, wherever you may be, how did you glitter in your home of ether, when the two Miss Pecksniffs put forth, each her lily hand, and gave the same, with mantling cheeks, to Martin!' (72). The characters frequently use it: ' "Oh Calf, Calf! . . . Oh Baal, Baal!" cried Mr Pecksniff mournfully' (147); ' "Oh, Tom Pinch, Tom Pinch!" said Martin . . . "Oh, Dragon, Dragon!" said Mark.' (254).[43] This is done quite self-consciously, as the frequent use of the term 'apostrophe' or one of its derivatives in the novel shows: ' "Ah, envy, envy what a passion you are!" Uttering this apostrophe . . . Pecksniff left the room' (290); ' "Go your ways," said Tom Pinch, apostrophizing the coach: "I can hardly persuade myself but you're alive" ' (23); attempting to seduce Mary Graham, Pecksniff exclaims ' "Ah, naughty hand!" . . . apostrophizing the reluctant prize, "why did you take me prisoner! Go, go!" ' (414–15).

As Culler remarks, apostrophe 'makes its point by troping not on the meaning of a word but on the circuit or situation of communication itself'.[44] 'To apostrophize is to will a state of affairs, an attempt to call it into being by asking inanimate objects to bend themselves to desire . . . to make the objects of the universe potentially responsive forces' and 'to construct encounters with the world as relations between subjects'.[45] For Paul de Man, this makes it the most uncanny of rhetorical figures, the place where the living and the dead meet and exchange roles. In this novel, it is used in ways that are particularly disturbing to the book's ethical design. The most important act of prosopopoeia in the

---

[43] There are many more examples: ' "Oh, Mammon, Mammon!" cried Mr Pecksniff' (47); 'Oh late remembered, much forgotten, mouthing, braggart duty . . . Oh ermined judge . . . Oh prelate, prelate . . . Oh magistrate' (428); 'Oh woman, God beloved in old Jerusalem! The best among us need deal lightly with thy faults' (396); 'But then, outlaughs the stern philosopher, and saith to the Grotesque, "What ho! arrest for me that Agency. Go bring it here!" And so the vision fadeth' (467).

[44] Culler, *The Pursuit of Signs*, 135.   [45] Ibid., 139, 141.

book (apart perhaps from Mrs Gamp's creation of Mrs Harris) and where it becomes most clearly a matter of serious ethical consideration, is Tom Pinch's creation of Pecksniff as a moral man. Indeed, Pecksniff's morality only exists because of other people's willingness to ascribe virtue to him, a point strikingly made by old Martin in his encounter with Pecksniff at the Blue Dragon, when he insists, in a complex, satirical act of masking and apostrophe, on addressing Pecksniff as 'kind stranger' (36). Slightly earlier, on Pecksniff's first appearance, the reader is told that the stream smiles and the church spire glints 'in sympathy' with its surroundings (6), but the novel ascribes no such intention to Pecksniff himself. We are obliged to infer his intentions from his appearances, and to assume that he is alive and human, not a thing or a monster. But we have no solid grounds for doing so.

This universal prosopopoeia creates a world of endless metamorphoses, in which Tigg Montague can become Montague Tigg as readily as the name of Mrs Todgers's little servant can change, in a potentially endless chain of metaphoric and metonymic displacements from 'Benjamin', 'Uncle Ben', 'Barnwell', 'Mr Pitt' to 'Young Brownrigg' and 'Bailey junior' (125). When the Pecksniffs leave Todgers's, the gentlemen sing for them 'a requiem, a dirge, a moan, a howl, a wail, a lament' (161). The world at such moments becomes, like Mrs Todgers's boarding house itself, a matter of displacement and seriality, a world of turns:

a gentleman of a sporting turn . . . a gentleman of a theatrical turn . . . a gentleman of a debating turn . . . and a gentleman of a literary turn . . . a gentleman of a vocal turn, and a gentleman of a smoking turn, and a gentleman of a convivial turn . . . a turn for whist . . . a strong turn for billiards . . . a turn for business . . . a decided turn for pleasure . . . a fashionable turn . . . a witty turn. (126–7)

'Turn' is another word for trope, and here the turn both fixes and tropes (or turns) identity (126). At such moments the novel seems to glimpse the possibility that all social life is a matter of prosopopoeia, tropes, and turns. If this is so, it has a number of disturbing consequences, not least the way it troubles our ability to distinguish the human from the non-human, and the good from the bad. In recent literary theory, the analysis of rhetoric has often been concerned with its 'inhuman' qualities, the ways in which it seems to float free of any guiding human intention.[46] *Martin Chuzzlewit* too is concerned by this, most clearly in Pecksniff. If one boundary that it subverts is the one between human beings and the natural world, another is between the human and the animal.[47] Many people in the book are called monsters: Pecksniff and Gamp are monsters, Jonas is described as a 'monster' and a 'griffin' (341) by Mercy Pecksniff, Old Martin too is called a 'monster' (343), and Tom Pinch even thinks of the coach that takes John Westlock away as 'a great monster' (23). Dickens is often thought to be a great humanist writer, but *Martin Chuzzlewit* is a text persistently troubled by the limits of the human, by people who may be monsters or animals or machines.

In the 1849 preface to the Cheap edition, Dickens claims that his purpose was 'to show how Selfishness propagates itself'. This has often been seen as Dickens making an essentially moral point, allying himself to a satirical tradition of 'humour' comedy or moral allegory.[48] But this is to ignore the particular resonance that 'self' and 'selfishness' had in the 1830s and 1840s, when they were central terms in utilitarian ethical theory. Indeed, in the same year that *Martin Chuzzlewit* was appearing in serial form, the eleven posthumous volumes of the *Works* of Jeremy Bentham were published.[49] Utilitarianism is a moral as well as a social theory, and *Martin Chuzzlewit* articulates a critique of utilitarian ethical norms, in particular Bentham's central assertion, in the prefatory section of the *Constitutional Code*, that 'in the general tenor of life, in every human breast, self-regarding interest is predominant over all other interests put together'.[50] There are three kinds of human motive for Bentham:

---

[46] Paul de Man, 'Autobiography as De-facement,' *Modern Language Notes*, 94 (1979) 919–30. Culler, *The Pursuit of Signs*, 154.

[47] The most troubling political manifestation of the distinction between human and animal is in the book's concern with slavery: 'As if there were nothing in suffering and slavery grim enough to cast a solemn air on any human animal; though it were as ridiculous, physically, as the most grotesque of apes; or, morally, as the mildest Nimrod among tuft-hunting republicans!' (246).

[48] Barbara Hardy, 'The Change of Heart in Dickens' Novels', in Martin Price (ed.), *Dickens: Twentieth Century Views* (New Jersey: Prentice Hall, 1967), 48.

[49] Jeremy Bentham, *The Works of Jeremy Bentham*, ed. John Bowring (Edinburgh, 1843).

[50] Bentham, *The Works*, ix, 5, cited in John Dinwiddy, *Bentham* (Oxford: Oxford University Press, 1989), 24. Bentham does not identify this with 'self-interest' in a narrow sense, but it is clear that it could easily be construed in this way by a hostile critic.

social motives, such as goodwill; semi-social ones, which include love of reputation, desire of amity, and the motive of religion; and self-regarding motives of physical desire, pecuniary interest, love of power, and self-preservation.[51] It is the latter group that motivates most people in the book and old Martin might well have been reading Bentham when he exclaims, striking the key-note of the book, ' "Oh self, self, self! Every man for himself, and no creature for me!" ' (40). At the heart of this concern with selfishness is the presentation of Pecksniff. Like Mrs Gamp, he has a significance well beyond the pages of the book, as his rapid passage into the dictionary shows: 'Pecksniffery', 'Pecksniffism', and 'Pecksniffian' are all in the OED. He is a character in a novel, to be sure, but he is also a 'character' in the more extended sense that Alasdair MacIntyre uses the term, to describe figures who are 'moral representatives of their culture . . . because of the way in which moral and metaphysical ideas and theories assume through them an embodied existence in the social world. They are the masks worn by moral philosophies.'[52] For Pecksniff, as for Mrs Gamp and Jonas Chuzzlewit, all social relationships are manipulative and instrumental. It is hard not to think of Pecksniff when reading Bentham's list of motives—Pecksniff's are physical desire (part of the brilliance of his characterization is his sensuality in the attempted seductions of Mrs Todgers and Mary Graham), love of money (with his premiums, his meanness, his partnership with Jonas, his courtship of old Martin), and love of power—over Tom, his daughters, and others. '[I]n Bentham's discussion of private ethics . . . there was a strong emphasis on calculation',[53] as there was indeed in Mr Pecksniff's, who after declaring that he is ' "a Benefactor to my kind!" ' is found by the reader 'exulting . . . in his moral utility' (108). Indeed, Pecksniff and Bentham at times can even share metaphors. Bentham

[51] Even the relatively sympathetic J. S. Mill, who defended Bentham against the charge that he 'intended to impute universal selfishness to mankind', nevertheless contends that 'habitually . . . the more he has shown a man's selfish interest would prompt him to a particular action, the more he lays it down without further parley that the man's interest lies that way', quoted in Dinwiddy, Bentham, 23. See also J. S. Mill, 'Remarks on Bentham's Philosophy', in Mill on Politics and Society, ed. Geraint L. Williams (London: Fontana, 1976) 110 and 'Bentham', in Essays on Politics and Culture, ed. Gertrude Himmelfarb (New York: Anchor, 1963), 97.
[52] MacIntyre, After Virtue, 28.   [53] Dinwiddy, Bentham, 32.

'went so far as to suggest in the *Deontology* that acts of benef-
icence that were of no immediate advantage to the agent might
be regarded as deposits paid into a savings bank or General
Good-will fund, from which the agent might be expected to
draw benefits in due course'.[54] Pecksniff calls up 'morality from
the great storehouse within his own breast' (261) and describes
his conscience as ' "my bank. I have a trifle invested there . . .
but I prize it as a store of value" ' (282). At such moments,
Martin Chuzzlewit becomes Dickens's *Genealogy of Morals*, but
even Nietzsche, at his most flourishing, only approaches the rim
of the crater called Pecksniff. Pecksniff is a hypocrite of course,
but in the sublime mode. He is the representative of a much
wider force in his and other societies, as Karl Marx suggested
in his ethnological notebooks when he annotated a citation of
Bentham's 'greatest happiness of the greatest number' principle
with the exclamation 'O you Pecksniff!'.[55]

Martin Chuzzlewit is troubled by the difficulty of behaving
ethically in a world whose representative figure is Mr Pecksniff,
whose representative family is the Chuzzlewits, and whose
representative institution is the Anglo-Bengalee, but the book's
ethical positives seem less convincing than its negatives. The
embodiment of moral virtue in the book is Tom Pinch. In
one way there could not be a more effective dramatization of
master–slave relations than that of Pinch and Pecksniff. One is
the epitome of the will-to-power, the other its selfless abnegation.
When Pinch for once asserts himself against Jonas, he can do so
only by accident. In another sense, Pecksniff and Pinch are both
versions of what Nietzsche was later to call 'slave morality':
Pinch's virtues are the Christian ones of charity, benevolence, and
humility; Pecksniff's power comes from his willingness to feign
these qualities. Pecksniff looks like Nietzsche's 'ascetic priest' as
he feigns Christian goodness, but acts like the blond-haired beast
in his conscience-less search for power; when John Westlock,
whom he has conned out of a good deal of money, offers to shake
hands, Pecksniff refuses to comply, but also claims the right to
forgive him, whether he wishes it or not. The Victorians' fond-
ness for the selfless Tom Pinch shows a strong desire not to

[54] Ibid.
[55] S. S. Prawer, *Karl Marx and World Literature* (Oxford: Oxford University
Press, 1976), 362.

acknowledge the disturbing implications of the book—that the self is fictional and moral life ungrounded and arbitrary—and their profound need to believe in the possibility of a disinterested moral goodness in the world.[56] Where Bentham counsels an 'economy of sacrifice . . . to sacrifice a lesser quantity of happiness for the sake of obtaining a greater quantity',[57] Tom practises a sacrifice without restraint, calculation, or reserve. Modern readers have been a good deal more sceptical about this than their Victorian precursors.

A more interesting attempt to create a centre of moral strength in the book is the character of Mark Tapley. Mark Tapley is dedicated to being 'jolly' (61). He does this, it seems, regardless of the evidence. He is not unaware of selfishness, for the more selfish those around him are, the more he 'comes out . . . strong' (61) and the more jolly he becomes. What he finds in the world is what he puts into it; he places himself in situations where he cannot find selflessness, then he puts it there and claims to find it. The psychic trope most closely associated with these processes is that of projection, that 'operation whereby qualities, feelings, wishes, or even "objects", which the subject refuses to recognise or rejects in himself, are expelled from the self and located in another person or thing'.[58] For Freud, it always entails 'a refusal to recognise something', but Tapley seems to be quite conscious of what he is doing, and his affirmative disavowal embodies a virtue of great importance to the novel: that of being 'jolly'. 'Jolliness' encompasses many qualities, including courage, steadfastness, practical reason, and compassion. When Mark eventually returns to Mrs Lupin, jolliness also includes love and domestic affection. It is the product of a natural dialectician: Tapley's virtue is self-ironizing—as when he tells Tom Pinch he would like to become a grave-digger, as it is a ' "good damp, wormy sort of business" ' (62) in which he would have a chance to gain credit—but carried out with complete commitment and seriousness. Tapley recognizes the arbitrary and ungrounded nature of his moral goodness, but the more arbitrary the decision to act in such a way is, the more determined he is to do so. It is a kind of reversed prosopopoeia,

---

[56] Collins, *Charles Dickens: The Critical Heritage*, 185.
[57] Dinwiddy, *Bentham*, 32.
[58] Laplanche and Pontalis, *The Language of Psychoanalysis*, 349–52.

in the service of a happy ethical goodness which transforms patience and passive suffering into active virtue. Tapley's jollity is both an aesthetic concept, to do with the pleasure and enjoyment of popular life (this is one reason that he is so successful at the Blue Dragon and in steerage), and a moral one, which enables Martin and Mark to survive the worst that Eden can throw at them. Tapley can be serious at times, particularly in Eden and when he encounters slavery, but jollity is an essentially festive and communal virtue, which ends its days in the novel on the signpost of a public house renamed 'The Jolly Tapley', the mark of the arbitrariness of the sign and signification, to be sure, but also the invitation to a convincing, if wholly fictional, popular celebration.

V

What are we to do with the plot of *Martin Chuzzlewit*? No one would say that it is a maturely plotted work, formed after long and careful deliberation, which has renounced infantile delights for the calmer joys of adult control. The opposite in fact. *Martin Chuzzlewit* has been consistently punished over the years for its silliness, lack of common sense, and general misbehaviour, for being 'unfocused', 'random', 'juvenile', and full of 'blustering absurdities'.[59] Its plot is by common consent both non-existent and a mess. Modern criticism of Dickens has on the whole preferred the later novels, where the pleasure principle in both life and its fictional analogues yields to a logic of recurrence, stasis, and renunciation, and in which a protagonist like Pip in *Great Expectations* fails to grasp the plot he is really entangled in, and can only end his days in a half-life beyond life, in that strange clerkship at Clarriker's.[60] *Martin Chuzzlewit*, by contrast, is

[59] Lucas, *The Melancholy Man*, 136; Monod, *Martin Chuzzlewit*, 20; Hardy, 'Martin Chuzzlewit', 108.
[60] On the analysis of plot in Dickens's later fiction, see Peter Brooks, *Reading for the Plot: Design and Intention in Narrative* (Cambridge: Harvard University Press, 1992), 113–42. See also Allon White's analysis of the plot of *Bleak House* as 'the retrospective recapture of a bond already established but temporarily obscured': 'Language and Location in *Bleak House*', in *Carnival, Hysteria and Writing: Collected Essays and Autobiography* (Oxford: Clarendon, 1993), 89. *Martin Chuzzlewit* has almost nothing of this homeostatic pattern.

much closer to the impulses of the pleasure principle than the dark exigencies of Thanatos. It is a book of play and pleasure in language, a freely associative novel of the contingencies of character, its making and unmasking. The energies of the book seek to evade the bindings of plot in order to permit the many extraordinary events and encounters of the text, not just those between fictional characters, but between fictional readers and fictional characters (who may also be things), fictional things (which may also be characters), humans, readers, monsters, and everything beyond and in between.

This is another way of saying that *Martin Chuzzlewit* is a very funny book, written in Dickens's least utilitarian prose. Pecksniff, for instance, is a grotesquely playful, almost camp figure, as he warbles ' "Playful—playful warbler" ' (13) to his daughter Mercy, apostrophizes Mary Graham's hand: ' "Ah naughty Hand! . . . why did you take me prisoner! Go, go!" ' (414–15), or reproaches Tigg: ' "Oh fie! Oh fie! Oh, fie for shame! . . . Oh fie, fie! . . . Oh, fie! Oh fie, for shame!" ' (582–3). For Baudelaire, 'human laughter is intimately connected with the accident of an ancient fall',[61] and we first meet Pecksniff pratfalling, like a slapstick clown, seeing stars. This prepares us for his later, greater fall when Tom Pinch rumbles him and he falls '[f]rom that lofty height on which poor Tom had placed his idol . . . and . . . legions of Titans couldn't have got him out of the mud' (424) and for his final descent at the end of the book into a 'drunken, begging, squalid-letter-writing man' (715).

The greatest of the turns in the book is Mrs Gamp, who gathers together much that has gone before and is at play elsewhere in the novel. A carnival figure, an embodied grammar and thesaurus of carnival language and practice, her familiarity with the unborn and the dead gives us what Bakhtin calls 'simultaneously the two poles of becoming: that which is receding and dying, and that which is being born'.[62] She tells us of Mrs Harris's dead niece, whom

"she see at Greenwich Fair, a travellin in company vith the pink-eyed lady, Prooshan dwarf, and livin skelinton, which judge her feelins

---

[61] Baudelaire, 'On the Essence of Laughter', in *The Painter of Modern Life and Other Essays*, 149.
[62] Mikhail Bakhtin, *Rabelais and his World* (Bloomington: Indiana University Press), 520.

wen the barrel organ played, and she was shown her own dear sister's child, the same not bein expected from the outside picter, where it was painted quite contrairy in a livin state, a many sizes larger, and performing beautiful upon the Arp, which never did that dear child know or do: since breathe it never did, to speak on, in this wale!" (696)

At such moments, we are in the slipstream of a remarkable force of language, where in the most 'contrairy' representation of a representation, wholly at odds with itself, we read of a picture 'in a livin state' which is of, but does not resemble, a dead child, the imaginary niece of an imaginary character (Mrs Harris) of an imaginary character (Mrs Gamp) doing something that she never did (playing the Arp). Yet much else in the book has prepared us for these astonishing Gamp performances, which elaborate and repeat the leading tropes and figures of speech of the rest of the book. She is an allegorist, a voyager in 'this Piljian's projiss of a mortal wale' (347) who loves paradox and oxymoron, as when she admires the Mould children 'playing at berryins' (348), notes that Lewsome would make a 'lovely corpse' (376) or 'mingled sweetness and slyness' in her own manner (354). She, like other characters, is split or divided, becoming at one point 'two people . . . as if she were in the act of being embraced by one of the old patrol' (355). She is hyperbolic, 'the soberest person, and the best of blessings in a sick room' (350), but it is in prosopopoeia and 'apostrophe' (536) that she most excels. Pecksniff, tired and emotional, had summoned up the speech of his late wife to further his attempted seduction of Mrs Todgers: ' "Has a voice from the grave no influence? . . . It's not me" said Mr Pecksniff. "Don't suppose it's me; it's the voice; it's her voice" ' (132). Mrs Gamp, who resembles Pecksniff in many ways (both are great moralizers; both reassure people that they are not deceiving them; both are intensely self-conscious rhetoricians, hypocrites beyond hypocrisy, dissemblers beyond semblance) is a more shamelessly gifted user of prosopopoeia. What she does in her 'visionary dialogues' (348) with Mrs Harris is profoundly akin to what a novelist, such as Dickens himself, does, a strange doubling and repetition of the self and its language in virtual form, a simulacrum of ghostly sociability.

Mrs Gamp is, as Michael Slater has shown, a parody of

several important Victorian feminine ideals, such as the Angel of Death and the bereaved mother, but she is much more than a mere 'anti-woman joke', for Gamp is also the deconstructionist of the novel, an affirmative force.[63] Allegedly a servant, she is mistress of the book. Her multiple associations, her free semiosis, her wild jaculations, her 'unctuous and sumptuous conversation' full of portmanteau words and syntactical aberration carry off the novel to places it would not visit again until Joyce.[64] Even Mrs Nickleby pales beside her. She is a phallic woman, with her umbrella sticking out 'its battered brass nozzle from improper crevices and chinks, to the great terror of the other passengers' (402–3), but 'the ecstasies of Gamp' (600), and her large appetites—for gin, pickled salmon, cucumbers, and the celebrated staggering ale—defy sexual identity and measure. It is thus she compels our desire, makes us her familiars and *fetches* us, like one of the unborn, or one of the dead, or some of her old clothes. She is also, of course, a complete monster, except that monsters, particularly this one, are never complete, or completely anything.[65]

For Gamp, like the novel, is a triumph of language, of a speech that is also and only writing. Sylvère Monod is wrong to say that when Mrs Gamp turns 'police' to 'pelisse' (534), or 'conquer' into 'conker', it 'is good fun, but fun that the author is having on his own'.[66] It is no more Dickens's fun than any of the other coinages of Gamp, but it shows how troubling is language's and Gamp's ability to create terms, such as Derrida's 'différance' or her 'pelisse' and 'conker', that tread the boundary and subvert the distinction between speech and writing.[67] The book has often been criticized for incoherence,[68] but it is better to think of *Martin Chuzzlewit* as a great moddled thing, both modelled and muddled and in a state beyond them both. It is therefore appropriate that almost the last words in the book are in the form of a letter from Augustus Moddle, which makes

---

[63] Michael Slater, *Dickens and Women* (London: Dent, 1983), 224.

[64] Chesterton, *Chesterton on Dickens*, 101.

[65] On the monstrous, see Jacques Derrida, *Points . . . Interviews, 1974–1994*, 385–6.

[66] Monod, *Martin Chuzzlewit*, 61.

[67] Jacques Derrida, 'Différance', in *Margins of Philosophy* (Sussex: Harvester Wheatsheaf, 1982), 1–27.

[68] Chesterton, *Charles Dickens*, 242.

his farewell to Mercy Pecksniff.[69] Writing from the schooner *Cupid* on the way to Van Diemen's land he tells us that his '*inscrutable* and *gloomy* Fate' 'was written—in the Talmud'. It is not written in the Talmud, that book of the law and moral doctrine, but in these other, wilder, freer ethical texts, Dickens's and his own. Despairing of a world of constant figurative displacements, the prey of absurd allegories, puns, and unsustainable tropes, hopelessly bound and free to Cupid and to Mercy, writing within writing, 'totally unhinged', he carries himself off to a far distant land, 'if not a corpse' at least 'never' to be 'taken alive', singing his final, hopeless, hilarious song of farewell: ' "I love another. She is Another's. Everything appears to be somebody else's" ' (714).

[69] 'Everything and everyone is undecidably *modelled*—parasitical and contaminated—subject at once to "a catechising infection" and to "an infection of absurdity" ': Nicholas Royle, 'Our Mutual Friend', in John Schad (ed.), *Dickens Refigured: Bodies, Desires and Other Histories* (Manchester: Manchester University Press, 1996), 48.

Index